"At long last we are beginning to see Thomas Merton's correspondence with significant women who exchanged letters with him during his short life. Sr. Thérèse Lentfoehr stands out as an example of one who encouraged Merton, the young poet and writer, and actually collected and catalogued his voluminous writing over the years until his death in 1968. Kudos to Fr. Robert Nugent, for making this exchange better known and appreciated."

Patrick Hart, OCSO
Abbey of Gethsemani

"Drawing on a vast trove of published and unpublished letters and other materials spanning two decades, Robert Nugent has fashioned a richly detailed, insightful record the relationship between Thomas Merton and one of his most faithful correspondents and most devoted admirers. Sr. Thérèse Lentfoehr emerges as a fascinating, at times exasperating, fiercely loyal and generous friend, a complex and creative person in her own right, and Merton himself as a sensitive, supportive, (usually) patient and empathetic listener and advisor. This engaging volume makes a substantial and original contribution to our knowledge of the work and the world of Thomas Merton."

Patrick F. O'Connell
Editor, *The Merton Seasonal*

"Thanks to Robert Nugent, we now have available to us in this book the very human story of the relationship between Thomas Merton and his longtime friend, confidante, and, as it were, extern secretary, Thérèse Lentfoehr. Their correspondence, which forms the basis of his study, also gives us illuminating access as well to Roman Catholic life in the United States in the period of their friendship, as does Carol Thresher's excellent Afterword. The book serves an encouragement to the rest of us, with Merton's death no barrier, to enter in to the riches of the same friendship."  Donald Grayston
Past President of the Thomas Merton Society of Canada
and the International Thomas Merton Society

"Refreshingly unhagiographical, Nugent's book not only documents a friendship between two gifted and complex people, but provides a fascinating bit of the history of the preservation of Merton's manuscripts and an engaging glimpse of him as a spiritual director."  Bonnie Thurston
Editor of *Merton & Buddhism*
Founder and Past President of the
International Thomas Merton Society

THOMAS MERTON & THÉRÈSE LENTFOEHR

Visit our web site at
www.albahouse.org
(for orders www.stpauls.us)

or call 1-800-343-2522 (ALBA)
and request current catalog

# Thomas Merton & Thérèse Lentfoehr:
# The Story of a Friendship

ROBERT NUGENT

Library of Congress Cataloging-in-Publication Data

Nugent, Robert, SDS.
  Thomas Merton & Thérèse Lentfoehr : the story of a friendship / Robert Nugent.
       p. cm.
  ISBN 978-0-8189-1339-6
  1. Merton, Thomas, 1915-1968—Correspondence. 2. Lentfoehr, Thérèse,
1902-1981—Correspondence. I. Title. II. Title: Thomas Merton and Thérèse Lentfoehr.
  BX4705.M542A4 2012
  271'.12502—dc23
  [B]
                                              2011043697

Produced and designed in the United States of America by the
Fathers and Brothers of the Society of St. Paul,
2187 Victory Boulevard, Staten Island, New York 10314-6603
as part of their communications apostolate.

ISBN 10: 0-8189-1339-8
ISBN 13: 978-0-8189-1339-6

© Copyright 2012 by the Society of St. Paul / Alba House

**Printing Information:**

Current Printing - first digit    1    2    3    4    5    6    7    8    9    1 0

Year of Current Printing - first year shown

2012    2013    2014    2015    2016    2017    2018    2019    2020    2021

## DEDICATION

To my Salvatorian Family:
Priests and Brothers of the Society of the Divine Savior;
Sisters of the Congregation of the Divine Savior;
Lay Salvatorians
and to the Baltimore Province of the De LaSalle Brothers of the Christian Schools
who played significant roles in sustaining and nourishing my priesthood and ministry
at crucial turning points in my life journey.

# CONTENTS

Preface: Dr. Paul M. Pearson ..................................................... xv

Introduction: Listening In ......................................................... xix

Chapter 1: Thérèse Mae Lentfoehr ............................................ 1

Chapter 2: The Stuff of Legends ............................................... 15

Chapter 3: Early Contacts: 1948-1949 ..................................... 39

Chapter 4: Becoming a Sister: 1950-1954 ............................... 57

Chapter 5: Difficult Years: 1955-1959 ..................................... 89

Chapter 6: Maturity and Growth: 1960-1964 ....................... 105

Chapter 7: The Final Years: 1965-1968 ................................ 131

Afterword: Carol Thresher, SDS ............................................ 173

Appendix: *Song For A Marriage* ........................................... 177

Endnotes ................................................................................ 179

# EPIGRAPHS

"I do not hesitate to confess that letters from my friends have always and will always mean a great deal to me."
Thomas Merton<br>Letter to Thérèse Lentfoehr<br>September 26, 1956

"...there is a spontaneous consciousness of beauty; and my experience has proved that apart from a prayerful union with God, nothing so inspires and enriches one, both humanly and spiritually, as contact with a beautiful soul."
Thérèse Lentfoehr

"He believed his story would be revealed in his letters. 'It has ever been a hobby of mine (unless it be a truism and not a hobby) that a man's life lies in his letters.'... Newman's unrelenting literary obsession was the story of his own life; he was the ultimate self-absorbed autobiographer. He was increasingly absorbed in textual, literary self-referential preoccupation. Yet his was no narcissistic endeavor. Every detail of his story, his relationships, his feelings and insights, at every stage of his life, were noted, identified and contemplated in the light of the mystery of God's Creation, Revelation and Redemption. Newman's undying 'unforgotten voice' is nothing less than an insistent search for ultimate meaning, through the telling of the story of his own life."
Newman's Unquiet Grave: The Reluctant Saint<br>John Cornwell, Continuum International<br>Publishing Group, 2010

In this <u>now</u> day
of resurrection, these with him we
celebrate, praising

*the Creator who in so brief and
desperate a season
shaped us a friend who reached into our
solitudes and with
the finger of a word touch in us the deep
places of the living God*

Thérèse Lentfoehr
OUT OF A CLOUD
(in memory of Thomas Merton) *America*, December 13, 1969

"Merton's letters offer a rich and nuanced portrait of the monk whose life and writings spoke so eloquently to his contemporaries and continue to speak to readers today.... Merton's one and only way of reaching his friends, was, normally through his writings.... He loved people and craved human contact. His letters helped to fill that need and... created an extraordinary record of Merton's life and the development of his thought.... Exchanging letters make it possible for him to keep in touch with people who were important to him.... They reveal aspects of his character and thought that do not appear... with the same... personal touch, in his published works."

*Thomas Merton: A Life in Letters*
William H. Shannon and Christine M. Bochen

"Any reader of his journals and letters will quickly realize that Merton was no stranger to insecurity, nor was he ever tempted to send himself any fan letters. Like us, he was a product of the modern world with all its attractions and distractions. But in the end, by an amazing working of grace, he was able to maintain his search for true wisdom. He attracts us because he is more than a gifted theologian and brilliant writer. He is a brother in Christ who was — and through his writings still is — able to show us the way."

*Living With Wisdom: A Life of Thomas Merton*
Jim Forest

"...Friendship is the first and most important thing, and is the true cement of the Church built by Christ...."

Thomas Merton

# ACKNOWLEDGMENTS

I would like to express my thanks to the following individuals – in no particular order – for their assistance and encouragement in helping to bring this story to life:

Paul M. Pearson, Carol Thresher, SDS, Mark C. Meade, Tommie O'Callaghan, Steve Avella, Paul Portland, SDS, Karlyn Cauley, SDS, James Rieden, SDS, Roger Nelson, SDS, John Barry Stutt, Katie Freund, Dan Pekarske, SDS, Paul Portland, SDS, Margaret and Anthony Scola, John Yockey, Michael Hoffmann, SDS, Edward Havlovic, SDS, Susan Staff, SDS, Patrick Hart, OCSO, Bonnie Thurston, Barry McCabe, Paul E. Dinter, Marvin Kluesner, SDS, the Merton Legacy Trust: Peggy L. Fox, Anne H. McCormick and Mary R. Somerville; Richard Hite, Diocese of St. Cloud, Hugh Birdsall, SDS, Dennis Frank, St. Bonaventure University, David Gentry-Akin, Thomas Novak, SDS, Patrick O'Connell, Columbia University, Patrick Lawlor, Jennifer B. Lee, Maureen Coughlin, SC, Maureen Daugherty, SC, David Miros, the Polish Dominican Fathers at Notre Dame Parish, New York City; Robert Hamm, Edmund Lane, SSP, John Eudes Bamberger, OCSO, Michael J. Drury, Susanna Kendall, Donald Grayston, Marcia Kelly, Roberto Bonazzi, College of Notre Dame of Maryland, St. Mary's Seminary and College, Baltimore, Thomas Raszewski, Patricia Brown, the University of Scranton, Mark Scott, OCSO, Robert Boley, O.Carm., Joseph Delaney, Keith J. Egan, Neal Panzarella, Maryann Engelhardt, SDS, Liturgical Press, Beverly Heitke, SDS, Virginia Erickson, Deborah Gephardt and Marilyn Banach.

I am especially honored by and indebted to Dr. Paul M. Pearson, Director and Archivist of the Thomas Merton Center at Bellarmine University in Louisville, Kentucky for his Foreword. He has been a valuable resource both for his encouragement and support from the first time I mentioned this project to him. He has been extremely generous with his time and advice and always patient in answering questions, locating materials and providing suggestions. A renowned Merton scholar, author and lecturer in his own right, he is always ready to assist both experts and beginners in Merton research with his encyclopedic knowledge of the vast field of Merton studies which he has mastered more than anyone else I know. The Merton Center at Bellarmine University and Merton scholars are blessed in having access to this talented and dedicated scholar who embodies the very best of Merton's own intellectual qualities and warm, human approachability.

The Sisters of the Divine Savior in the person of Sister Aquin Gilles, archivist of the US Province and former Provincial (1959-1965) were fully supportive of the recounting of this story of one of their own. Sr. Aquin was Thérèse's Superior in Milwaukee for several years and served for twenty-five years in various capacities on the staff of her congregational headquarters in Rome. Sister Aquin was a knowledgeable and professional first-class historian and guide in supplying crucial information, correcting errors and offering valuable suggestions. She died on Holy Saturday evening, April 23, 2011 and so did not live to see this book in print. She read several drafts along the way, however, and was extremely instrumental in helping shape a more accurate and coherent account. She is missed by many people. The Salvatorian Sisters have made this project both possible and pleasurable by opening their archives to me and providing me with permission to include many of the photographs that appear in this book and some documents through the generous assistance of Sister Aquin's co-worker, Susan Staff, SDS. Sister Carol Thresher's Afterword nicely puts into context Thérèse's membership in the Congregation at a particular historical period and her living out of the timeless Salvatorian charism with her own unique personality. I am grateful to Sister Carol for her valuable contribution to this effort and for her visionary leadership of the Congregation of the Sisters of the Divine Savior today.

*C. Robert Nugent, SDS*
The Nativity of the Blessed Virgin Mary
September 8, 2011

COPYRIGHTED MATERIAL

Quotations from previously unpublished letters by Thomas Merton, Copyright © 2012 by the Trustees of the Merton Legacy Trust; used by permission of the Trustees.

Excerpts from *The Road to Joy: Letters to New and Old Friends* by Thomas Merton, selected and edited by Robert E. Daggy. Copyright © 1989 by the Merton Legacy Trust. Reprinted by permission of Farrar, Straus and Giroux, LLC.

Letters of Thérèse Lentfoehr quoted with the permission of Paul Dinter.

Letters from the Thomas Merton Papers, Rare Book and Manuscript Library, Columbia University quoted with permission of Columbia University Library.

Documents and photographs of Thérèse Lentfoehr used with permission of the Congregation of the Sisters of the Divine Savior, USA Province Archives.

Quotations from the previously unpublished letters of James Laughlin, Copyright © 2010 by the Trustees of the New Directions Ownership Trust, used with by permission of Daniel Javitch and Peggy L. Fox, Literary Executors and Trustees.

Quotation from Robert Lax letter used with permission from the Robert Lax Literary Trust.

Photographs of Thomas Merton used with permission of the Merton Legacy Trust and the Thomas Merton Center at Bellarmine University.

Photograph of Fr. Barry Griffin used with permission of the Society of the Divine Savior, USA Province Archives.

Photograph of Thérèse Lentfoehr with permission of Wicks Photo Center, Racine, WI.

Photograph of Thérèse Lentfoehr with permission of Ray Toburen.

Photograph of Thérèse Lentfoehr with permission of Karlyn Cauley, SDS.

Photograph of Merton hermitage with permission of Deborah Gephardt.

# PREFACE

Over the years readers of the ever-growing library of books by and about Thomas Merton have become aware of innumerable aspects of his life and thought. Merton's friendships, especially his lifelong ones with figures such as Bob Lax, Ed Rice, Ad Reinhardt, Dan Walsh, Robert Giroux, James Laughlin and others have been well documented not just in the many biographies of Merton but in dedicated studies including works such as *Merton and Friends: A Joint Biography of Thomas Merton, Robert Lax and Edward Rice* by James Harford, and in volumes of their letters such as *When Prophecy Had a Voice: The Letters of Thomas Merton and Robert Lax*, *Thomas Merton and James Laughlin: Selected Letters* and, hopefully soon to appear, Merton's correspondence with Robert Giroux. Clearly missing from this list though are Merton's friendships with women. Some attention has been given to some of those relationships from the sixties such as Mary Luke Tobin, Rosemary Radford Ruether and, of course, the nurse he fell in love with in 1966. But his lifelong friendships with women have been overlooked thus far, and I think in particular of his friendships with women such as Naomi Burton and the subject of this volume, Sr. Thérèse Lentfoehr. So this book marks the first step in reversing this trend. As with his Columbia friends his relationships with Naomi Burton and Thérèse Lentfoehr date back to the same period and, again like his Columbia friends, continue, relatively unbroken to his final days, writing to both Naomi Burton and Thérèse Lentfoehr in the final months of his life.

Merton's contact with Naomi Burton began in either 1939 or

1940 when he appeared in her office at the Curtis Brown Literary Agency seeking a publisher for his early pre-monastic novels, in particular *The Labyrinth*. At this time Burton was a fairly green junior at Curtis Brown, fresh off the boat from England. Burton recalls she sent the typescript of *The Labyrinth* to over a dozen publishing houses all of which would reject it, though not unfavorably. Editors saw Merton's talent and, as Stanley P. Young, a senior editor at Harcourt Brace would write to him, "our interest in you is sufficiently galvanized by your manuscript to make us want to see anything you may do… we don't feel this is the one to launch you with, but let me hear from you." After a brief gap during Merton's early years in the monastery his contact with Naomi Burton resumed once again when on October 21, 1946 Merton sent her the manuscript that would not just launch his literary career but make him a household name, *The Seven Storey Mountain*.

The beginnings of Merton's correspondence with Thérèse Lentfoehr are not quite so clear and, at times, Thérèse would contradict herself as to who had initiated the correspondence. Nevertheless, that aside, it appears to begin after either Merton had seen poems by Lentfoehr in *Spirit* or she had seen one of his poems, most likely "Fable for a War" which was published by *The New York Times* in June 1939. However, contact was made in approximately 1939, and in one interview Lentfoehr recalls that they exchanged "a few notes, postcards or something like that" though adding that she never kept any of those early exchanges. As with Naomi Burton this correspondence would cease during Merton's early years at Gethsemani commencing once again when Lentfoehr wrote to Merton in 1948 to take issue with a review he had written of her Marian compilation, *I Sing of a Maiden*. From Merton's response to that letter onwards she would keep every letter Merton sent her, indeed every scrap and, like Burton, would correspond with him right up until 1968 when he would write his final missive to her, a postcard from India on November 21, 1968.

Thérèse would, once their correspondence resumed, become

*Preface*

one of Merton's most avid collectors, and one with access to the very spring that regularly flowed from Merton to her bearing priceless treasures for her collection. Although Merton at times appeared dismissive of her fervor in collecting, as in the development of other collections that emerged from the forties onwards, he cooperated in their growth and development. At the end of the day Merton was as keen as Thérèse to ensure the preservation of his work, as he writes in his journal, "whole-heartedly because I imagine it is for real. That I will last. That I will be a person studied and commented on." Indeed, although Merton says a number of times that he destroyed certain materials, for example his pre-monastic novels before his entry to Gethsemani, a surprising number of them have been preserved. Or again, though recording in his journal his burning of letters from his nurse, he still made sure it was recorded and saved in the pages of his personal journals, in the poems and letters he entrusted to James Laughlin and even in his correspondence with Thérèse, no doubt expecting her, as was her wont, to preserve every scrap he sent her. However, in overly protective mode, she felt, as she records in 1966, the necessity to destroy certain letters Merton sent her that year.

Thomas Merton's friendship with Thérèse Lentfoehr was quite different from that with his other lifelong friends. Although Lentfoehr resumed her correspondence with Merton in 1948 by taking him to task for his review, she very quickly became one of his foremost admirers and would never really criticize him again, whether in reviews of his books, or in her letters to him that have survived, or in her talks and articles about him. Their correspondence always maintained a formality that was rare in Merton's correspondence where, with most correspondents, he would quickly move from the formal Father Thomas Merton (or Louis) to Tom Merton, or quite often, just Tom. Not so with Thérèse. His letters to her were always addressed to "Sister Thérèse" and nearly always, with just a few exceptions in 1968, signed "f. m. Louis"; similarly her letters to him were equally formal.

So what was the nature of their relationship? William H. Shannon has suggested that Merton's relationship with Naomi Burton was at times like that of a brother towards a sister, or as a son to his mother even, Shannon suggests, valuing the "scoldings" she sometimes gave him. However, in reading Merton's correspondence with Thérèse Lentfoehr, neither sister nor mother comes to mind. Rather, I am more reminded of correspondence with an old-fashioned and prim maiden aunt whose life revolves around her only nephew — concerned about each other but at a certain distance; collecting every minute scrap of information about her famous nephew to be shared with, indeed shown off to, anyone interested. Their correspondence certainly lacks both the chumminess that existed with his Columbia friends and the honesty that could scold him and take him to task evident in his correspondence with Naomi Burton or Rosemary Radford Ruether.

We are indebted to Robert Nugent for his careful telling of the lifelong friendship of Thomas Merton and Thérèse Lentfoehr, in particular his careful reconstruction of their story based solely on Merton's letters to Lentfoehr for the years that he didn't keep her letters to him. *Thomas Merton and Thérèse Lentfoehr: The Story of a Friendship* provides the reader with an important aspect of Thomas Merton's life that has, for far too long, been overlooked, and is certainly therefore a keystone in the ever-growing Merton Library.

> Paul M. Pearson, Ph.D.
> Director and Archivist
> The Thomas Merton Center
> Bellarmine University
> Louisville, Kentucky

INTRODUCTION

# LISTENING IN

On November 9, 1981, shortly after the death of Sister Thérèse Lentfoehr, SDS, her close friend and former Salvatorian Sister, Kathryn Freund, wrote to Sister Mary Paul Rouse, the Provincial of the Sisters of the Divine Savior: "I am sure someone will want to do a book on her relationship to Merton... in her own right she was such a survivalist and such a good poet (not to mention her idiosyncrasies), that I feel sure someone will crawl out from somewhere and want to see all her stuff and write about her alone too."[1] After many years thinking about a book on Thérèse's friendship with Merton, I have finally decided to "crawl out" and do it! James Laughlin, Merton's publisher for many years at New Directions, who often consulted Thérèse about publishing Merton's poetry after his death, told Thérèse that she was "certainly as close to Tom as anybody in this world."[2] According to her own testimony, she "had a beautiful sharing" in the aspects of Merton's spiritual living.[3]

This book, however, is not about Sister Thérèse Lentfoehr alone. Perhaps someone else will take up that particular project one day. While her personality was very different from Merton's, her literary career as a poet was very much related to his. She will be mostly remembered, however, because of her friendship with "Fr. Louis." New Directions published all of Merton's poetry and Thérèse's own book analyzing his work, but was not interested in her own papers. Her papers are now part of the Merton Collection at Columbia University, although Marquette University offered to house her own papers in their collection. The question of whether her importance as a literary figure stems from her own accomplishments (which were impressive in their own right) or from her relationship with Merton, I leave to the reader to determine. I am sure she would not contest the conclusion that her significance as the subject of a book is intimately tied to her friendship with Merton, and would be delighted to bask in Merton's sun now as she did from the late forties to her death in 1981 and even beyond.

This book is also about Thomas Merton. As prominent Merton authorities William Shannon and Christian Bochen have pointed out, "Merton's letters to particular individuals, especially those with whom he corresponded often and with some regularity, reveal something of his own character and the special regard he held for his correspondents as evidenced in tone and, oftentimes, in humor as well. Who Merton was in himself and in relationships comes through best in sustained correspondences."[4] Among his hundreds of correspondents, Merton wrote to no one more frequently and with more regularity than Thérèse Lentfoehr. He was the one who generally initiated his own letter writing with well-known correspondents in the literary, political, ecclesiastical and intellectual fields and they responded: "He had a realistic notion of his reputation: it was altogether sufficient to ensure a good possibility that persons he invited to correspond would welcome the relation."[5]

This was not the case, however, with Lentfoehr: she was the one who initiated correspondence with him long before his reputation as an influential author and intellectual had developed and spread among a vast variety of writers, thinkers, activists, and influential people in church and society. According to Jim Forest, "Merton began opening more and more lines of contact and dialogue with people beyond the monastery" after his awakening experience in Louisville at the corner of Fourth and Walnut in 1958. He had been corresponding with Thérèse, however, on a regular basis ten years before this event. He had great respect and care for her as the tone and content of his correspondence indicates, including his way of chiding her with gentle humor. Even his occasional harshness and pleading are evidence of the value he placed on their friendship.

I am not a poet nor have I read all of Thérèse's published poetry. Therefore, I am not in a position to judge the quality of her oeuvre. From her own publications, teaching and lectures, however, I think it safe to say that she was among a recognized and acclaimed group of Catholic poets of a certain historical period and literary taste. One reviewer said of her: "Sister Thérèse has already taken her place beside Sister Madeleva among the foremost of convent poets, which is not to say that her reputation is bounded by the convent wall nor restricted to the pious if unimposing literary world vaguely defined by the term 'Catholic.' Her talent isn't measured by her theme but by her achievement; and this achievement, though not in any way startling, is still real and undeniably poetic."[6] Another was more fulsome: "Sister Thérèse is not, as the literary world judges, a great poet. She has, however, certain unusual gifts and talents that have caused her to make a strong impact on this modern world.... In certain respects she is the outstanding nun-poet — even the outstanding woman-poet of our century — not even excepting the near-great Sister Madeleva, C.S.C."[7]

It was a common interest in poetry that sustained and nourished her relationship with Merton. Yet she consistently gave much more prominence to his poetry and writings than to her own. It was his poetry that people came to hear her read. It was her perspectives on his life and work that attracted her audiences and friends. It was her friendship and experiences with him that they wanted to hear about; and she was more than happy to meet their expectations. She once described herself as a "nationally known expert on the works of the Trappist writer Thomas Merton, especially his poetry, for it was through that mutual interest that we first came to know each other some thirty years ago."[8]

My own personal interest in her life and work is connected to my acquaintance with Merton's *Seeds of Contemplation* that I first discovered in 1955 when I entered St. Charles Borromeo Seminary in Philadelphia. I first visited Gethsemani and Merton's grave when in Louisville visiting long-time friends from my first parish in Pennsylvania. Since then I have visited the monastery several times and in the early eighties had the rare privilege of being permitted to make a five-day retreat in his hermitage. While studying in Belgium from 1983-1984, I met Marilyn McTague in the Netherlands, a Catholic woman in the New York publishing world who later gave me a signed copy of Merton's *Original Child Bomb*. In researching this book I was given what I was told was Merton's brown, ceramic two-handled mug with the coat of arms of the Abbey imprinted on the front — identical with those used by all the monks at Gethsemani in his time.

It was through his writings and a growing interest in his life and relationships that many others and I first heard the name Thérèse Lentfoehr. His personal friends and Merton scholars in the "inner circle" during his lifetime certainly were aware of her long friendship with Merton more than the general reading public. Although she occupied "a very special position in the Merton family," most of them were probably not familiar with her distinct accomplishments as a published poet in her own right.[9] Merton, however, related to her as an artist and colleague — not just as one of the thousands of "fans" he accumulated over the years. His critique of her work was both sensitively offered and generously received. Merton was not, however, her only mentor. She had developed numerous personal contacts with other writers and poets including some noteworthy and recognizable names in the Catholic literary world of the time such as the poets Jessica Powers, Marianne Moore, Daniel Berrigan, John Ciardi, John L'Heureux, Sister Madeleva and literary figures like J.F. Powers, Jacques Maritain, Evelyn Waugh, Jim Forest and Naomi Burton.

Robert E. Daggy, who initially edited their correspondence and published some of it, totally from Merton's side, described her in a brief memoir as "soft spoken with eyes averted, reserved, even reticent, each word precise and carefully chosen. Yet she always came

*Introduction*

alive as she talked about Merton and, when she read his poetry and talked about it, her eyes flicked straight forward, the voice became firm, the figure, if possible, grew more erect and straighter, and a vibrancy came over her which captured attention."[10] Thérèse was more interested in capturing attention for Merton than for herself. Roy Larson, a columnist from the *Chicago Sun-Times*, met Thérèse in 1979 at a Common Ground gathering focused on Merton's poetry: "For me, the spirit of Merton was embodied... by Sister Thérèse Lentfoehr... the soft-spoken nun would be the despair of talk-show producers. When asked a question, she took long pauses until she found in the center of her being the thoughts she eventually expressed with her 'accurate tongue'... When I observed how carefully she listened and how thoughtfully she spoke, I thought she evoked what Merton once described as 'the grace-inspired desire for newness of life.'"[11]

Readers will sense Merton's discomfort with her idolization of him that included the most extravagant praise and to a certain obsession about collecting every little scrap of his writings. Yet despite his frustration, he decided to maintain and continue their relationship and, in his own way, fed her appetite for all things Merton by writing to her regularly and sending her more materials than anyone else in his personal or professional life. She, in turn, provided invaluable services for him, not only in her willingness to fulfill any formal request or even mere suggestion, but also by serving as his first and earliest unofficial archivist. He realized that his writings would be of interest and value in the future, though he sometimes down-played the idea. Nevertheless, as years went by he carefully preserved everything he wrote, though much of it he dispersed to various individuals and institutions. In Thérèse, however, he found someone who would not only preserve his materials meticulously, but also respect and protect his privacy.

While the relationship was never a "tit for tat" kind of affair, over the years each was recompensed in different ways for their gifts to one another — for Merton, relics, secretarial services, publicity and constant affirmation; and for Thérèse, a constant stream of "Mertoniana," his personal letters to her and the feeling that she had a very special relationship with Thomas Merton enjoyed by none other. This, undoubtedly, was her greatest treasure. Daggy describes their kind of friendship as "rare in our times, an almost atavistic kind of relationship. It was a friendship based on mutual interest expressed through letters, a friendship which did not need and which did not flourish on the strokes and assurances of personal contact."[12]

It is my hope that readers will enjoy "listening in" on their conversations, will gain some insight into a more informal side of Merton and will meet and come to know one of his closest friends, who, in my estimation, has never received the due recognition for the part she played in his life and work. His friendship with her was only one minor part of his multi-faceted life and I agree wholeheartedly with Christine Bochen: "The best work on Merton has been characterized by humility and a sense of limits of the ability of any one biographer, scholar, interpreter or reader of Merton to capture the *whole* Merton."[13]

THOMAS MERTON & THÉRÈSE LENTFOEHR

# 1

## THÉRÈSE MAE LENTFOEHR
### 1902-1981

Most readers will already be familiar with the general outlines of the life and literary work of Thomas Merton. Only a small number, however, will have any awareness of the person and career of Thérèse Lentfoehr and her twenty-year friendship with Merton carried on solely through voluminous correspondence and two personal meetings. While this book might be of some interest to Merton scholars, it is directed primarily to the many Merton aficionados who might enjoy seeing one more side of the multi-layered personality of the monk whose impact on the spiritual lives of countless people of all and no religious faiths continues to grow since his death in 1968.

Their friendship, which developed and matured over the years, was not always as idyllic as that portrayed by Robert Daggy in the only background article on Thérèse cited in the author's Introduction. One Merton scholar feels that Merton might have taken advantage of the relationship, humoring her so that she would continue typing his manuscripts, sending him information he could not otherwise obtain and providing constant adulation and ego stroking that, while making him uncomfortable, was not sufficient for him to discontinue the correspondence or break off the friendship. Readers will have to judge for themselves whether this is an accurate evaluation. Obviously his friendship with her was not of the same relaxed quality of his interactions with the "old boys" from

Columbia days; but that is to be expected. While his friendship with her might be called "intimate," it did not have the same history of the give and take associated with lifelong friends like Bob Lax, Ad Reinhardt, James Laughlin, Ed Rice, Bob Giroux, Dan Walsh or Sy Freedgood. Thérèse, after all, was a woman, a nun, and a shy person by nature to begin with and not given to strong expressions of emotions in her professional and personal relationships. She treated him from the very beginning with a deep sense of reverence and respect, if not idolization. Merton, over the years, grew from relating to her initially as "the good little nun" to an adult, professional peer in her own right.

Her spontaneous and rather unorthodox personal encounter with Merton at Gethsemani in 1951, her persistence in importuning a librarian at St. Bonaventure College for Merton journals and photographs and other assertive behavior, are proof that when the cause involved advocacy on his behalf, she could pursue her goals with tenacious determination and practiced cleverness. If Merton, consciously or unconsciously, humored her to benefit from her undaunted devotion and valuable assistance, then Thérèse, in turn, reaped other benefits for herself from their long association. Like most individuals with artistic gifts, she had a need to feel "special," even "important." And while she might have attained that status from her own writing talents and her professional teaching and lecturing career, it was primarily from her relationship with Merton and the aura it carried in certain Church and literary circles that she became a recognizable name and sought-after speaker. Thérèse and Merton benefited from the friendship on both a personal and professional level. To know her, then, is to gain some insight into another facet of Thomas Merton through the dynamics of his friendship with this "would-be sister" for twenty years.

Her full baptismal name was Florence Mae Brooks Lentfoehr and she grew up in a strong Catholic family. She was born on July 18, 1902 in Oconto Falls, Wisconsin and named after her mother whose maiden name was Brooks. Thérèse's father was George whom she described in her dedication of a poem to his memory as a person who "for a lifetime span busied with brush and pigment disciplined neutral surfaces to beauty's clarity and proportion."[14] This might lead one to believe he was a painter like Merton's father; but he was actually a painting contractor. She had two sisters, Veronica and Beatrice. Her own twin sister, Mae Florence, died at birth. A twin of her sister Beatrice also died as an infant. There were four brothers: Gordon, Henry and twins, Claude and Clyde. It was Gordon who later became a priest of the Society of the Divine Savior.

Her mother was an artist and, as a child, Thérèse spent many hours in the studio where her mother's canvases provided inspiration for her early attempts at poetry: "As for my own writing, it was my mother, an artist and educator, who fostered in me a love for the 'sister-arts' of music and poetry. I began writing poems as a child, moved by nature scenes upon my mother's canvases. She encouraged me, and having set me at the piano at the age of six, planned that I later go on to study under her uncle, the American composer George Whitfield Chadwick, who was director of the New England Conservatory of Music. Her early death changed all this, but I continued writing poems, and when my first submission was accepted by Michael Williams at *Commonweal*, and an early sonnet by H. Mencken for the *American Mercury*, I was greatly encouraged."[15] In a poem entitled "Spirit of Place," she reminisces: "And I think of you my mother (who has long gone into the pristine morning) as you sat at your easels while I, playing beneath them snatched the bright tubes of gamboge and vermilion, leaving your rug a miniature Pollock."[16] Ever since she was a small child she had wanted to be a concert pianist: "I was really trained to be a musician and studied piano, organ and violin. However, as a small child my sole desire was to become an artist, like my mother."[17] When she started to express herself, however, she found her voice in poetry. When she was eight years old she wrote verse in which she once described a Thanksgiving turkey as "fat as fat can be."[18] Her father wanted to send it to a local newspaper, but her mother, who wanted to encourage but not to push her, was against it. As a child she was fond of swimming, boating, skating and other outdoor sports and also interested in amateur dramatics.

She was educated in schools in Webeno, Gilette and Green Bay, Wisconsin and studied at the Wisconsin Conservatory of Music before entering the Congregation of the Sisters of the Divine Savior in Milwaukee on August 21, 1933. Known as Salvatorians, the Congregation is an international apostolic Religious Order founded in Rome in 1888 by John Baptist Jordan (Venerable Francis Mary of the Cross). Theresa von Wullenweber (Blessed Mother Mary of the Apostles) worked with Jordan in founding the Salvatorian Sisters who first arrived in the United States in 1895 as nursing Sisters in the city of Milwaukee. Currently there are about 1,200 professed Sisters in some 29 countries worldwide.

After completing a candidature period, she was invested with the habit of the Congregation on July 14, 1924 and given the name "Thérèse." She then began the Order's canonical novitiate period of one year. She professed first vows on July 15, 1925 for one year, and made her perpetual profession as a Salvatorian Sister on July 15, 1931, thus living her life as a member of the Congregation for 56 years. Her patron was St. Thérèse of Lisieux and her name day was October 3rd, the feast of "The Little Flower." In later years she sometimes signed her name "Sister M. Thérèse," including "M" for Mary as the Sisters were allowed to do if they so chose. In the late 1930's she signed her published poems "Sister M. Thérèse, SOR.D.S.," for the Latin, "Sisters of the Divine Savior." [Merton's name in religious life also included "Mary" as was the Trappist custom.]

In 1926 she taught music and poetry to the candidates and young Sisters at the Motherhouse of the Sisters of the Divine Savior at 35th and Center Streets, and studied at the St. Joseph Conservatory (presently Alverno College) in Milwaukee graduating in 1926. She once spoke of the influence of music on her poetry: "I have always found myself more comfortable in some kind of form, no matter how flexible. Much of my later writing has been in 'syllabics' in which

I create my own pattern, and when writing in free verse I seem to hear and follow some inner cadence."[19]

In 1933, she earned a B.A. in philosophy *magna cum laude* and an M.A. in English in 1938 from Marquette University. In 1946 she returned to Marquette to lecture in English until 1951. By 1937 she was a member of the faculty of the Congregation's Motherhouse in Milwaukee and taught composition and rhetoric. She had a room in the section of the building that housed the candidates, although she was not involved in their formation. Thérèse was highly regarded by Mother Ottilia Haeckel who had been elected Provincial of the American Province in 1935. Haeckel thought Thérèse was an exceptional musician and authorized her to select the books and music for the community. While at Marquette she had written a poem for an English class, "Interval," that the teacher considered so good he urged her to submit it to *The American Mercury* magazine. The editor, H.L. Mencken, accepted it for publication and wrote her a complimentary note. Later in life her poems were published in such prestigious publications as *The New Yorker, The New York Times, New York Herald Tribune, America, Commonweal, Catholic World, Saturday Review of Literature,* the *American Benedictine Review* and the *Anglican Theological Review*. Her work is also included in an updated edition of Joyce Kilmer's *Anthology of Catholic Poets* (James Edward Tobin, ed.). She was a regular reviewer of books on poetry for the *Milwaukee Journal*. She continued to write and publish poems, reviews and essays in a variety of Catholic and secular journals all her life. In 1944 she was asked to teach a class in poetry at St. Clare College that later became Cardinal Stritch University in Milwaukee.

Her first of five published volumes of poetry, *Now There is Beauty* (Macmillan, 1940), grew out of her master thesis of 35 unpublished poems and was dedicated to her mother "who with her brush on canvas first showed me the beauty God had made."[20] In March 1940 the book was included in a book survey published by the Cardinal's Literary Committee of the Archdiocese of New York.

Other books followed: *Give Joan a Sword* (Macmillan, 1944), dedicated to her brother and inspired by a trip to Rome with a preface by Jacques Maritain; *I Sing of a Maiden* (Macmillan, 1947); *Moment in Ostia* (Doubleday, 1959), dedicated to her brother Gordon (Fr. Theophane), who had entered the Society of the Divine Savior in 1933.

Reviews of her books of poetry were generally favorable, but not always without criticism. Reviewing her *Give Joan a Sword* in *Spirit*, Kevin Sullivan echoes Merton's criticism when he says: "Almost all the good things in this volume are busheled and casked in the front. Perhaps this is because here is more of the nun and less of the poet in the later poems — to be explained (hastily) by the increasing proportion of religious and spiritual themes... the latter verses... do not measure up to the first part of the volume...."[21]

William Slavick says that in the 1940's and 1950's Catholic poetry was identified with a small group of nuns like Sister Madeleva and Sister Thérèse [and Jessica Powers, also], but that they were later overshadowed by the poets John Frederick Nims, John Logan and Robert Lowell. As for her poetry: "Sentimentality slides along the pages of Sr. Thérèse's first two volumes, but reviewers of her final volume praise her intellectual reach, enlarged vision, wider lyrical range, the richness of her allusions, and her command of the craft."[22]

It was her book of poetry, *I Sing of a Maiden*, which first brought her to the attention of Thomas Merton in 1948, though their initial and brief first contact had occurred much earlier. From 1951 to 1952 she lectured in English at Divine Savior College, Milwaukee; and in 1952, she was assigned to live in a convent of Salvatorian Sisters in Wausau, Wisconsin attached to St. Mary's Hospital run by the Order. Ostensibly, the transfer was an extended furlough for rest from a rigorous teaching schedule. There is no doubt that at least she was a very busy woman in 1949 even long before her days of Merton fame as one reviewer recounts: "Sister Thérèse is a teacher at Marquette University in Milwaukee.... She is also called upon almost constantly to lecture about poetry, or more rarely and delightfully, to present a recital of her own work she responds with a much more than ordinary gi ing, as she does, with a humble recognition of t patterning of God in every human soul, that into is given a *word*, and that 'each created soul reflects in its own induplicable way some fact of the beauty of God' with 'its own unique preciousness, its own revelation of God' to others. And so, with a prideless dignity she shares her *word* with all who seek."[23]

It was in northern Wisconsin that she honed her appreciation of nature and animals. One sister recalls that she and another nun were breaking branches off a tree for decorating the convent when Thérèse spotted them from her room in the north wing of the hospital. Opening the window, she informed they there were destroying the tree and damaging the birds and went immediately to the superior and informed her of their actions.

By this time she had been in contact with Merton since 1948 and was writing about him in various journals while amassing the foundation for her collection of Mertoniana. It was during her time in the woods of northern Wisconsin that she developed her love for nature and affection for small animals evident in so many of her poems and letters to Merton. Many people remember her affection for animals including a pet rabbit. One of her Salvatorian students from Mount Saint Paul in Waukesha, Wisconsin, occasionally took care of the rabbit she had named "Gerard" after the convert Jesuit poet Gerard Manley Hopkins. He recalls how surprised she was when the rabbit gave birth to a litter of bunnies and realized that a more appropriate name for the rabbit would have been "Geraldine."

In 1965, she was reassigned by a new Provincial to the Sisters' headquarters in Milwaukee, having been offered a teaching position at Mount St. Paul College, operated by the Salvatorian Fathers and Brothers in Waukesha, Wisconsin. From 1965 to 1969 she commuted to the suburban college from her Milwaukee residence. In 1969, she was given permission from the Generalate (governing body) of the Sisters' Congregation in Rome to live, as a matter of onvenience, in a private residence in Waukesha and closer to the college. Mount St. Paul closed in 1971 and merged with Dominican College in Racine, Wisconsin, and she moved there as an associate professor of English and poet-in-residence until 1974. In 1973 the Dominican College became the College of Racine, but closed just a year later in June 1974. The permission to reside in Racine, where she found the living situation conducive to her work of tutoring, writing and lecturing on Merton, was renewed. Fr. Barry McCabe, SDS, a Salvatorian priest, was her close friend and advisor. He had been a teacher, counselor and administrator at Mount St. Paul College from 1968 to 1970 when Thérèse taught there and, later, the Vice-President and Dean of the College of Racine, where she also taught. McCabe and Jean Blais, SDS, another Salvatorian priest, had been the former occupants of the Racine apartment she called her "hermitage." She had visited the apartment previously and liked it because she could be in touch with nature through the large sliding glass patio doors and still feel it was private and secluded. Visitors remember her parakeets ("Sunshine" and "April") that had free run of the apartment and a cat ("Casper"). After one of her favorite pet birds died, she had it stuffed and kept it at the apartment for several years.

Marilyn Banach was only fourteen in the late seventies when she visited her grandparents' apartment in Racine during summer vacations. They lived next to Thérèse on the ground floor level and she remembers meeting her when Thérèse was invited over to share an evening of "delightful conversations" and drinks with her neighbors. At the time she was writing her book on Merton and needed peace and quiet. Her neighbors often noticed that Thérèse's lights were on all hours of the day and night. Thérèse spoke of Merton as her "pen-pal" and regaled them with stories about him. Marilyn remembers that Thérèse would bloom and radiate when she spoke of Merton and thought at times she might even levitate! Marilyn's intellectual father, whose religious background was Catholic and Church of the Nazarene, knew of the Trappists and Merton, but the

*Thérèse Mae Lentfoehr*

young teenager wanted to hear about her relationship with Merton directly from Thérèse. Their conversations roamed over topics from theology and philosophy to literature "on that lovely patio of your mother's apartment" as Thérèse mentioned when inscribing a copy of her book to her Racine neighbors.

Between 1962 and 1968 she participated in some of the annual writers' conferences at Georgetown University and wrote a poem about her experience there called "Poet at Georgetown" published in the *Catholic Worker* in December 1964. During the Racine period after Merton's death she continued with Merton poetry readings and lectures in different venues. She also participated in various Merton academic commemorations including one on the 10th anniversary of his death in 1978 and a Merton Symposium at the Fordham Lincoln Center campus in New York City on March 30th, 1970, where she read his poetry and exhibited some of her vast collection of Merton materials. During her life, she was a guest lecturer in many institutions of higher learning, including Cardinal Stritch College in Milwaukee where in 1973 she spoke on Merton at a meeting of Wisconsin Writers. As late as September 25, 1980, twelve years after Merton's death, she traveled to the Holiday City Convention Center in Louisville for a Maritain-Merton Symposium moderated by Dan Berrigan. She contributed a paper on "Thomas Merton: Poet of the 'Inner Experience'" and gave a sampling of Merton's Zen-mystical poems. After the program, some of the participants were taken to the Abbey at Gethsemani for a visit to Merton's grave and hermitage. (A photograph of this event where she and Bob Lax gave poetry readings on the porch of the hermitage is included in this book.) It was at this event that she met Michael Mott with whom she had been corresponding about the official Merton biography. Apparently, she had written several letters before hearing from Mott, but when he finally wrote in July 1980, he said that what she had written in her letters had been most helpful. He was looking forward to meeting her in Louisville and the chance to talk with the possibility of planning a later visit.

She died on October 31, 1981 at St. Mary's Medical Center in Racine after a three-week illness, according to the official obituary, from complications due to the flu. Kathryn and Nick Freund, close friends of Thérèse for many years, for whom she had written "Song for a Marriage" on their wedding day (in the Appendix), had discovered her one day collapsed in her apartment. They think she might also have suffered a stroke either in her apartment or at the hospital, which contributed to her death. Robert Lax, a close friend of Merton, had mentioned "Sister Thérèse's stroke" in an October 19, 1981 letter to a friend. Apparently, she had a number of falls including one at the September symposium in Louisville in 1980, and often complained of her bursitis. A niece later commented that Thérèse was too busy even to attend her own sister's birthday party: "Her calendar and conversations with me made me feel that there was urgency about finishing the collection — that perhaps she felt she was coming down with something, or that the end would be sooner than she wanted to believe."[24]

She lay in state at the Divine Savior Community House, 4311 N. 100th St., Milwaukee, on Tuesday, November 3rd with a memorial service for family and friends at 7:30 that evening. A Mass of the Resurrection was celebrated by Fr. Thomas Novak, SDS on November 4th at 10:00 a.m. at Mother of Good Counsel parish on Lisbon Avenue, a parish staffed by the Salvatorian Fathers and Brothers. Fr. Andre Papineau, noted Salvatorian author and homiletics professor at Sacred Heart School of Theology, Hales Corners, Wisconsin, preached the eulogy. She was interred in Holy Cross Cemetery, Milwaukee.

At her funeral Mass one of her former teachers at Marquette, Dr. Victor Hamm, paid tribute: "Our Sister Thérèse has flown away, back to the God whose praises she sang like a bird among her roomful of birds.... All her poems, published in volumes slender and delicate like herself and like her verses, take wing and soar... but finally we must treasure the memory of Sister Thérèse as a handmaid of the Lord who remains with us in the presence of her own lovely poems.

## Thérèse Mae Lentfoehr

Let me read a few verses which her friend Merton — 'Father Louis' in religion — wrote in the language of the country of his birth:

> 'Je suis un oiseau
> Enchanté
> Amour que Dieu
> A inventé.'

Why are we all afraid of love? Why should we who are greater than grains, / Fear to fall in the ground and die?' Her words have ceased. The rest is silence. *Requiescat in pace, soror amata nostra.*"[25] He described her as one of a small group of people "who wrote verses and read them at meetings once a month, a shy little lady garbed in the habit of the Sisters of the Divine Savior. She listened to what most of that group read, rather hoping it would pass for poetry, without showing any sign of boredom or annoyance. That was more than courtesy I think. Was she mortifying herself?"[26] It was not, I think any kind of mortification, but her natural respect for other people as one reviewer notes: "Quite irrelevant to the subject of her writing, perhaps — and yet not so, for the poet's song is a reflection of all that the poet is — was Sister Thérèse's generosity toward struggling young writers. She gives liberally of her time and talent, to criticize and encourage them."[27]

Kathryn Freund, a former Salvatorian Sister and close friend of Thérèse since 1943, played the organ at the funeral Mass and provides a more personal account of Thérèse's last days and burial: "On the 27th she was not good in the A.M., but when I returned after lunch she was quite lucid. I told her we had seen the ms. that she was trying to get published with Merton's help [prior to his death in December, 1968], and we tried to ask her the important questions.[28] We then had the Eucharist, and she repeatedly [sic] put her face up to be kissed. It was then I asked her if she would like Barry [McCabe, who by that time had left the Society of the Divine Savior] to come and Nick [Freund] called and laid the trip on him. I told her Barry was coming, and when we said good-bye we know she 'knew.' Barry was there in the morning, and she had a good day... we were pleased with the funeral arrangements. There were a couple of things Sister may have 'blanched' at, like 'canned' music, but she would have been happy with the services, with all the numbers of our former students that got together... and they did a fine job on the 'Salve Regina.'"[29]

Freund also speculates about Thérèse's apparent indecision when the College of Racine closed, and those Salvatorian Fathers and seminarians so close to her moved on: "She was faced with a decision of remaining on or of returning to Milwaukee. Barry [McCabe] convinced her that she should stay there and continue her own work.... I think she probably was in a difficult position. I had no Merton legacy, nor was I a public figure that had a reputation of my own, so I was able to leave the Order. She was disheartened by the way things were going, but she had to keep faith with her own past."[30]

Thérèse would also have been delighted with Freund's observation so similar to one that Merton's official biographer, Michael Mott, made about Merton's funeral Mass at Gethsemani: "What might have amused Merton most were the different 'Mertons' others brought to his burial."[31] Of Thérèse's funeral, Freund observes: "Everyone seems to have known her on a different level and at the services all these levels were coming to me in different ways as well."[32] This would have been one more link connecting Thérèse with her beloved "Fr. Louis."

Keith J. Egan, President of the Carmelite Institute and emeritus professor of theology at St. Mary's College, Notre Dame, was another of Thérèse's close friends who first made contact with her in 1954, the Marian Year, when he was researching a project on Marian poems: "My friendship with Thérèse was sparked by the kindness of Gervase Toelle years ago when he suggested her as a resource for two projected surveys of Marian literature. In recent years it was possible to visit with her more frequently, especially near the feast of Our Lady of Mt. Carmel, a day especially sacred to her friendship with Thomas Merton. Sr. Thérèse much enriched the lives of my family and I count it a special blessing that I was able to bring to her a relic of St. Thérèse, her patroness, just before she died at 6:40 in St. Mary's Medical Center, Racine, Wis."[33]

As a Carmelite priest, he taught with her at Marquette and invited her to speak to his students as part of his course on Merton. In 1978 he organized a tenth year anniversary commemorative event on Merton's death at Marquette and Thérèse, along with Archbishop Rembert Weakland, Dom Jean Leclercq and Dan Berrigan, was a featured speaker. After Egan left the Carmelites with a dispensation, Thérèse visited his family in Milwaukee and wrote a poem in honor of his daughter, Bridget, calling it "Bridget's House is a Window," a takeoff on Merton's "Grace's House." Thérèse had given Egan an inscribed prayer book for Bridget that had been given to her by Jacques and Räissa Maritain. Egan and his wife Connie often visited Thérèse at her apartment and took her to lunch on her birthday. They were with her on the afternoon of her death and Keith was a pallbearer at her funeral. Egan recalls that Dan Berrigan once advised Thérèse not to leave her Merton collection to an "Institution," and notes a "myth" that Fr. Gerard Smith, S.J., her philosopher friend and colleague at Marquette, wanted Thérèse to study at Oxford, but the Congregation declined. "Thérèse has never received the recognition that she deserves," commented Egan.[34]

During her life Sr. Thérèse held a number of teaching positions in Catholic institutions including Divine Savior High School, Divine Savior Junior College, Marquette University and Alverno College in Milwaukee, Mount Saint Paul College in Waukesha, Wisconsin and Dominican College in Racine. She also lectured at numerous colleges and universities in the United States including Loretto Heights College, Denver, Fordham University, New York, Georgetown University, Washington, D.C., the University of Wisconsin, Milwaukee and Oberlin College, Ohio. At Marquette she was the first nun to teach in that institution's Liberal Arts School during a regular term. For a time she was poet-in-residence at Georgetown

University in Washington, D.C., the first woman to be so honored. Among her other recognitions were the Golden Keys award for High Scholastic Standing, 1930-1931; "Poet Laureate" of her Alma Mater, Marquette University in 1933; and a citation from Marquette University in 1963 on the occasion of her 25th anniversary of graduation. She was also the founder of the Milwaukee unity of the Catholic Poetry Society of America in 1935 and spoke at the 15th anniversary celebration of the national organization in the spring of 1946 at Hunter College. She received the Boreston Mountain Poetry Anthology award in 1963 and 1965 for the category, "Best Poems," and was selected by the Poetry Consultant at the Library of Congress to come to Washington to record her poems in 1968 and 1969. She was also on the board of *Jubilee* magazine, no doubt through her friendship with staff member Robert Lax, a close friend of Merton's from their days together at Columbia. During her lifetime she was a member of a number of professional organizations including the Aquinas Society, the (Milwaukee) Mayor's Council of the Arts, Gallery of Living Catholic Authors, The Poetry Society (London), the Modern Poetry Association, a charter member of the Catholic Poetry Society and an honorary member of Sigma Tau Delta. She was also listed in the "Who's Who of American Women" and in "Outstanding Educator of 1970." There are entries about her in the *Handbook of American Women's History* (Garland Publishing, 1990) and the *Biographical Dictionary of Contemporary Catholic Writing* (Greenwood Press, 1989). In 1979, she was given an award from the Council of Wisconsin Writers for her book, *Words and Silence: On the Poetry of Thomas Merton.*

# 2

## THE STUFF OF LEGENDS

The name Thérèse Lentfoehr appears in the index of almost every book written about Thomas Merton. It might be a mere mention as his lifelong friend and correspondent; or she may be credited for having played a significant role in his life both as a writer and confidant with whom he could freely share feelings and experiences — as could she with him. Despite the uniqueness of this enduring spiritual relationship of twenty years with Merton, no one has ever undertaken to document the story of what Robert E. Daggy, former Director of the Thomas Merton Center, once described as "the stuff of which legends are made."[35]

Thérèse always insisted that her religious name be pronounced correctly in the French Thérèse (as in Thérèse of Lisieux), and not the English, Teresa or even Theresa or Therese. Among Merton's many women friends during the years of his monastic life were Räissa Maritain, poet and mystic, Rosemary Radford Ruether, theologian and writer, Angela Collins (Carmelite Prioress), Naomi Burton, Dorothy Day, and Mary Luke Tobin, former Superior General of the Sisters of Loretto, Joan Baez, composer and folk singer, Hildegard Goss-Mayr, peace activist, Etta Gullick, spiritual writer, scholar and expert on monasticism and June Yungblut, civil rights activist. His friendship with Thérèse, however, was one of his longest ongoing relationships with a woman maintained exclusively through letters. Merton seemed to have found in Sr. Thérèse, as one writer put it, "the sister he never had."[36] As for the women in his life before his monastic vocation, they were "by and large according to his own admission, not those of love but — again in his words — 'adulterous.'"[37] Her letters are always addressed to "Dear Father Louis," and, when speaking of him to others he was always "Father Merton" or "Father Louis." She referred to him only rarely as "Tom," with close friends; and never "Merton," as did most who knew him. As their friendship matured, she began to sign her letters, "Your sister" before her more formal name. He always addressed his letters to her "Dear Sister in Christ," or, more commonly, "Dear Sr. Thérèse."

She was an accomplished musician, poet, literary critic, lecturer, teacher and author who had already published her first book (*Now There is Beauty*) in 1940, long before Thomas Merton became a Catholic household name. There are conflicting and confusing accounts of her initial contact with Merton. It occurred either in 1939 or 1940, before he entered the Abbey of Gethsemani in 1941. He spent both of those summers in Olean, New York, but he did not begin teaching at St. Bonaventure College until September, 1940.

Daggy claims that Thérèse wrote to Merton in 1939 to express her admiration about a poem he had written, but he does not identify the poem or the source. In June 1939, before he entered the monastery, Merton's poem, "Fable for a War," appeared in *The New York Times* and another, "Song" in the *Experimental Review*, in November 1940. A newspaper interview with Thérèse in the 1960's stated that they both had poems in a Catholic poetry magazine called *Spirit* around the same time and wrote to each other. Thérèse's first poem in *Spirit* was published in 1938. Merton's earliest poem in *Spirit*, however, was not until May 1941. In September 1941, however, their poems did appear on opposite pages in *Spirit*.

Another newspaper account claims that Merton had written to Thérèse in 1940 when he was teaching at St. Bonaventure because of a poem about Mary that she had published, perhaps in her first book *Now There is Beauty* in 1940. She later acknowledged that Merton claimed he had written to her at the time of her first book,

## The Stuff of Legends

but Thérèse had no memory of that. Yet, in a recorded interview with Thérèse at Gethsemani in April 1978, she responded to a question about their first contact by saying that when Merton was living in Greenwich Village he had contacted her about one of her published poems. She was not able to track down the poem or where it appeared. In any case, she wrote back to him about some of his own poems and they had a little correspondence — mostly notes and postcards — which she did not preserve.

Merton, a recent convert to Catholicism, had been baptized conditionally on November 16, 1938 in Manhattan's Corpus Christi Church by Fr. Moore. His sponsor and Godfather was Ed Rice. Merton was confirmed on May 29, 1939, taking the name, James. Merton's great-grandfather was James, but Merton knew little about him until later in life. Prior to his confirmation he was using "F" (for Feverell) as a middle initial. In May and July of 1941 Merton had two poems published in *Spirit* and signed them "Thomas James Merton." In February 1939, he had received a Masters of Arts from Columbia University. He was also in the midst of discerning a religious vocation and their first contact occurred just two years before he entered the Trappist Abbey of Our Lady of Gethsemani, in Kentucky, on December 10, 1941 at the age of 26.

Almost ten years elapsed before she contacted him again in 1948 to respond to his critical review of her book, *I Sing of a Maiden*, an anthology of Marian poems by Catholic writers that was published in 1947. His review had appeared in *Commonweal* magazine February 20, 1948. By this time Merton was already a Trappist monk in solemn vows. Thérèse had actually included Merton's "The Blessed Virgin Mary Compared to a Window" in the collection. He described her book in the review as actually two anthologies of varying quality and scope. He also questioned why she had not included the poet Robert Lowell.[38] His question about her omitting Lowell might have arisen from the fact that in a review of Merton's first published book, *Thirty Poems* (1944), Lowell called Merton "the most promising of our Catholic poets, and possibly the most consequential Catholic poet to write in English since the death of Francis Thompson" and termed Merton's poems as both subtle and intense: "So small and genuine an achievement is worth consideration."[39]

Then Merton made the comment that provoked Thérèse and prompted her first letter: "And one begins to wonder if the great amount of 'Mary poetry' written in our times is to be ascribed to faith or merely to the fact that there exist so many small colleges where English teachers find a moment here and there to write down an imitation of the models they have been displaying to the young."[40] At the time Thérèse was teaching English at Marquette University in Milwaukee. She was not at all pleased with his remark, which she characterized as unnecessary and sophomoric, and wrote to Merton telling him so. On October 4, 1948 Merton's autobiography, *The Seven Storey Mountain*, was published and Thérèse wrote him again expressing her admiration for the book.

He responded on November 18th by sending her an original typescript of the manuscript containing some parts that had been deleted from the published version: "I thought you might be curious to see a manuscript of the 'MOUNTAIN,' since it was much cut.... It is of no value to anyone, and when you have looked at it you can do whatever you like with it. I only hope it isn't a nuisance. But in case it is, I'll make matters worse by sending you one or two other little things I did for the monastery."[41] That typescript — one of three copies Merton gave away: carbon copies to her and Father Terence Connolly, SJ of Boston College and the original typescript to his publisher, Robert Giroux — was the seed of what she always called her "Merton collection." His response also included a half-hearted apology for the tone of the review and thus commenced a clockwork correspondence and personal friendship that endured for twenty years until his death in Bangkok, on December 10, 1968.

Throughout the years of their relationship, Merton regularly sent her drafts of his articles for her comments, a steady stream of his notes, journals, diaries and other assorted writings. When she died in 1981 at the age of 79, she was the owner of the single largest private collection of Mertoniana that included the corrected typescript of *The Seven Storey Mountain*, fragments of his novitiate journals, notebooks and journals used in *The Sign of Jonas*, numerous drafts of poems, most of his conference notes as master of scholastics (students who were preparing for ordination to the priesthood) and master of novices (beginners in the monastic life), and an extensive collection of his mimeographed articles inscribed to her. She, in turn, deluged him with copies of her own books and articles, literary reviews, newspaper clippings, books, relics and other gifts.

Sometime in the summer of 1950, as his writing career grew and demands on his time increased, she offered to help him by typing his handwritten notes. The "Orientation" notes were from his yearly series of talks to the students and eventually amounted to some 700 pages. His tiny, close, nearly illegible handwriting is difficult for most people to read; and he once acknowledged that even he had problems reading it at times. Thérèse gradually became something of a personal secretary, expert in deciphering and typing his cryptic scrawl. Merton asked her to do much more than just type his notes. He sent her his journals for reading and comment and she was, perhaps, the first outsider to get a glimpse of his inner life reflected in the journals. He also urged her to correct his typing errors, spelling mistakes, unclear statements and unintelligible expressions not only in his notes but also in the drafts of manuscripts he sent her for publication. She did not hesitate to offer suggestions as to arrangement, layout and design for the printing of his yearly class notes.

During their twenty-year correspondence she reviewed almost every book he wrote during that period, but not always with the required objectivity, according to Robert Daggy: "Her friendship with Merton was lasting, her admiration unbounded. In fact, her admiration was so great that it prevented her… from being truly critical. Her many reviews… were flowing and full of the adjectives of praise, accepting without question the worth of what he had written. She was always quick to point out the beauty of his poetry, but rarely saw or wished to see its flaws and shortcomings."[42] Her reviews were consistently positive, if not adulatory. For her, Merton could not write anything that was not brilliant and insightful. It was only in 1975 that she spoke of Merton as a man rather than a monk in her review of *Thomas Merton Monk* by Patrick Hart: "This is a most important book for the Merton shelf, and especially so since it focuses not only on the monk... but also and most strikingly on the *man*, with his individual idiosyncrasies and shortcomings that bring him close to us all."[43]

Most of the time she was correct in her professional judgments since she was a nationally recognized published poet and author in her own right. Although she once told a former student that she and Merton went "back and forth" about things, it is obvious that there were no major disagreements between them. She rarely challenged him on anything, although she did not hesitate at times to offer suggestions and advice about his personal life and work. Mott says that Thérèse was always Merton's advisor on his poetry. Whether she included herself in a judgment she once made about the quality of the studies of Merton's poetry, is not known: "...there has been a minimum of anything approaching balanced criticism of the Merton poetry oeuvre."[44] *Words and Silence: On the Poetry of Thomas Merton* was perhaps her attempt to supply such a balance.

Kevin Lewis reviewing her book described her as the "most knowledgeable text critic of a sprawling body of poetry greatly in need of further critical assessment and winnowing."[45] He called her work a "primer" and said: "Students of Merton's best poetry must await a more discriminating treatment of that poetry and a more commanding treatment of his religious and secular sources."[46]

Jay Martin, reviewing the work in *American Literature,* recognizes that by her long association with Merton for over twenty years she, "in a very direct and particularized manner, watched his individual poems, and ultimately his poetic career develop."[47] He praises her for offering "thoroughly sympathetic and sensitive commentaries on Merton's poetic development. Her book is unpretentious in the best sense: the poet-subject, not the critic, is steadily in the forefront."[48] Another reviewer of her first major study of the complete poetic corpus echoes Daggy's observation in more detail: "...the author seems unable, or at least unwilling, to entertain any substantive criticism of Merton. She hardly mentions the unfavorable evaluations, which have been frequent and sometimes sharp. The common judgment that Merton wrote too much [poetry, biography, autobiography, history, philosophy, theology, social criticism, fiction and meditations] is not answered. ('He needed a[n] [Ezra] Pound to cut him to size,' said Daniel Berrigan)."[49] Yet Robert Lax, one of Merton's closest friends once wrote to Thérèse: "Your feeling for them [Merton's poems] is loving (not idolatrous) — you tend them, as he tended them, like a garden."[50]

The harshest review appeared in *America* by Thomas P. McDonnell, the editor of *A Thomas Merton Reader* in 1962. McDonnell claims that she ignores the fact that while Merton's social concerns may have been first rate, "his poetry at all times may not have been."[51] While she quotes much of Merton's poetry, she does so "without the slightest indication... of their possible deficiencies."[52] In 1978 she contributed "Social Concerns in the Poetry of Thomas Merton" to *Thomas Merton: Prophet in the Belly of a Paradox*, edited by Gerald Twomey. McDonnell speculated that the chapter might well have been material that she rejected for inclusion in *Words and Silence* but which would have enhanced the work. She claimed that the secular-critical response to Merton's poetry was unfair because of his Catholic faith and theology, and McDonnell agrees. On the other hand, "Sister Lentfoehr's problem... is that she can't get Merton's 'beliefs' out of the way in order to see his poetry. Where the secular critics are blind to Merton's virtues as a poet, Sister Lentfoehr is almost equally blind to his faults."[53]

Despite the sometimes lengthy, two-page letters containing unique materials not found in Merton's more than 3,500 published letters to public figures and close friends, Merton and Thérèse met face to face only twice. On August 2, 1951, she arrived unannounced at the monastery gatehouse in Kentucky asking to see Merton, but was refused admittance. The abbot was away at the time but she somehow convinced the prior (the second in charge) to summon Merton, and convinced him to take a photograph of them in their full religious habits outside the monastery. The second visit occurred on November 7, 1967, at a picnic on the monastery grounds that had been arranged by Merton's close Louisville friend, Tommie O'Callaghan. Merton had written to Thérèse about the possibility of a meeting and followed up with a phone call to the convent. In her response she waxed eloquent about the invitation, and then the surprise of hearing his voice on the phone. The much-reproduced photograph of Merton in slacks and sweater, and Thérèse in a modified religious habit and red poncho Merton had pressed her to wear, kneeling on a picnic blanket on the Gethsemani property, documents the personal encounter. Although she had inquired about the possibility of a visit many years earlier, Merton had demurred, knowing that his superiors would never have approved of such a visit, even before he entered the hermitage in 1965.

Their friendship was primarily one between two poets. Much of their correspondence centers on poetry and literature, but also includes references to contemporary events, happenings in their daily lives and news of their mutual friends. As Merton's interests and writings expanded to contemporary Catholic issues like ecumenism, liturgical renewal and Eastern religions, and to larger social questions of racism, nuclear war and peace, so did hers. She was primarily a popularizer of Merton's work through her readings and analyses rather than an equal partner in a conversation that helped shape and formulate his positions on contemporary social issues. She was an accomplished and competent interpreter of his poetry including his work between 1962 and 1968 when he prepared four volumes of poetry for publication that included many Zen poems and his less accessible anti-poetry. Thérèse lectured and wrote on such difficult topics as "Zen Mystical Transparencies" and "The Zen-Mystical-Poetry of Thomas Merton."

## The Stuff of Legends

She was a tireless collector of every scrap of his writing despite his somewhat ambivalent attitude towards the whole enterprise of various collections of his writings, and even questioned their future usefulness. In his July 1967 journal, Merton criticized Abbot James Fox who had recently announced his retirement. Merton had a stormy relationship with Fox and in one of his more caustic moods said that Fox would probably go around asking the monks what they thought so that they would plead with him not to resign: "I can see how Dom James is cheating: but so what? What good does that do me? And what good can I do *him*? The more important thing is that I too am cheating and perhaps more than the others. Perhaps monstrously. For instance — the collection at Bellarmine, the collection of Sister Thérèse [Lentfoehr] — and all the business of filing and cataloging every little slip of paper I ever wrote on! What a comedy! But I like it and cooperate wholeheartedly because I imagine it is for real. That I will last. That I will be a person studied and commented on... This is a problem, man," he wrote in 1967.[54]

They also had a mutual love of nature so obvious in many of their letters. Thérèse once told a reporter interviewing her: "Inspiration often comes from observation of wild things — birds, squirrels, chipmunks. I watch them up in the woods in Wausau, where we have a convent. It is a quiet, lovely place to work."[55] Her letters to Merton almost always contained mention of deer, chipmunks, squirrels, rabbits and birds. At her funeral Mass, Andre Papineau, the Salvatorian priest-professor of preaching at Sacred Heart Seminary, Hales Corners, Wisconsin, quoted from a poem she had written about a chipmunk. Merton was also very observant of nature around him and his journals are also filled with references to deer, birds, etc., even the "bastard" snake he sometimes encountered in the hermitage outhouse. He tried to encourage her love for animal life whenever he could.

A former student and personal friend of Thérèse, Dr. Steven Avella, recalls receiving a frantic call from her one night at 11:00 p.m. She had discovered ants in the bathroom at her Racine apartment. When he arrived to help, she insisted that he lift each ant out individually and safely onto the front lawn. Another student recalls an incident when she was teaching at Mount St. Paul College in Waukesha, Wisconsin. Some of the students were preparing to leave for a hunting trip and their gear, including guns, was lying in the school's lobby. When Thérèse happened by, she became visibly upset by what she saw.

I knew nothing about Thérèse Lentfoehr other than her name and friendship with Merton in 1981. I was Co-Director of New Ways Ministry, a Catholic-oriented research and advocacy group for homosexual Catholics and their families in Mt. Rainier, Maryland. At the time I was doing research for an article on Merton's attitudes on sexuality and homosexuality. I had come across Sr. Thérèse's name many times in my Merton reading over the years since I first discovered him in 1955 when I entered St. Charles Borromeo Seminary in Philadelphia. I was ordained for the Archdiocese of Philadelphia in 1965, and, ten years later, entered the Society of the Divine Savior, popularly known as Salvatorians. One of the Society's priests who knew my interest in Merton mentioned to me that a Salvatorian Sister had been one of Merton's longtime personal friends.

I decided to consult Sr. Thérèse about my research and wrote to her on March 13, 1981 asking if I might visit her and explaining my project. At the time, she was living in what she called her "hermitage" in imitation of Merton, which was in reality a small suburban apartment in Racine, Wisconsin. I asked for suggestions of relevant books, articles, manuscripts or even her personal insights from her analyses of Merton's writings that might relate to the issue of sexuality. I knew that many of the poets Merton admired such as W.H. Auden and Rainer Maria Rilke were involved in romantic affairs with men during their lifetimes. Gerard Manley Hopkins was among these poets although, as a convert to Catholicism and Jesuit priest, he lived a celibate life. There is some speculation that Merton's own father, Owen, might have been, at least, bisexual.[56]

In early August I visited Thérèse in Racine and found her trying frantically to catch a chirping bird that had somehow escaped from its cage in her apartment. According to some, she was in the habit of letting them out now and then. She managed to enlist me in a half-hour rescue effort before she finally abandoned the search. We chatted about Merton for a bit and I tried to explain my research. She was frail and a bit confused at the time, and did not seem to realize who I was or why I was there. She was more preoccupied with the welfare of the stray bird. Suddenly she plunged her arms under the bed and surfaced with an original typescript of Merton's *The Seven Storey Mountain* that had been published in 1948. I immediately envisioned all kinds of other valuable Mertoniana scattered haphazardly around the apartment. Being a librarian by training and an archivist by instinct, I feared the worst. Little did I know at the time that for the past twenty years she had devoted herself to gathering, enlarging, preserving and professionally cataloging her incredible "collection," and had already decided where it was to go after her death, though not before changing her mind several times.

I wrote on August 18th thanking her for her time and for the privilege of being in such close contact with Merton through his manuscript. I also volunteered to work, at my own expense, for a month or so, to help her with the sorting, cataloging and preserving the Merton collection. To strengthen my case I told her I had a degree in Library Science and was an excellent typist. Most of all, "I feel strongly that the material is so precious that the treasure should be cared for as much as possible so that eventually others may have the opportunity to share its riches as easily and productively as possible."[57] I can only imagine her wondering, in more lucid moments, about the naiveté of this upstart Salvatorian priest!

The story of her disposal of the Merton collection forms an interesting part of her relationship with Thomas Merton. In July 1925 Thérèse had willed all her property of whatever nature to the Sisters of the Divine Savior, as is required by Church law for members of religious orders with a vow of poverty. This was renewed again on August 5, 1940. Then in October 1974, by which time she had accumulated a massive amount of Merton materials, she was given permission to make a new will, bequeathing her entire collection, which she judged to be of considerable literary value, to Georgetown University where she had lectured in several summer programs and served as Poet-in-Residence. As early as August 1966, Joseph E. Jeffs, the librarian at Georgetown, had made an overture for her collection and, for several years it was her intention to bequeath it to Georgetown.

The new October 2nd will specified that the personal letters to her from Merton were not to be read or made public until twenty-five years after her death, unless the trustee named in the will should decide otherwise. She had named her priest-friend and confidant, Fr. Barry McCabe, as the personal representative of her estate and trustee of the Merton Trust she established in her new will. McCabe, however, only learned of this after her death and, since she had later drawn up a new will naming another representative, he was not involved in the final disposition of her collection. McCabe was at the time a Salvatorian priest and President of Mount St. Paul College where Thérèse taught and, later, Academic Dean of Dominican (Racine) College where she also taught for a short time. He was also her close personal friend and advisor, and traveled from California in 1981 to see her shortly before her death. Fr. John Yockey, a priest of the Archdiocese of Milwaukee and a member of the faculty of De Sales Seminary in Milwaukee, was named as an alternative trustee in the event that McCabe should decline or resign. Yockey had been a student of Thérèse at Mount St. Paul between 1965 and 1967 when he was with the Cistercians and was one of two Cistercian students Thérèse had in class over the years. She was particularly impressed with the Cistercians, no doubt because of the Merton connection, and wrote Merton how proud and happy she was to see them sitting before her in class in their black and white habits.

By 1980, when the "Merton industry" of publishing works by and about Merton was beginning, her collection had increased considerably both in scholarly and monetary value since Merton's

*The Stuff of Legends*

death in 1968.⁵⁸ In early 1980, she was considering changing her will and leaving her Merton collection to the recently founded Thomas Merton Studies Center, part of the Columbia University Campus Ministry of Columbia University. Two years earlier in 1978 she had met the charismatic and controversial Fr. Paul Dinter when he invited her to speak on Merton's poetry at the Merton Commemoration at Columbia, a two-week series of events at the University's St. Paul's Chapel, on December 10th (the anniversary of Merton's death in 1968) framed by sermons by the Trappist Fr. John Eudes Bamberger (at Corpus Christi Church where Merton had been baptized) and the Dutch priest, Fr. Henri Nouwen. One of these events, on Friday December 1st, served as the inaugural Thomas Merton Lecture and the keynote of the annual meeting of Pax Christi USA. It featured Br. David Steindl-Rast, OSB as the lecturer. At that event, Terence Cardinal Cooke announced the founding of the Merton Center which was to be located in the neighboring Notre Dame Church and Rectory where Dinter resided at the time.

It was at this gathering that she told Brother Patrick Hart, a monk of Gethsemani and Merton's secretary for several months, that Merton had whispered to her, "This is where it belongs."⁵⁹ The Merton Center was housed at the Notre Dame rectory on 114th Street, just off the main campus. At the time Dinter was a priest of the Archdiocese of New York ministering to the Catholic population at Columbia University while in residence in Notre Dame Church on the Upper East Side from 1978 to 1982. He was also an activist in many social justice causes, and a devotee of Merton.⁶⁰ A gift of $45,000 from Mrs. Jane Blaffer Owen of Houston, Texas, another Merton fan, to help promote Merton's influences on society, enabled the Center to renovate space for the collection and provide programs for the public. The project had the approval of New York's Terence Cardinal Cooke but no financial support from the Archdiocese. In March 1980, Thérèse informed Dinter of her decision to leave her collection of Merton's manuscripts, papers, journals and artifacts to the Merton Center, and asked Dinter to serve as executor of her estate. On March 22nd, he wrote to express his shock and joy at being asked to serve as executor. While others had doubted and demurred about the feasibility of his Merton Center project, he said, she was most encouraging.

On September 22, 1980, Thérèse had a codicil added amending the 1974 will and naming Dinter her personal representative for the estate. Hart was named the alternate personal representative. The codicil bequeathed the entire collection to Dinter's Thomas Merton Studies Center and continued to restrict the public use of certain Merton letters to and from various persons. The public announcement of the bequest was made in the same month. On October 10th, Dinter visited Thérèse in Milwaukee to discuss the provisions of the codicil, the transfer of the materials at the proper time and to clarify any claims on the materials that Thérèse's Order, the Congregation of the Sisters of the Divine Savior, might make. In a letter on October 24th thanking her for the collection, he waxed eloquent about seeing and handling some of the Merton material, admitting that he "fairly salivated over them."[61] The centerpiece of the 500-page catalogue of her holdings was an original typescript of *The Seven Storey Mountain*, Merton's best-selling autobiography. Although Thérèse had restricted the use of the materials, she was usually generous in allowing Merton scholars fairly free access to her collection, a practice that caused much anxiety for the Merton Legacy Trust. In May 1972, Naomi Burton (now Mrs. Melville Stone), Merton's first literary agent and one of the original Legacy trustees, had written to Thérèse about Thérèse's copy of Merton's manuscript, *The Inner Experience*. Merton had mentioned specifically in his Literary Trust agreement that he did not want published: "Any drafts of books existing in manuscript and not yet published, with the exception of two books: *The Inner Experience* and *The School of the Spirit*."[62]

Burton felt that *The Inner Experience* manuscript should not be shown to anyone at that time, other than to some scholars who could consult it with permission from the Trust. Merton himself had given copies to people who were unaware of the restrictions. She did think that it should be published in the future and it was, in 2003. She also asked Thérèse if Merton had ever indicated to her why he did not want it published. Then she asked Thérèse to have a sealed copy of the work sent to the Center at Bellarmine. The library at Gethsemani, she revealed, had been keeping it on their open shelves and showing it to anyone who asked. Stone assured Thérèse that the Trustees "have now had to put a stop to that but with much pain to scholars who had been shown it and, naturally, think the Trustees are fiends."[63] Thérèse was being asked by the Trustees to send a copy of another manuscript, *The School of the Spirit*, to Bellarmine and, although Burton had been designated to ask, she does not see any reason for Thérèse to do so, but "…thought that you would rather I did [i.e., ask] than Tommie [O'Callaghan]!!!"[64]

Why Thérèse's collection went to Dinter (from whom Columbia University purchased it in 1988) rather than to the Thomas Merton Center in Bellarmine University's library is still largely a matter of conjecture. A Merton scholar said that when he asked Thérèse why her collection was going to Columbia instead of the Merton Center, she paused, and then replied with a Cheshire cat smile, "They were very nice to me."

The official Merton Collection in Louisville was initiated in September 1963 and the Merton Room was opened and dedicated on November 8, 1964. Merton had ongoing professional contacts with Bellarmine and personal relationships with the original Trustees who were appointed in 1967 when he designated Bellarmine as the official Merton repository. It remains today the epicenter of original Merton materials and scholarly research that includes a holding of 10,000 Merton letters to some 2,100 correspondents, 3,500 of which have been published. The number of letters continues to grow yearly with donations to the Center. An accurate number of letters would also have to include other academic institutions housing Merton-related collections including the universities of Kentucky, Buffalo, Marquette, Boston College, Notre Dame, Columbia,

Harvard, St. Bonaventure, Syracuse, Georgetown, Northwestern and Dartmouth.

A year before his death Merton asked Tommie O'Callaghan to suggest to Thérèse that she leave her collection to Bellarmine. O'Callaghan, one of the original members of the Merton Legacy Trust, is one of the few living members of the Merton "inner circle" as is Hart. According to Dinter, Hart, who had been Abbot James Fox's secretary for ten years, supported Thérèse's eventual decision to give the collection to Columbia. Hart, who took care of Merton's mail while he was traveling in the East, confirms this: "I remember telling her at that time that it belonged to her and she must make the final decision, although I did add if she decided to leave it to the new Thomas Merton Studies Center at Columbia in New York, it was a most appropriate place for it! She agreed and shortly afterwards had re-arranged her will. Again, I think she had real insight in this decision, realizing that it would be taken care of properly at Columbia, where there was a lot of interest in Merton and his work."[65]

On February 15, 1982, Robert E. Daggy, then Curator of the Merton Studies Center and Chief of Research for the Merton Legacy Trust, wrote to Kathryn Van de Kamp Freund, a former Salvatorian Sister and close friend of Thérèse mentioned earlier. Freund had written to Daggy on February 8, 1982, to thank him for the 1981 autumn issue of *The Merton Seasonal*, a quarterly publication of the Thomas Merton Studies Center, which was dedicated to Sister Thérèse. The issue contained an article by Daggy titled "Sister Thérèse Lentfoehr, S.D.S.: Custodian of 'Grace's House' and Other Mertoniana," quoted earlier. Daggy wrote: "I am most interested in Sister Thérèse's literary effects. If you think I could be of help or service in any way, do not hesitate to call on me. I think her journals especially should be preserved and available for future scholarly use — as Merton's are or will be. I am sure too that her correspondence would be most interesting and enlightening."[66]

Not long after her death on October 31, 1981, Thérèse's personal belongings were moved to the Motherhouse of the Salvatorian

*The Stuff of Legends*

Sisters in Milwaukee where Sister Margaret Shekleton, the Salvatorian Provincial, completed an inventory of all the articles in Thérèse's possession at the time of her death. The Merton collection had been moved for safety to the home of John Barry Stutt, a former student of Thérèse at Mount St. Paul and a lawyer in Milwaukee. Dinter later drove to Milwaukee personally to secure the materials for Columbia. Some of Thérèse's personal and professional correspondence and papers are now also part of the Columbia collection. The Salvatorian Sisters in Milwaukee also have a collection of Thérèse's works.

On January 22, 1982, Robert Wilmot of the Milwaukee law firm of Purtell, Purcell, Wilmot and Burroughs informed Dinter that Thérèse's will had been probated on January 12th. As previously arranged, the collection passed to the Thomas Merton Center at Columbia University with Dinter acting as personal representative and trustee of the collection. The collection was divided into five categories: the collection, letters, personal letters from Merton, special items and other property. Wilmot also advised Dinter that the retention covering Merton's personal letters to Thérèse for 25 years in the 1974 will would be cumbersome, and that "the discretion invested in you gives you the authority to read the letters involved to enable you to determine, according to the stated criteria, what options should be exercised."[67] The criteria listed by Thérèse for future public use of the collection included "the continuing study of Thomas Merton, his life, philosophy and his literary and spiritual contribution to all mankind."[68] Since Thérèse had modified the qualification of the 25-year moratorium in the codicil, the trustee (Dinter) could determine when the personal letters from Merton to her could be read and made public.

Unpublished selections of the more than one hundred extant letters from Merton to Thérèse make up the bulk of the material in this book. Excerpts of some of these letters have already appeared in edited form in Robert E. Daggy's 1989 *The Road to Joy: Letters to New and Old Friends*, and are appropriately referenced in this work.[69] Daggy, understandably, was primarily interested in Merton's life and thoughts and *The Road to Joy* did not include the more personal exchanges between Merton and Thérèse or any of her letters, notes and cards to Merton. Their voluminous correspondence runs from November 3, 1948 to November 21, 1968, spanning and documenting twenty years of a very special relationship between two creative artists and religious figures. What is unique about this work is that it includes substantial, unpublished portions from more than a dozen extant letters and postcards from Thérèse to Merton, from March 1962 to March 1968. The first full-length extant letter of Thérèse to Merton is dated March 17, 1963, although several postcards and notes from various places prior to that date have been preserved. The last communication between them is a postcard from Merton in India dated November 21, 1968, just a few weeks before his accidental death on December 10, 1968.

Most of Thérèse's letters to Merton excerpted in this work are from the originals that Merton himself preserved and are now in the Bellarmine collection. His letters to her, numbering more than 200 over the years, though not all extant, are part of the Merton collection at Columbia University. A substantial number but not all are available since Merton did not start preserving letters to him (and carbon copies of his responses) until about 1963 when the staff at Bellarmine urged him to retain all those materials. Whether there are other extant originals or copies of letters from Thérèse to Merton remains unknown. If she did keep copies of her letters to Merton, she most likely would have destroyed them at some time out of respect for both the privacy and confidentiality of the principals. We do know from her own testimony that she destroyed several of Merton's letters to her that dealt with his relationship with the nurse with whom he had fallen in love. It is highly unlikely that Thérèse gave any letters to a third party for safekeeping. It is this writer's belief that she most likely did not keep copies of her letters to Merton, but did preserve most of his correspondence to her.

From Merton's letters to Thérèse we can discern the events and moods of her professional and personal life including physical and emotional health issues, difficulties with religious superiors, writing and teaching projects, and, above all, a continuing and growing devotion to Merton. Despite the lack of her letters to Merton in the forties and fifties, we are not left with a one-sided conversation by any means. From her extant letters and notes to Merton, her own professional writings, lectures, newspaper reports and other relevant sources, we can fill in many of the blanks in order to hear more from her side of the ongoing conversation. From Merton's responses to her letters, we are able to garner a substantial picture of what she wrote to him.

We must be cautious, however, in accepting too readily as objective, or even balanced, Thérèse's portrayals of certain religious superiors about whom we know only from Merton's responses to what she writes about her dealings with them. We do not know in any great detail what kind of difficulties Thérèse was experiencing, or specifically what she wrote him about certain authority figures that evoked strong, if not angry, sentiments in his letters. We have only *her* view of the situations and personalities and only as reflected indirectly through Merton's emotional responses. We should also remember that Merton would use very strong language when writing about what he saw as abuses of authority in the Church, such as in the case of Charles Davis, a popular and influential British Jesuit theologian who left the priesthood to marry in 1967. Merton did not think Davis's very drastic criticisms were either baseless or unjust.

Merton, perhaps, was aware of the dangers of someone in her position and once advised her against taking on the "attitude of a martyr" — always a temptation for someone who feels wronged or treated unjustly. At the same time, some individuals in positions of authority in the Church and in religious life at the time of her writing, were not always noted for their compassion and understanding, especially at a time in the Church when unquestioning obedience was seen as the most important virtue of a good religious. On the other hand, it is quite possible that Thérèse, as an artist, felt herself unduly constrained by the demands of religious life and not subject to the traditional expectations of communal life in that period of the Church's history. She might have seen herself as a progressive thinker chaffing under the authority of more traditional superiors.

Thérèse was an artist with a sensitive temperament and like many creative people not always easy to fathom. Those who knew her have described her as something of a "free spirit," and an individual of strong opinions who was not always easy to live with. Superiors might have seen her as not providing a good example for younger nuns. Her absence from traditional community gatherings, for example, due to conflicts with her teaching and lecturing schedules, must have provoked some tension among those with whom she lived in community. She was, some said, habitually late for meetings and seemingly unaware of the impact this behavior had on others. One former Sister who took piano lessons from Thérèse at the Milwaukee St. Mary Community recalls that she was a "good teacher when she was there," but there were many times when she simply failed to show up for the lesson. According to a close friend, she had a need to be a "star," as apparently she had been while teaching at Marquette.

An incident in 1939 might indicate this need to shine resulted, at times, in her imagination running away. The General Chapter of the Salvatorian Sisters began on August 18, 1939. Thérèse had traveled to Rome with her Provincial Superior, Sister Ottilia, and Sisters M. Olympia and M. Sophie for their General Chapter and also to be present for her brother Theophane's ordination and first Mass. The group left the USA on June 22nd, visiting England, France and Italy. In a letter dated August 10, 1939, to the readers of *Spirit* magazine, she describes her reactions to her visit to Rome; "From the loveliness of the English countryside, London, Oxford, Paris, and Lisieux, I have come to this mecca of the soul — Rome! Its charm and spiritual beauty cannot be defined. I have found it everywhere — in the swaying of a lonely daisy between broken columns in the Forum, in the austerity and otherworldliness of a First Holy Mass (my brother's) in the Papal crypt, in the catacombs of St. Callistus, and in the cool quiet of St. Peter's and the Vatican with their vision of a lyric figure in white with the face of a nimbused saint, who gives blessings as Christ must have given them in Galilee. Here in Rome the soul can sing but a song of thanks for being *filia Ecclesiae*."[70]

One newspaper account of the trip claims that she had three audiences and two conversations with Pope Pius XII, including one at the Papal summer villa of Castel Gandolfo outside the city of Rome. In the August 10th letter to the members of the Catholic Poetry Society of America she says she had been received in audience by the Pope and was personally presented to him. She took the occasion, she says, to speak about the Society and ask for a special blessing on the members. She then quoted the Pope as saying, "Tell the members of the Catholic Poetry Society of America that I bless them and their work." She told the Pope about a recent volume of poetry published by the Society called *From the Four Winds* and promised to send a copy.

The story grew with the telling. One newspaper account has the Pope meeting the two Salvatorian sisters in a little circle during a private audience. As he went on to greet the next pilgrims he supposedly turned back and repeated twice, "The Americans are a pious people." In 1945, an introduction of her as a guest on a local radio program, says she had presented the Pope with the original copy of her poem, "Prayer for the Pontiff" and that the Pope rewarded her by giving her his own silver pencil, which she used for special occasions, including autographing her books. These embellishments of the experience, perhaps, can be credited in part to her desire to edify and encourage the members of the Catholic Poetry Society. But also as a strong four on the Enneagram, she needed something special, a more than ordinary account to share about her trip to Rome and encounter with the Pope.

An article written by Margaret Lawler, a laywoman who was also in the group of visitors from Milwaukee, describes a general papal audience in the Hall of Benedictions with hundreds of other people when the Pope was carried in on a high mobile throne blessing the crowd as he went along. This might have been the reality of

Thérèse's "papal audiences." In a letter dated September 6, 1939 the Papal Secretary of State, Cardinal Luigi Maglione, wrote to Thérèse to thank her on behalf of the Pope for her letter of August 6th and a copy of her poem "Prayer for the Pontiff." The Pope was pleased to learn of "your great interest in the Catholic Poetry Society of America, which He holds in highest regard, and He bids me inform you that He will receive with sincere satisfaction the volume [*From the Four Winds*]... which you have promised to forward to Him."[71] A later newspaper account has the Pope *asking* for a special copy of the anthology at the audience. The Cardinal's letter concludes: "It was hoped that it maght [sic] have been possible to arrange an audience for you with His Holiness but, unfortunately, present circumstances render this impossible."[72]

Thomas Merton died on December 10, 1968 — 27 years to the day since he had entered the Trappist Abbey of Our Lady of Gethsemani. Since his death, many have speculated about how he would have developed intellectually and religiously and what his response would have been to contemporary social and ecclesial issues had he lived longer. One Merton scholar conjectures: "From our earthly point of view, his was an unfinished life, as it still had so much promise, so much waiting to be accomplished, totally 'open' to new possibilities that could have been. We are left with questions of 'what if...' or 'if only...' and have only our imaginations to fill in the blanks on 'what could have been.'"[73]

In 1974, Raphael Simon, a Trappist monk from St. Joseph's Abbey in Spencer, Massachusetts, wrote to Thérèse about the "timeliness" or "untimeliness" of Merton's death. He suggested that since Merton's prayer and charity had reached its acme, he did not need the East for a further expansion and, therefore, his death was timely. Thérèse did not agree: "In this I really cannot agree since it concerns only Merton *personally*. And even then, does one ever attain his full spiritual potential.... Given his Christ, and his security in Him, Merton, with a rich maturity of spirit, and theological and monastic poise, could well take his stance, not only ecumenically, but

## The Stuff of Legends

with a certain conaturality of spirit with any sincere search for the Infinite, however experienced and expressed, and especially when it touched on the dimension of contemplative wisdom in which he was adept. This is the *real* Merton... during the years of our friendship, Merton was accustomed to send me his journals and diaries when each was filled (even the most personal notebooks), and in reading these I thought I had reached the very spiritual and human depths of the 'living' man. But what came through in the *Asian Journal*, though unexplainable, far surpassed them. I touched the *total* man, in a way that I had never done before, a man who had reached a fulfillment and maturity that few of us dare hope for. To speak of the "untimeliness" of his death, therefore, hinges on precisely this dimension. Had he lived, this added richness of vision would have been incorporated into his writings, in which sense there were 'miles to go before I sleep.' (And you will grant that 53 by modern computing is *young*!)."[74] McCabe says Thérèse felt that Merton's interest in Eastern philosophies "would someday lead to a fuller understanding of Christianity by Christians. Accordingly, she was devastated first by his death and secondly by the termination of his exploration of Eastern philosophies... she was particularly taken by Merton's *Zen and the Birds of Appetite*."[75]

Merton never stopped thanking Thérèse for her secretarial and archival skills and for her views and opinions that he valued and sought on Church and literary matters. He supported her emotionally and spiritually during bouts of depression, feelings of being treated unfairly, and misunderstandings with superiors. He encouraged her professionally in her own poetry writing and enjoyment of nature as he advised her to be her own person and to follow her bliss. The Anglican priest and Canadian Merton scholar, Donald Grayston, once visited John Eudes Bamberger. Bamberger had entered Gethsemani in 1950 and was a student of Merton. He later became a psychiatrist and was elected Abbot of Our Lady of the Genesee Monastery in Piffard, New York in 1971. Merton often consulted him about particular applicants to Gethsemani when

Merton was part of the reviewing process. In October 1976, Bamberger, who at the time was the abbot at Genesee, wrote to Thérèse for help in preparing an article he was writing on Merton and near the end of the letter inquired about her collection: "Have you made any definite plans for the MSS of Fr. Louis' works for the future? Will you be arranging to have them deposed [sic] in some library or monastery eventually?"[76] In an undated letter to Thérèse about his own visit with Bamberger after Merton's death, Grayston relayed a statement that Bamberger had made about her friendship with Merton: "I think it was the most *peaceful* relationship he [Merton] ever had" and, continued Grayston, "I know he meant that in the biblical sense of the word peace."[77] Peace was a gift that she seemed able to give to others: "Sister Thérèse is unmistakably a twentieth century woman, vibrantly alive to all the world about her; yet she has learned the ancient secret of the cloistered, listening heart, that has learned to live wholly in peace in the presence of God."[78]

This unique and mostly very private friendship that Thérèse herself once described as "warm and close," is a gift that we can share in some limited degree as we listen in on their intimate and revealing conversations carried on through their letters over the years.[79] The letters, as Daggy so accurately and fittingly described them, are truly "poetry in prose at times."[80]

# 3

## EARLY YEARS
### 1948-1949

As has been recounted in Chapter Two, on February 20, 1948, Thomas Merton's critical review of Thérèse Lentfoehr's 1947 anthology of poetry, *I Sing of a Maiden*, appeared in the *Commonweal* magazine and she wrote to him about his review, but there is no record of his response, if there was one. In October 1948, Merton's bestselling autobiography, *The Seven Storey Mountain*, was published by Harcourt Brace. Thérèse wrote again to Merton this time praising the book extravagantly and he responded to her enthusiastic letter on November 3, 1948: "No book written by me could be possibly that good!"[81] In a postscript he admits that he only accepted the job of reviewing her book because he wanted a free copy for the library at Gethsemani, and chided himself for what he had written: "I felt rather cheap after having made the statement reflecting on all Catholic poets in the U.S. *en masse*. I shouldn't have said what I did if I did not believe it."[82]

The publication of *The Seven Storey Mountain* elicited tons of mail for Merton: "Letters come in from everywhere, Park Avenue and San Quentin Prison, the sanctuary and the studio, and the thing that most strikes me is the wonderful beauty there is in all these souls, even the ones who suffer and are wretched because of what seem to them to be sins. But what is most wonderful of all is to see Jesus in these beautiful hearts. Most of them do not realize Who they are, or Whose love prompted them to write. From the composite picture that I have pulled out of the mail-bag this Christmas I have seen Him born and I know now for certain that He is in possession of the poor, chaotic world, dwelling in the midst of it in the infinite peace and security of his Kingship, no less unknown, relatively, than he was a[t] Bethlehem, but no less in command."[83]

In a letter to Bob Lax a few days earlier, Merton had written again about the many personal and moving letters from people who had read the autobiography: "I have been getting a great lot of letters and all of them very sane and very holy except only two which were not sane but were nevertheless holy anyway and some of them simply are so sane that they require better answers than I can give, but I have to try and give some answer. And, like I said, all over the letters you can see the handwriting of Christ."[84] To most of his letter writers, Merton sent a standard form response on a pre-printed card, but Thérèse received a more personal response and, eventually, much more than that.

She wrote back almost immediately and sent him copies of her own published books of poetry. In his November 18th response to the gifts, he says he has been reading Thérèse's *Give Joan a Sword*. Her poems are, he thinks, full of serenity and peace, which his were not, and he talks mostly about the challenges and difficulties in writing good poetry. In a previous letter she had suggested that he send something to the Holy Father, Pope Pius XII, probably a copy of *Mountain*. He likes the idea and intends to ask Father Abbot, who was away at the time, for permission. Thérèse was in the practice of sending copies of her own books to the Pope and between 1939 and 1949 received several acknowledgments from the Vatican City's Secretary of State.

Merton repays her gift of books with what he terms a little token: "I thought you might be curious to see a manuscript of the *Mountain*, since it was much cut. So I'll give you the carbon instead of burning it up. It is of no value to anyone, and when you have looked at it you can do whatever you like with it. I only hope it isn't

## Early Years

a nuisance. But in case it is, I'll make matters worse by sending you one or two other little things I did for the monastery."[85] The day Merton's two packages containing the manuscripts were dropped at Thérèse's office door in the convent her good friend, Sr. Cecilia [Katie Freund], recalls that they heard her scream when she opened them and realized what they contained. The return address read simply "Louis, Trappist Kentucky." The *Mountain* manuscript was 800 pages long.

Thérèse sent Merton a relic of St. Thérèse, the first of many relics of various saints she would give him over the next twenty years. No doubt she procured some of them from Rome through her brother Gordon, a Salvatorian priest, who studied for the priesthood there. On December 27, 1948 Merton notes in his journal: "One of the biggest graces of this or any Christmas — Sister Thérèse at Marquette sent me a first class relic of the Little Flower."[86] He was afraid that "Father Abbot might insist on putting it with the relics here, in the Church. But no: he said, with a sigh of relief and an expression that contained a ray of hope: 'Frater Louis, you *need* something like that.'"[87] The abbot had insisted that Merton wear the relic and Merton concurs: "Really, I will be *her* monk. She is reminding me of my pact with her, and I am terribly grateful to her — and to you — for the fact that she has decided, in her own simple way, to walk in and take possession. I have the relic over my heart. From now on, when I sing in choir, it will be a duet. I always meditate with my hands over my heart, the way one does when he is trying to keep a match from blowing out in a high wind. From now on, it will be a bonfire with her there to tend the flame and unite it with her own wonderful love for Jesus: and we will both burn together in His Spirit. And the flame will be part of the same great fire that burns throughout the whole Christ, and in your own dear, generous heart. Be sure that you have not lost her by sending her to me. You will be in all those prayers, just as if the relic were still with you."[88] Merton had the St. Thérèse relic along with seven others, including some from Thérèse, in his shaving kit when he left for his fatal visit to Bangkok in 1968. He also informs Thérèse that he had been ordained a sub-deacon on the feast of St. Thomas and that he had functioned for the first time at the monastery's Midnight Christmas Mass. Merton was ordained a deacon on March 19th, but does not mention this to Thérèse in his letters at the time.

In his January 18, 1949 letter he referred to her inquiry in a previous letter about the role of a person's natural temperament in the contemplative life. Merton had written an article on active and contemplative religious orders in *Commonweal* that had appeared the previous December, and was criticized by John Fearon, a Dominican priest, in the January 1949 issue of *The Thomist*: "So I sit down to figure out an article... which has gone to the great trouble of refuting something I must have said somewhere about contemplation. I am flattered at being refuted by learned men. It almost makes me feel as if my opinions were important — almost, but not quite."[89] Elsewhere, referring to the same incident, he recorded that he was flattered as a third year theology student to be refuted by one of the foremost magazines in the country. Merton was thinking of writing a response to *The Thomist* article because he thought he could defend his thesis that had been challenged by quoting other writings from Dominicans. He eventually did and received a conciliatory response from Fearon. He was also planning to write a theological study of the contemplative life and asks Thérèse to send him any leads or materials on the topic she might come across.

Early on in their correspondence and increasingly through the years, Thérèse was intent on pursuing any and all photographs of Merton she could get her hands on. She had asked him for one very early on in the relationship, but he tells her that none is available. When Merton first began writing articles and books, one of the restrictions placed upon him by the Trappist authorities was that his photograph could not be used in conjunction with any of his publications. For many years Merton's growing Catholic audience had no idea what the world famous author actually looked like, but Thérèse was set on changing that. At the celebration of Gethsemani's

*Early Years*

centenary, on June 1, 1949, Merton was unintentionally captured on film and would later be recognized, but only by those who already knew what he looked like. Gradually, the restriction about personal photographs was relaxed and his photograph appeared on the dust covers of some of his works and, eventually, in Catholic newspapers and magazines.

In response to his inquiry about works on contemplation, Thérèse had sent him notes from Giovanni Batista Scaramelli, a Jesuit ascetical writer, and a pamphlet about contemplation by a French Jesuit, Jean de la Taille. On February 19th Merton says he needs time to read the materials before making any judgment, but he thinks that de la Taille's statement that women enjoy retirement and solitude more than men is false: "I think they get lonely much easier than men; or am I wrong?" he asks.[90] There is no record of her response to his question.

At the time Merton was working on a book about the mystical life he titled *The Cloud and the Fire* [alternatively, *Fire Cloud and Darkness*], which was eventually published as *The Ascent to Truth*: "I have had to scrap fifty pages and start the new book over again on a much simpler plan. My whole attraction is to get away from the psychological approach to mysticism and return to the dogmatic treatment which the Fathers used. Not that this would mean ignoring the experimental side of prayer altogether, but I'd like to situate it in a patristic setting. In fact, what I am dreaming of now is a book on the mystical life, with a solid dogmatic foundation, plenty of material from the Fathers, but communicated to the reader through a scriptural and liturgical medium: take part of the liturgical cycle and work out everything there is in it about the mystical life… not only by individuals but also collectively by the Church."[91]

Merton had sent one carbon copy of *The Seven Storey Mountain* to Fr. Terence Connolly at Boston College and one to Thérèse. Referring to the uncut copy of *Mountain* in her possession, he tells her to "feel free to make use of your copy in any way you please. I give you all rights over it, in so far as I can, with Father Abbot's permission."[92] He asks her to keep a lookout for references to Adam as a contemplative, but adds he doesn't "want to put you to any special trouble on my account: really you have more important things to do."[93] Throughout their long correspondence and his frequent requests to Thérèse to type various materials for him, he is always careful not to overburden her with work or pressure her to complete the tasks by certain deadlines.

At Easter, Thérèse had sent Merton a rosary with an indulgenced cross containing earth from the Roman catacombs. He thanks her on April 26th and mentions a postcard she had sent him from New York sometime between February and March: "One thing distresses me: it is the thought that you may have been led to ferret around in the Columbia library until you unearthed some skeleton in the closets of the Columbia of fifteen years or so ago. If you did, then I have no need to assure you that those skeletons are certainly skeletons and there is nothing in those closets to edify a religious. I am only thinking of your own sensibilities."[94] He feared she might be prowling around Columbia University library and had found some skeleton in the closet from his student days some fifteen years previously. Merton had drawn a series of risqué cartoons in 1935 for the Columbia's student publication, *The Jester*.

He is preparing for ordination to the priesthood scheduled for May 26th, the feast of the Ascension: "I am trying to immerse myself in the Mass — and the more I do so, the more I feel that Holy Sacrifice is the purest and most perfect of prayers and that all contemplation is to be found therein. It is the fountain of everything and the short way to the heights. I did not make this discovery until I began associating ceremonies with prayers. I had used a missal for years, of course, but really, the making of gestures and movements in harmony with the words and *doing* all the things that are said makes a tremendous difference. Of course it brings your whole being into play, and that has the effect of a liberation, psychologically. What will it be when I can actually consecrate! Pray that I may keep my feet on the ground, dear Sister. I am the enemy of all exaltation and I want nothing more than to offer our dear Lord, with His own sacrifice, the sacrifice of a perfectly pure and simple and humble heart."[95]

Merton was saddened, he wrote, by what Thérèse had told him about the poet Robert Lowell who so admired Merton as a poet. Lowell was a Pulitzer Prize winning writer and a member of the upstate New York artistic community known as Yaddo where he created a controversy that has come to be called "The Lowell Affair." It involved his almost fanatical campaign against supposed Communist sympathizers at Yaddo and his manic breakdown following the whole affair. "What a terrible thing that such a real poet should be silenced by the devil. After all, he is one who can say that poetry is his vocation, whereas the rest of us have other and far more important things to do than write verse."[96] Elsewhere he had written: "Lowell is in some ways better than Hopkins. Though he is not as deep spiritually, he is sometimes more of a poet.... He is a better poet than Dylan Thomas because he is Catholic and grown up and not drunk. I thank God for this good poet who is really great and I pray for him to write more. I'd like to write to him but I guess it would be smarter if I didn't."[97] He is sending her a copy of *Seeds of Contemplation* and then he scolds her for sending him too many presents: "Dear Sister. You must not send me any more gifts because I am now one of the idle rich of this community, a man of great possessions, and it does not really please Our dear Lord. But I do value your precious notes."[98]

Merton was right about her snooping at Columbia. She actually had discovered the Columbia cartoons, described by one writer as soft pornography, Merton mentioned and he is now apologetic, if not embarrassed: "About the Columbia *Jester*, the years 1938 and '39 contain less objectionable material than the years when I was an undergraduate. As for the *Columbian* [yearbook]... and those inane pictures. Well, I deserve punishment."[99] By this time Thérèse had confided in Merton some of her own personal difficulties and he responds sensitively: "Do redouble your prayers, dear Sister. That is all that counts: that we may be saints. I expect Our Lord is teaching you confidence in a way you don't quite grasp. Never spoil His work by leaning on a broken reed. But I won't repay your kindness by dry sermonizing... as soon as I start to preach I have the feeling that I am talking through our cowl."[100]

Thérèse had inquired about her visiting Gethsemani for his upcoming ordination to the priesthood in May or his First Mass which she thought would be celebrated in a local parish church, but Merton demurs: "Father Abbot [James Fox] wants everything to be very, very quiet and simple... we have absolutely no accomodations [sic] for lady visitors. One or two friends — the close ones mentioned in the book [*The Seven Storey Mountain*] — will be here, I expect. No, we never go out to say a First Mass. That is strictly forbidden. I know that with the slightest encouragement you would probably be willing to camp in a tree with the Kentucky possums."[101]

Merton had recently sent her a copy of a special edition of his *Seeds of Contemplation* that had been published in March 1949. Thérèse had arranged to review Merton's *Seeds* and on May 13th he tells her he is pleased she will be reviewing the work and adds: "I do not know what to say about chapter 15 of *Seeds*. In the abstract, I still think I am right, since despair is the obverse of pride. For the rest I am delighted that you are to review it: but please, Sister, do not overlook the *faults*."[102]

On May 27th, the day after his ordination, Merton celebrated his First Mass and, the following day, May 28th, his first Solemn High Mass in the monastic community and reflected on these events in a journal entry of the 29th. Thérèse had heard a rumor, probably through the growing Merton grapevine, that Clare Boothe Luce, the wife of the newspaper magnate and a generous benefactor of Gethsemani, had been present for Merton's ordination. It was Luce who had given Merton a typewriter. The Luce family had also donated a three thousand acre site of the family estate in Aiken, South Carolina to the Abbey of Gethsemani. In 1949, that property eventually became the site for the foundation of a new monastery, Our Lady of Mepkin Abbey. Merton assures her on June 17th, however, that it is only a rumor — Luce was not present at the ordination. His only visitors were some close friends from Columbia days and his two living aunts.

On June 2nd, Thérèse had sent Merton a chaplet (a string of beads used for prayer) and asked for his rosary in return, but he told her it is quite large and would not be able to be used. A short time later, on the 17th, following a visit by the Abbot General Dom Dominique Nogues, he informs her that "…the iron curtain is coming down again."[103] He had already far exceeded the quota of letters permitted to the other monks. At certain seasons of the year, like Christmas, Easter, All Saints and the Assumption, the monks were allowed to write only four, half-page letters. One of Merton's legal four pieces of correspondence was always to Thérèse. Daggy claims that Merton wrote to Thérèse consistently more than to any other person, and that he was permitted to write to her even when his general correspondence was severely restricted. By July, his time to answer correspondence had been reduced to two hours a week and, while this might be a good thing, he mused, it still cramped his style for letter writing.

He tells Thérèse on July 15th that he had sent books to the Holy Father (*Mountain* and *Seeds*) as she suggested, and thanks her for her glowing review of *Seeds*: "How like you it is! You have seen deeply into the book and have been very kind to the author, and have neglected the faults of a brash young writer who is perhaps too bold and too careless.… I am not surprised that some of the clergy are annoyed at me. There will always be careful and conscientious folk who travel strictly beaten track who will be upset by people like myself who have too little respect for convention. I do not think they are jealous, they are just temperamentally different. But I have seen a couple of stinging letters written by a priest in New York about both the *Mountain* and *Seeds*. They were more extremely bitter and savage than any criticism I have ever got from Protestants or unbelievers.… I shall certainly not be such a fool as to defend myself."[104] He is preparing a second edition of *Seeds* and asks for her suggestions as well as those of "dear saintly" Father Ellard.[105]

Thérèse was planning to ask the well-known nun-poet, Sister M. Madeleva of the Sisters of the Holy Cross, to write an article about Merton, but he pleads: "Don't ask her to write *another* article on the poet Merton: she has done at least four articles and reviews, all of them so generous.... By all means reprint what you wish from the *Mountain*.... I'd like to ask that you soft pedal the mystic note a little, as it gets people too excited. There is certainly nothing extraordinary about a contemplative religious having the beginnings of contemplative prayer: but nevertheless the word 'mystic' carries the connotation 'unusual' and the best thing I can do is to appear to be very usual, which, in fact, I am."[106] Thérèse herself had already written three articles about Merton. He is flattered but is also afraid of her unbounded enthusiasm which he gently, at first, tries constantly to dampen but with little apparent success: "I am glad and flattered that you have written three articles and I hope to see them, but I am afraid you are probably too enthusiastic. You are too generous a soul."[107]

Replying to her inquiry about some missing pages from her *Mountain* manuscript, Merton suggests she consult another copy of the manuscript he had sent to Fr. Connolly at Boston College. That copy was more complete and not worked over, although it contained material Merton preferred not be published. He had deliberately tossed out one section to make sure that nothing was left of it in any manuscript. The myth that the Trappist censors made him delete all the racy or scandalous parts of the autobiography is sometimes overdrawn.[108] Naomi Burton, his first literary agent, balances the record: "In April, 1947, Merton wrote me that the censors wanted changes (though even in the letter, he wrote me that the censor had 'capitulated') and had written a letter with some excellent suggestions."[109] Merton himself thought that the book was too long, and that the British version, *Elected Silence*, edited by Evelyn Waugh, was much better.[110] Waugh's revised title came from a poem by Gerard

## Early Years

Manley Hopkins. In March 1949 Therese met Waugh when he came to speak at Marquette University. Following a buffet Waugh asked her questions about what had been cut from the original manuscript because of length or objections from the Trappist censors. Waugh had visited Merton in the fall of 1948. Thérèse published "First Christmas at Gethsemani" in the *Catholic World* in December 1949 and sent Merton the excerpts she had used for the piece from her uncut, original typescript of *Mountain*. More material from the original manuscript appeared in *Catholic World* in May and September 1950 and in *Renascence* in the spring of 1951. Waugh told her he had cut out Merton's trip to the dentist and references to the Long Island Railroad and had sent Merton a copy of Fowler's *Dictionary of Modern English Usage*.

One of Thérèse's students when she was teaching in Milwaukee was a Cistercian seminarian. She had described him to Merton as a "Trappist" in one of her letters, but not from the same branch of Trappists as Merton. She thought he was a member of the Trappist foundations that had been established from the French Abbey of Cîteaux. Merton corrects her: "I am interested in your Cistercian: but he can hardly be an OCR (Order of Reformed Cistercians) because that is what I am (it is identical with OCSO (Order of Cistercians of the Strict Observance) — same Order, and we are not allowed to go to universities — except the Gregorianum [in Rome]. He sounds like a Cistercian of the Immaculate Conception, the Lerins congregation. And now I chide you. *We* are the ones who stem direct from Cîteaux. Anyway, he would be welcome here at any time."[111]

In her letters to Merton over the years, Thérèse often confided personal struggles relating to her prayer life and her life in religious community. While some of these will become more pronounced in the coming years, from the very start of their relationship and throughout the years of their friendship and correspondence Merton continued to offer both encouragement and informal spiritual direction. Once again he comforts her in her difficulties: "May Our Lady bless you and keep you and give you her deepest peace.

All things pass, and only God remains, and no matter how we may feel, sometimes, He is always God and that is all that matters. It is sufficient to turn to Him and look at Him and He will do the rest because we cannot even turn to Him without Him, and the fact that we should even want to do so is the pledge of all the rest!"[112]

Along with relics, Thérèse began to send Merton books she thought he might want. In a journal entry of August 11th, he records that she had sent him Dom Chapman's letters and a copy of *Priest-Workman in Germany*. While he is anxious to read the letters, the book will have to wait because he is so busy, but maybe he can manage to have it read in the monks' refectory. The book, by Henri Perrin, was published in 1947 by Sheed and Ward, and recounts the ministry of a worker-priest in Germany during World War II.

In a brief note dated August 26th he comments on an article about him that she was trying to have published, but wanted his approval first. He characterizes the article as both "restrained" and "temperate" and suggests a few changes. Then he adds: "On the whole it seems to me rather impossible for me to utter an official 'approval' of such a nice article. Of course I approve, most heartily. I love compliments. But it is not quite fitting that I should utter my approval pontifically, so for the others I trust your judgment entirely."[113] He then suggests she try *Catholic World*, or the Catholic British journal, *The Month*, as possible venues for publication!

On August 28th Merton sends a lengthy four-page letter responding to hers of August 6th. He is busy correcting *Seeds (of Contemplation)* for a new edition and writing the life of St. Lutgarde, a Cistercian mystic and stigmatic. Thérèse's letter had mentioned a problem in her prayer life bordering on despair and he advises: "When you feel particularly low, and are convinced that you have been abandoned by God because of your weaknesses, remember that He is nearer then than in many an hour of consolation. Console yourself with the thought that it cannot help being that way, because God tries those whom He loves and He is close to them that are in tribulation."[114] She told him that she was going to recite the Little

## Early Years

Office of the Blessed Virgin Mary a second time on any day she received a letter from him, but he strongly disapproves: "I thought it was a very bad idea, but did not say anything. Now I <u>know</u> it is, and I do hope you will not be so unwise. Our Lady does not want that of you! If prayer, and especially vocal prayer, is such a strain for you, this is the last thing in the world you should be doing: saying your office <u>twice!</u>"[115] What she is experiencing, he says, is not despair but "a perfectly natural consequence of jagged nerves and a sensibility that easily gets exhausted. It is a form of mental and moral weariness, nothing more. You must pay no attention to it whatever except to take it peacefully as a standard trial and go through it restfully, if possible, without reflecting on your state in any way.... He has permitted it because He knows it will ultimately <u>contribute</u> much to your union with Him, if only you do not spoil it by restlessness and by trying to shake it off when it simply won't shake. It is the form the dark night takes in your case... don't force things, and don't strain yourself and all will be well. When you feel particularly low, and are convinced that you have been abandoned by God because of your weaknesses, remember that He is nearer then than in many an hour of consolation. Console yourself with the thought that it cannot help being that way, because God tries those whom He loves and He is close to them that are in tribulation... have you a garden or somewhere that you can walk in, by yourself? Take half an hour, or fifteen minutes a day and just walk up and down among the flowerbeds with the intention of offering this walk up as a meditation and a prayer."[116]

Merton had finally identified the "Trappist" student she had mentioned in a previous letter as an OCR: "I am surprised that he won't acknowledge us as members of the same Order! And why did he go knocking on the door of the Common Observance? Perhaps we have a reputation for being a bit tough, down here in the woods of Kentucky. His being with you is, indeed, most unusual! Still, when one has to raise money for a destroyed monastery...."[117]

Thérèse, still intent on procuring some photographs of Merton had sent him several photographs of Trappist monks from Gethsemani asking if he was pictured in any of them. Although he isn't, she is rewarded for her persistence: "The pictures are returned herewith. They are <u>all</u> off the target. Some are Father Placid, some are Father Timothy. I am sending a couple of my ordination and first Mass. They are not very good. Please, please, please never print them or make them public — show them to special friends if you like but you know what I mean, not in a big exhibition, please."[118] Thérèse's zeal for procuring photographs of her idol will play a significant role in one minor crisis years later in her attempt to respect Merton's restrictions on publishing photographs of the author.

On her feast day, October 3rd, Merton sends greetings in response to her two last letters full of ideas and helpful things and informs her that the relic of St. Thérèse of Lisieux she had given him was solemnly exposed in the archives on the feast day of St. Thérèse with candles and flowers. He comments on the reviews of *Seeds* she had sent him from *Thought* and *The Tablet* in London. He had also heard a rumor about a recent Papal pronouncement on the contemplative life, but has no real information. Would she send him whatever she can find? The editor of the British Jesuit journal, *The Month*, wanted to reprint her already published Christmas excerpt from *Mountain*, but only the part on mystical prayer. The editors had asked Merton to persuade her to allow them to have it, but he suggests she might want to sell the whole article to some American magazine, and then let *The Month* have the excerpt they want to use. He assures her that he had not written any novels on material from *Mountain* and that Bob Giroux, who had mentioned a Merton novel to her, was referring to a novel Merton had written at Olean while he was teaching at St. Bonaventure College.

Near the end of the October 3rd letter Merton tries to assuage Thérèse's anxiety about what he thinks of her confiding in him her personal difficulties: "Far from being shocked at the spiritual parts of your letter (I mean the personal problems) I am most deeply moved by them. How you must have suffered, poor Sister! But you simply must not think of yourself as estranged from God. You have been hurt badly and your nerves have reacted in such a way that they will no longer permit you to pray like other people. Well, pray in some other way… just mentally say the word 'Yes.' And this will be full acceptance… most of my own prayers are completely inarticulate. I walk around saying 'Love!' Or I just mentally keep slipping the catch that yields my soul to Love. You might do that too, one way or another. Or you might just mentally wish to keep uniting yourself to whatever prayer St. Thérèse is praying in heaven. Your short sharp cries to our Lady are amply sufficient."[119]

Merton devotes a good portion of some letters advising Thérèse to cope with her situation, and offers concrete suggestions to handle what she had, apparently, called bitterness toward God: "If you feel bitter toward God — perhaps it is only that you feel bitter to the God that once existed in your sensibility. Only a very pale and remote reflection. If you have had to go without the comfort of that reflection, be glad and do not worry about the pain. It necessarily involves pain, but it is good for you that He should go, because then you will not become attached to the reflection and perhaps forget about the reality. He is now much closer to you than any image or feeling and that is why your acts must always remain supremely simple… remember that I am an unwise and inexperienced director and know nothing… there is quite a bit of that fire devouring me too, at the moment and I have my problems."[120]

Thérèse is still after more photographs of Merton and, even of his younger brother, John Paul. Merton refers her to a publication called *Gethsemani Magnificat*, the official 1949 Centenary Book of Gethsemani Abbey. There was a rumor that the monk pictured in the Cistercian Literature page of the book with his monastic cowl pulled up to conceal his identity was Merton, and he seems to confirm it by pointing her towards it. Thérèse will settle for the original, but he tells her they do not have it. She can write, however, to Father Irenaeus Herscher, the librarian at St. Bonaventure in Olean, New York for some notebooks Merton had left with him after graduation.

Merton recorded elsewhere that he had destroyed or given away all but one of his novels, but kept his notebooks and journals that would eventually form the basis for his published journals such as *The Secular Journal*.

She had already written to Irenaeus on April 6th seeking photographs of Merton for the Marquette Merton exhibit she was planning for that November. She told Irenaeus that Merton owed it to his reading public to let them see a photograph of him, and she is willing to pay anything for the one St. Bonaventure has. By August she was still waiting for a response to her letters to Irenaeus and, as inducement for his cooperation, she offered to loan them her *Mountain* manuscript if they ever want to mount their own Merton exhibit.

On August 24th, after several more pleas, she finally received a photograph of Merton with some Franciscan Fathers. Although grateful for the materials, she is still not fully satisfied and writes back asking for the photograph of Merton from the 1939 Columbia yearbook that Irenaeus had mentioned. Might he have some idea of where she can purchase a copy of the yearbook itself — but not for more than ten dollars! Robert Giroux, Merton's first editor who edited his contributions in the 1930's to *The Columbia Review*, had sent her some of the original photographs, but none of Merton, from *The Waters of Siloe*, a history of Trappist foundations, and the original manuscript itself: "I almost fainted when I received his letter."[121] Finally, she received a shipment of Merton's photographs, books and notebooks from St. Bonaventure, including Merton's 1939 journal, on loan for her exhibition.

On November 12th Merton tells Thérèse about a retreat given to the monks at Gethsemani by Msgr. Fulton Sheen who sometimes preached for an hour and a half! Though the retreat was over when Merton was writing, he still has little time to answer her last letter with its requests, because a group of monks was preparing to leave Gethsemani to begin a new foundation in Aiken, South Carolina on land given to Gethsemani by Clare Boothe Luce. He thanks her

*Early Years*

for the information on the Papal pronouncement on contemplation that turned out to be just a rumor. The handwriting on the back of a photograph of his brother, John Paul, that he had sent is, he explains, that of his uncle, Harold Brewster Jenkins, on his mother's side. He also encloses an October 13, 1949 letter from Monsignor Giovanni Battista Montini (later Pope Paul VI) thanking him for copies of *The Seven Storey Mountain* and *Seeds of Contemplation* he had sent to Pius XII at Thérèse's suggestion. He is planning to teach scripture and mystical theology as well as an orientation course for the novices.

Thérèse had questioned him about the provenance of the *Mountain* typescript now in her possession, but Merton is not quite sure which one it is — the one he had first sent to the publisher (Harcourt Brace) or the carbon copy he had amended. Hers was one of these and, probably, the one that he had corrected himself. She also had asked Merton for the Roman breviary he used as a new priest for the November Marquette exhibit, but he tells her they were not available since they were being used in the retreat house for visiting priests who had forgotten theirs. She later wrote to the Franciscans at St. Bonaventure for the breviaries Merton used when he was teaching there as a layman.[122] He closes by assuring her that his health is good, even excellent. Throughout the years she was in the habit of inquiring regularly about his health, despite Merton's continued reassurances that he was well. Merton rarely told her of all his trips to the hospitals in Bardstown or Louisville to be treated for various ailments of one kind or another.

On November 17th Thérèse writes to thank Fr. Irenaeus for the books, pictures and notebook he had sent on loan for the Merton exhibit at Marquette. At this time, Merton's 1939 journal had not yet been published, and would have been in great demand by Merton's growing readership. Apparently, Thérèse had already experienced attempts to get her to divulge some private information about the monk writer Thomas Merton, so she assures Irenaeus that "no one else shall get his fingers on the precious volume. I have had such a holy fear of editors, etc., who want to scoop and print.... I have had one unpleasant experience apropos of this matter since the matter of the Seven Storey ms came into my hands, so your treasure shall be kept well out of their way."[123]

In her persistent quest for photographs of Merton, Thérèse had also contacted Edward Rice, Merton's good friend from Columbia days. Rice must have told Merton of her contact because Merton mentions it in a letter to Bob Lax on November 27th: "The same Sister Thérèse wrote to Rice asking for pictures and went into ecstasy over his answer asking her to pray for his wife. If you ever go to Milwaukee go and see her. She will light vigil lights all around you. But she is very nice."[124]

By December, Merton was already beginning regularly to send Thérèse numerous packets of materials as he records in his journal: "I spent the whole day, morning and afternoon work, trying to reestablish the appearance of order in the vault. It took all that time to clean up the piles of ragged envelopes full of notes and manuscripts.... Turned in some twenty books to the library, sent off a lot of old galley proofs to Sister Thérèse and Fr. Connolly [Boston College] to save myself the trouble of burning them, and finally the place began to look neat."[125]

# 4

## BECOMING A SISTER
### 1950-1954

On July 17, 1949, Merton fainted while singing the Gospel as the deacon at the Solemn High Mass at Gethsemani. It might have been the hot summer, or it might have been emotions at play on the Feast of Our Lady of Mt. Carmel observed on that date in the Cistercian Order. During his visit to Cuba in 1940, before entering the monastery and while still exploring his religious vocation, Merton had a profound religious experience in the church of St. Francis in Havana, and in the church of Our Lady of Cobre outside Santiago, he had made a vow to offer his First Mass to Mary, the patron of his priestly vocation if he became a priest. He also made the second vow to Our Lady of Mt. Carmel when he returned one day to the Hotel Andino where he was staying and saw the church dedicated to her under that title reflected in the mirror of his room.

The first vow was fulfilled when he celebrated a low Mass following his ordination to the priesthood in 1949. Michael Mott, Merton's official biographer, however, says that in July of 1949 Merton felt himself growing further from fulfilling whatever the second vow was. Mott had access to all of Merton's last twelve restricted journals while writing the official biography. Since then, all of the personal journals have been published, but the nature of that vow is still not clear, although Mott thinks it may have had something to do with Merton's attraction to the vocation of solitude.[126] When he became a hermit, he dedicated the hermitage to Mary of Carmel.

Mott characterizes this period of Merton's monastic life as a time of stress and physical, if not spiritual, burnout. Merton had been pushing himself too hard: "The isolated collapse [July 1949] was not the beginning of a serious illness. It was a clear sign. A check. He had been straining himself too hard for too long. He had believed, too, that ordination would be a resolution, whereas it had become clear it was only a beginning at a higher plane.... In his prayer life there had been little or no solitude that spring and summer.... He was simply burnt out."[127] In 1944 he had published *Thirty Poems*, his first book of poetry, and in 1949 his fourth book of poetry in five years appeared. Only one Merton book was published in 1950, *What Are These Wounds?*, a book he had written five years earlier about the life of St. Lutgarde, a Cistercian mystic.

On January 7, 1950, Merton thanked Thérèse for her Christmas gifts that included relics of St. Joseph and St. Anne. He refers also to a relic of the True Cross she had given him. Was he referring to himself when he told Thérèse "...the relic of the True Cross is still in my keeping, against the day when it is to decorate an abbot"?[128] In June of 1949, however he had told her that the abbot wouldn't let him keep it because that right belongs only to an abbot or a bishop.

In 1952, when Gethsemani was planning to open a new foundation in Ohio, Merton was chosen for the group sent to explore suitable sites. Merton thought the abbot, James Fox, who had replaced Dunne, had picked him because he was expecting Merton to lead the new foundation. Merton later recorded the incident in his journal and not without some evidence of his disappointment that Fox had never seriously considered him for the position of Superior: "It seemed, at the moment, that I must be going to make a foundation in Ohio. Why else would Reverend Father get me to go all the way up there unless he intended me to be Superior of the foundation? Afterwards this turned out to be by no means certain."[129] The next day Merton records his feelings: "When we were coming into Dayton, Reverend Father told me he had no intention of making me superior of the foundation, if there was a foundation. So I threw

## Becoming a Sister

away all the plans I had been drawing up since the morning and felt as if I was making a sacrifice."[130] Fox did tell Merton, however, that someday a foundation might elect him (Merton) as their abbot. Mott says that there was some question of making Merton the abbot of the Genesee community. On October 8, 1952, Merton made a private vow never to accept the office because there was a serious reason barring him from that honor.

As late as 1968, when an election was held to replace Fox, Merton conjectured that there might be a move to elect him as abbot, and he made a comment in one of his conferences that he would not accept the position. Then he posted a statement for the community on a bulletin board ["MY CAMPAIGN PLATFORM for non-abbot and permanent keeper of the present doghouse"] explaining that he was incompetent for the position, and reminded them of the private vow he had made on October 8, 1952. He added as a further reason for not being elected the fact that the Abbey might be embarrassed if the child of the abbot turned up. Actually, he received a considerable number of votes despite his campaign "platform for non-Abbot" that angered some of the monks whom he had described as "one hundred and twenty-five slightly confused and anxiety ridden monks."[131] Whether Merton had ever had serious thoughts that someday he would be elected abbot is not known, although it seems he thought this might be a possibility in 1952 and again in 1968.

Thérèse's Merton exhibition in November and December 1949 at Marquette University was a great success and she sends him an account from a local Milwaukee newspaper that contained her photograph. He acknowledges that he has been publishing far too much, something that might have caused her to worry about his health. She also sent him some of her own notebooks and a copy of her December 1949 article on Merton from the *Catholic World* ("First Christmas at Gethsemani") which contained unpublished material from *Mountain* and an introduction by Thérèse: "Thank you especially for your notebooks. I have glanced at one or two of their beautiful pages and know enough to tell that I shall read the rest with great interest — and to say that probably you are much better off now then you were then. It is much better to go through aridity, with pure faith, serving God in peaceful dryness and without commotion, than to be consumed by an experience that is shattering and drains all one's energy."[132] He judges it as nicely presented, "... yet I cannot feel too happy about having let you become a regular press-agent for this poor sinner! I know you are doing it all for the love of Our dear Lord and that it feeds your love for Him, otherwise I could not consent to let you make anything of me and the things I write. But you know, you do seem to take an over optimistic view of this Thomas Merton.... Thank you then, not for the publicity but for the charity."[133]

Thérèse was worried about all the writing he was doing: "I have been publishing far too much and it is time to be quiet for a little. Preparing classes take up most of my time anyway, but the material will all go to make a book later on if God wills it. There is surely no great need for a spate of books from Gethsemani: and it is not our vocation. However, I shall hope to get something on paper once in a while."[134]

On January 21, 1950, Merton dashes off a short note about another of Thérèse's pieces on Merton, including an introduction and selections from his works that she had sent him for approval. He suggests some changes and then reminds her again: "I am scared of all this attention but — well, so what. The article says what the answer is so I had better keep quiet... but please do not go and insert any little words like heroic or magnificent or whatnot when I am not looking."[135]

Merton had asked Fr. Irenaeus at St. Bonaventure to send Thérèse some of the journals that he had left behind. Merton first started keeping secular journals at St. Bonaventure and continued the practice, on and off, beginning with his first monastic journal in 1945 and continuing until his death in 1968. Forty-six pages were torn from his 1949 journal for the months February to October. During this period, Mott explains, Merton was struggling to overcome self-consciousness in his writings and in the public aspect of his religious life. Thérèse had inquired about the location and missing parts of the early Cuban journal (published as *The Secular Journal*) and he tells her on February 18th that, although he does not know where it is, it definitely is either lost or strayed, but not stolen. The gap is explained by the fact that he was busy writing a novel, one of several prior to entering Gethsemani. Before leaving for Gethsemani he had destroyed some drafts of novels (except *My Escape from the Nazis*) and given another to Catherine de Hueck Doherty of Friendship House in New York City who had spoken at St. Bonaventure and with whom he had been in contact. He had preserved some other journals, notebooks and poems, but left them behind at St. Bonaventure when he left for the monastery.

Not all of Merton's writings were appreciated in some quarters, especially among the clergy. One of his literary critics was a Carmelite priest-poet from the Chicago Province, Gervase Toelle. In the 1940's Toelle, a frequent contributor to *Spirit*, a publication of the Catholic Poetry Society, had critiqued some of Merton's early poems. In 1949 he published an essay on Merton in *Spirit*, titled "Merton: His Problem and Solution."[136] Merton thought the article was fine, though he knew Thérèse was not at all pleased with Toelle's criticism. She was, he told her, too sensitive. He asked her to convey his thanks to Toelle through a written note or to tell Toelle personally herself, if that would not put her in an embarrassing situation. Thérèse must have done just the opposite: "Did you give Fr. Toelle the impression that I did not like his article? If you did, I hope you will correct it by letting him know from me that I thought it was excellent. I found nothing wrong with the tone of it. It was the right, sharp, objective sort of criticism that a self-respecting literary magazine demands these days: and it was certainly very humane and temperate in its treatment of my shortcomings"[137]

In January 1950, Toelle published a review of Merton's new book of poems, *The Tears of the Blind Lions*, in *Spirit*, describing some of them as "verbal gymnastics, feats of syntactical ingenuity" and a reaching for desperate metaphors that sometimes "degenerates into bathos."[138] He also noted that Merton had to modify his original description of Mary as a "priestly virgin" because someone had informed him that it was theologically inaccurate. Thérèse was having none of it: "And one dislikes the tone of the remark as to the theological inaccuracy of the epithet 'priestly virgin': 'meanwhile it must have been pointed out to him…' In this matter Merton is by no means the only offender. The term, and variants of it, occur in Marian poetry with surprising frequency, and that in the work of poets of much longer standing in the Church and in Orders than the young Trappist of Gethsemani."[139] In the same review Toelle had judged Merton's poem, "The Reader," as "unredeemed by single excellence," and "a mere vehicle for conceits."[140] The poem was one of Thérèse's favorites! Naturally, she rushed to Merton's side with a passionate defense in the March issue calling Toelle's review an "extremely facile and peripheral judgment to say the least."[141]

In 1982 Thérèse published a lengthy article in *The Sword*, a journal of the Carmelite Province of the Most Pure Heart of Mary, on Toelle's poetry. In an epilogue, Keith Egan says that Toelle, who died on January 22, 1967 at the age of 45 after an auto accident on May 9, 1966, would have appreciated Thérèse's article in a journal of which Toelle was once editor: "He would, moreover, have appreciated her keen attention to his poetry. On the occasion of the Marian Year (1954), Gervase replied to the question where he found his favorite Marian poetry, by saying that Sr. Thérèse's anthology, *I Sing of a Maiden*, 'wins with no trouble.'… I asked Sr. Thérèse, a long-time admirer of Gervase's poetic gifts, to write this essay on his poetry; she accepted the invitation readily and in this connection recalled a memorable visit she had with Gervase in Milwaukee."[142]

In 1950, Thérèse was not Merton's only self-appointed publicist. Another was Dan Walsh, a teacher and a close friend from Columbia days who had influenced his decision to enter Gethsemani. Walsh himself later became a priest for the Archdiocese of Louisville and taught at both Bellarmine University and Gethsemani, but not before he spent some time lecturing on Merton in various venues. When Merton asked him to cease, he readily agreed. As for Thérèse, Merton had little hope of effecting any change: "I shall not attempt to discourage you because I know you like the labor of it and that my advice would fall on deaf ears."[143]

On March 7th Thérèse wrote an emotional plea to Irenaeus in an attempt to acquire Merton's 1939 journal, which she had borrowed for the Merton Marquette exhibit in 1949: "<u>I only wish I could buy it from you for my collection</u>. But I suppose you wouldn't part with it, or <u>would</u> you? I keep telling myself you would <u>still have</u> the 1940 Notebook, which is much richer…. I wish too, that I could <u>buy one of his books,</u> at least <u>one</u>. Would you at all consider this?"[144] Reflecting on her request in a more sober mood, on Monday in Passion Week, 1950, she describes her plea for the journal as a "Merton moment" and a "preposterous question."[145] Thérèse was to have many such "Merton moments" in her life!

On Holy Saturday, April 8th, Merton writes to thank her for yet more relics. He had been walking in the woods picking daffodils for Mary and when he returned… "she [Mary] put your package in my lap. So that was quite a profitable bunch of daffodils, if you ask me. Besides that, some notes on Our Lady and the interior life from Fr. Paul Philippe who teaches Mystical Theo at the Angelicum. But the relic. Now I have unmasked you. You went and got all those relics together and had the people make a special reliquary! It is wonderful. You could not have picked them better. They went to Communion with me this morning."[146] At that time she was writing a poem, which he correctly surmised, might be about him and he was apprehensive: "I am looking forward to the poem… but if it has anything to do with me it will probably make me call out to the mountains to fall upon me and to the hills to cover me. I do wish you wouldn't praise me and treat me as if I were holy. It is just not that I am humble… but I just get embarrassed. After reading the Journal you know me well enough, I think, not to overestimate me. Thank you again and again for that typing job…. I am glad you are so easy to please, otherwise I would never dare to accept the wonderful presents you send."[147]

The state of his health continued to be of concern to Thérèse. On April 17th Merton assures her again that he is quite all right and, aside from the flu epidemic that had hit him and the whole monastery during Lent, he does not have tuberculosis, something that was part of his medical history, and he knows he has to be careful. She was apparently working on some revisions for him of *Mountain* at the time, and he tells her there is no hurry. If she is reviewing *What Are These Wounds?* — a book that he describes as awful — he hopes she "will give it the review — the panning — it deserves. You must be frank about it."[148] By May, Thérèse had begun to do some small typing jobs for Merton, mostly liturgy notes as she had done for the "Orientation notes." She had also had published, "I Will Be Your Monk" for the *Catholic World* (May, 1950), and on May 6th, Merton congratulates her on the piece and mentions another article of hers in *Renascence* (Spring, 1950), "Todo y Nada: Writing and Contemplation," that contained more of the unpublished material from Merton's *Mountain*.

As their friendship developed over the years, Thérèse sought out contacts either personally or through correspondence, with many of Merton's friends including Jim Forest, Naomi Burton, Robert Giroux, John Howard Griffin, Patrick Hart, Victor Hammer, Tommie O'Callaghan and Evelyn Waugh. She especially cultivated two of his closest friends from Columbia days, Robert Lax and Edward Rice, and was writing them frequently — something that Merton could not do because of monastic restrictions, so he heartily approved.

She was still solicitous for his health: "No I am not dying of TB. There is absolutely nothing picturesque about me. I had a bad dose of flu during Lent but so did everyone else around here. I certainly will not despise any prayers you say for my health, bodily or spiritual!"[149] He inquires whether she ever got to review his book he most disliked, *What Are These Wounds?*: "I suppose you were your usual kind self, with a blind eye for all the stupidities in the thing.

It is really badly done, this time, and we tried to persuade Bruce at any price not to publish it, but it was too late."[150] No matter how bad Merton judged the book, however, he still wanted it reviewed!

In May their letters had apparently crossed, and she was wondering why he had not answered her. On June 3rd, he explains that sometimes the Father Prior finds her letters so interesting that he puts them aside to read at his leisure. This means that Merton only receives them some weeks later: "Never be perturbed. Perhaps he has a letter of yours now. That is why I mention this."[151] Merton writes on July 10th in advance of what he mistakenly thinks is her big day — July 17th, the Feast of Our Lady of Mt. Carmel. Actually, the yearly anniversary of Thérèse's religious vows was July 16th, not the 17th as Merton thinks. He takes the opportunity to encourage her again: "He loves you very much, you know, and He has proved it by letting you suffer. You ought to thank Him for that more than for anything else. I will thank Him for you — and for whatever He has given me in that way and for whatever He has planned for me too. All these things should remind us that only He is good. And because that is the only thing that matters, why should we care what happens to us. Well, we do, and He understands that we do. He does not expect us to be inhuman or superhuman either, all in a rush. If there were one present I would really like to give you it would be this: that you be overwhelmed with the sense that whatever may be your infirmities they, and they most of all, are your most infallible claim upon His infinite love. That is one grace I want for myself too, I certainly have plenty of infirmity to cash in on."[152]

Thérèse had mentioned in one of her letters that she would like to continue typing for Merton and he jumps at the offer: "Can I take you up on it? Please do not feel yourself bound in any way if the project is unappealing.... If you feel like typing these up with a couple of carbon copies it would be a great service because someother [sic] monasteries want to see them. I suppose you might be interested in reading the notes otherwise I would not make the suggestion. Let me know if it would not bother you too much to do this — or part of it. If I get a copy I can let you keep the original. Is it a bargain? I feel very mean imposing on you in this way: but I am simply snowed under."[153] He adds that typing the orientation notes would give her a rest from writing all her articles putting him before the public. We can imagine Thérèse's delight with this request and her eagerness to be of service to Merton in any way she could. On July 11th he finally sends her a photograph taken by a professional photographer who had been photographing the monastery, and had asked to take his picture.

Thérèse had been on a summer speaking tour about Merton and by July 31st was back in Milwaukee: "I hope you did not put anything into the poet that wasn't there, but I am afraid this hope is not too solid. Now that you have spoken at some length about this particular poet, perhaps you will consider dropping him as a lecture subject.… He ought not to be over-publicized. It would be good for the kingdom of Heaven if he were kept a little more on the shelf. I do hope you are tired of such a topic."[154] On the way she had visited Ed Rice in Greenwich Village where he was working on his magazine, *Jubilee*.

Merton is now concerned about her health, and reminds her that Dan Walsh wore himself out talking about Merton, but eventually stopped at Merton's request. Merton was hoping she would grow tired of Merton the poet topic too: "If I find out by my secret service agents that you have in any way suffered from having written or spoken so much about me I shall get very earnest about trying to persuade you to go a little slower. The trouble is, I am getting to know you now and I am beginning to fear that persuasion would not be much use. But I do think of it, seriously."[155] She has been growing in union with God all along and he is grateful for her wanting to do the typing of the stencils for his talks to the novices: "A hundred copies would be wonderful. If there is any part of the process we can do from here, we will be glad to — anything to save you from too big a burden."[156]

Sometime in early August, Thérèse sent Merton an avalanche

of pictures, including those by Fra Angelico, Giotto and Picasso. He thanks her on August 19th again for typing his "Orientation" notes that he now wants titled "Lectures given to Choir Novices — Abbey of Gethsemani — 1950," and asks her to correct mistakes in spelling, typing errors and unclear or unintelligible statements. Merton's own typed letters are filled with numerous typos, entire lines crossed out with typed X's, misspellings and incorrect punctuation — something he never seemed to learn very well. Alluding to his tiny, cramped and almost indecipherable handwriting, he says he would be "eternally grateful if you could do something to bring a little light out of the darkness."[157]

Thérèse had described in a letter to Merton her July visit with Ed Rice in New York, when she was returning from a lecture tour and Merton says he was able to see Rice's apartment through her eyes. Apparently, she told him she had to knock on Rice's apartment window to get his attention and that Merton might be surprised at that: "I didn't bat an eyelash at your knocking on the window — except in surprise at the thought that you would think I would be surprised."[158] Rice later commented on her visit that she ought to be Pope! Merton sent Thérèse a manuscript on September 11th asking her to send it to Ed Rice so that he could run it by the diocesan censors in the Archdiocese of New York. Although this was not really necessary, Merton wanted to do it for safety. On September 26th, he informs Thérèse that the abbot wants any money the Abbey received from her articles about Merton (presumably through copyright payments), to be used to help cover her expenses of mimeographing Merton's notes. With any leftover funds she could have some copies bound permanently, including a copy of her own.

He alerts her to the fact that he had just returned from St. Anthony's Hospital in Louisville where he had been admitted for a checkup: "They found no ulcers or anything like that. But I am being treated for colitis."[159] He had registered at the hospital as "Fr. Ludovicus," the Latin for his religious name, Louis. One of the nuns at the hospital had asked who was the "Polish Trappist" Ludoviski on the third floor. His brother monks referred to him later as "Ludowhiskey." He asks her not to make that pseudonym,"Ludovicus," public because he might want to use it again. Was he thinking of future stays in the hospital or the possibility that he might one day be silenced and would have to write using a pen name? In the early sixties, when he was eventually prohibited from writing on issues of peace and nuclear war, he did publish several articles using various pen names.

Merton continuously sent Thérèse odds and ends of his writings on various occasions such as on September 30th in anticipation of her October 3rd name day, the Feast of St. Thérèse. That particular packet included a drawing of a saint, his schedule as a cleric and a note on an orientation talk that had not been typed: "Sorry present. But since you are so easily satisfied... if you wanted something better I could not give you a present."[160] On November 3rd Thérèse was in Chicago to exhibit her *Mountain* manuscript as part of the 20th anniversary celebration of the St. Benet Library and Bookshop. In one of her November letters Thérèse had invited Merton to visit her in Milwaukee: "You startle me with your delightful invitation to Milwaukee," he responded on November 29th: "We never get that far afield, and perhaps it is just as well. The hospital is far enough."[161]

He had been back to St. Joseph's Infirmary in Louisville from October 10th to the 21st and again on November 3rd for minor and successful nose surgery and treatment for spastic colitis due to strain and overwork. He also had a shady chest X-ray, probably a remnant of the tuberculosis he once had and he realizes that he has to be careful. He informs her on November 29th, 1950 that he had received a relic of St. John of the Cross from "someone" on the feast of St. John, which was November 24th. He hopes she was not looking for one for him — she was!

Thérèse had been working on a series of her own articles on Merton, and he inquires in November if they are nearly finished: "It is useless for me to tell you not to take so much trouble or wear yourself out. I know you enjoy doing the job, but really I feel that

*Becoming a Sister*

I ought to be less written about and would be relieved to be so."[162] For Thérèse, however, far from being less written about, she would see to it that Merton received as much publicity as she could generate. By this time she had become a fervent evangelist dedicated to spreading the name and writings of Thomas Merton as far and wide as possible.

A letter from Merton dated February 10, 1951, included what he described as a "horrible" photograph of him taken for his official papers as part of his application for U.S. citizenship. He eventually became a U.S. citizen on June 22, 1951, in Louisville. He had finally finished the book on the mystical life, *Fire Cloud and Darkness* [published as *The Ascent to Truth*], but while working on it he had experienced a writing block while hospitalized in October and November of the previous year (1950). In the letter he attributes the breakthrough to the relic of St. John of the Cross, which according to Mott, she had sent him in November 1950: "It was your St. John of the Cross relic that did the trick. The book is practically all about his doctrine. From the time I got the new relic [from her in November 1950?], I was so flooded with ideas… that the thing went like a breeze. It was when I got the other relic, incidentally (of St. John) that the book suddenly began to be all about him."[163]

Two years later, in 1953, however, he records in his journal that the "Mystery of the relic of St. John of the Cross solved. It came last Fall [1952] from a priest in Rome," although he told Thérèse he already had a relic of St. John as early as November 1950. Merton and/or Mott seem to have confused the origins and dates of the two relics of the same saint.

On March 1st, he tells her that with all the relics she is sending "you are going to turn me into a walking Basilica."[164] The extra ones were going to be taken to a new foundation in Genesee, New York where Fr. Gerard McGinley will be the new abbot.

Thérèse had been working on typing the *Journal* (*The Whale and the Ivy*, published as *The Sign of Jonas* covering the years 1946 to 1952) that she had meticulously deciphered from Merton's handwritten copy — a task he once described as "heroic."[165] He sent her the manuscript of the about-to-be-published *Fire Cloud and Darkness* (re-titled, *The Ascent to Truth*) by Harcourt Brace that was hers to keep. Merton continued to attempt to dampen her enthusiasm and resorted at times to convey his message with humor: "I know it does not do much good to reprove you. You will not listen. But I have a dilemma for you to deal with the horns of, Sister. If you think I am so smart, why don't you believe what I tell you? Why don't you agree with me, if I am such a wizard? You see, your admiration of me is a blatant self-contradiction. Yah."[166]

He was still trying to curb her boundless enthusiasm for all things Merton, no matter what the quality. Besides trying to keep up with her flood of letters and postcards sent even when she traveled, Merton still had to attend to his monastic responsibilities and to other personal and professional correspondence. One tactic he developed was to answer several of her letters with only one of his. He knew she thought everything he wrote should be published, but on April 28th he said: "I do not agree with you that everything should be printed. A lot of it is tripe.... please don't go overrating them. It makes me awful nervous to be the object of a cultus, you know. I wish you would find some way of being more nonchalant about my mediocre stuff."[167] By this time, however, Thérèse could never have judged any of his works as "mediocre." He is more concerned about his monastic vocation and the inroads he feels his writings have taken: "I have got to start doing something about being a better religious. Spring-cleaning has been going on for several months and there is more junk in my house than I care to think of. You know enough from the Journal. That someone with all the graces I have received should be as slow and sluggish as I am... God is very merciful and I am overwhelmed by His patience. Still I am beginning to hope that my days as a sort of monastic journalist are drawing to a close, that I may be more of a monk.... But it means a lot of things have to be cut down. The chief of them is magazine writing and correspondence — and slower on the books."[168]

## Becoming a Sister

Thérèse had indeed written a poem about Merton and sent it to him in the Spring of 1951, but had no reply. On May 21st he explains why. A Trappist father immediate, Abbot Louis Penneum from Trappist monastery in Melleray, in France was on an official visit to Gethsemani. Since he did not speak much English, Merton had been asked to act as his secretary and interpreter. Also his own correspondence had been cut back. On Trinity Sunday, 1951, he had been appointed master of scholastics (students) — a new position instituted as the result of the visit by Dom Louis — and a job that had to be designed from the ground up.

But there was another far more important reason for his not writing. It had to do with his continual but frustrated pleas to Thérèse to moderate her judgments and her rhetoric — pleas that went either unheard or misunderstood. He intended to be blunt and not beat around the bush: "About the poem... since I have to be serious and direct, I hope you will forgive me — and don't be hurt — if I ask you not to praise me. Just let me put it like that. I know you will understand. I have said the same thing before in many involved ways that were not clear. Please do not praise me. I esteem your friendship beyond words and this is nothing against it. I owe you more than I can say."[169] But her praise is doing him no favor: "Please stop telling me that I am wonderful, because that is not a favor. It is of no use to me and I believe it is no good for you either, for it is not based on the truth. Deceived by your own deep sincerity, you are in an illusion. I assure you of that."[170]

One can only imagine the feelings those words from her beloved idol must have evoked. Merton's brutal honesty was the only way he saw of shocking her into reality. The rest of the letter is more cheerful. He thanks her for the work on the *Journal* that is ready for publication thanks to her typing — the first legible manuscript his publishers have ever received from him! She ought to get part of the royalties! Returning at the end of his letter to his harsh words about the poem, he tries to soften the shock without retreating from his original, blunt position: "Do not think, by the way, that I did not appreciate the beauty of your poem. But the fact that it was about me spoiled it. To make up for being so churlish, I will pray extra hard for you — but I assure you I mean what I say."[171]

Merton returned again to what he called the "mean letter" on May 26th, perhaps because he was bothered by what he had written or because he discovered that, once again, he was forced to confront another of her illusions: "This must be your time to do penance... because here I come, Lady, with another one. After that mean letter I wrote you about your poem (...and I hold on to the essentials of that nasty message it contained, namely not to praise me) here is a disillusion."[172] Thérèse had mistakenly identified and praised Merton as the voice speaking on a recording of Gregorian chant, *Laudate Dominum*, which the monks at Gethsemani had recorded: "That voice is not mine.... My only commentary is contained in the written notes on the back of the envelope. The voice is that of one of our novices... really, you are full of illusions about me. Do get rid of them."[173]

Thérèse responded by telling Merton that his letter did not hurt her, though that is hard to imagine knowing her devotion to him and seeing that Merton himself had once characterized her as too sensitive: "I am happy that you were not too hurt by my reproaches about the poem in my honor," he wrote on June 5th: "I just feel as if I had no such thing as honor and to be praised makes me squirm so much that I haven't the mortification to sit still under it. Sorry you had to suffer. I notice that in any case it didn't change your wicked ways since you spent most of the letter telling me what a marvelous master of students I must be... only a saint — and I mean a <u>real</u> saint, someone who is completely dead to himself, can really help these monks. Now look: I am simply not a saint: I barely have the spirit of my Rule and I have been drifting along writing books and not really giving myself to God."[174]

Merton was taking his new job with the students and novices very seriously, perhaps, too much so: "I have to get out into the fields and give these kids a good example. The whole place might well go to pieces on account of me if I don't brush up and pull myself together and be a monk for once in my life. And I will never become one by writing a lot of books. Sorry to be so grim, but something simply has got to be done."[175] He is proofreading the galleys for *Ascent to Truth* and will send her the other journal (*Sign of Jonas*) to finish typing since the priest, Fr. Thomas, who was helping him is now occupied with the new foundation in Piffard, New York. After the stinging rebukes he asks her if she "might like to do the little that remains — although after being so nasty I hate to ask you another favor."[176]

Thérèse was still inundating him with relics, most recently of Pope Pius X about whom a book was being read to the monks, a book that Merton says is not too good, in the monastery refectory. The relics and a picture of the Pope Thérèse had sent occupied a prominent place in Merton's secluded writing vault where the "kids" came to him to talk about their problems: "I have the students on my hands and I feel like a different person. They certainly have problems. Keep praying that I may handle them properly.... I have nothing at all against being a spiritual director; in fact I quite like it: but every moment of it makes me wish I lived alone in the woods."[177] He had already sent her the first manuscript of a journal (*Sign of Jonas*) to complete the typing job, and more of his notes for her ever-expanding collection. He advises her again not to overwork herself, since teaching in summer school will occupy most of her time. Also, there is no hurry for the manuscript, as he wants more time to think it over before publishing it.

In July, Thérèse visited the Trappist Abbey of Our Lady of the Genesee in Piffard, New York to visit her friend and former Gethsemani monk, Abbot Gerard. Many years later she published "Our Lady of the Genesee" in *Commonweal* for January 18, 1957. On the same trip she visited her long-time Jesuit friend, Father Augustine Ellard. Among her papers is a brochure from the visit on "Cistercian Life in Upstate New York" autographed by Henri Nouwen, a Dutch priest-psychologist and popular spiritual writer, though she could not have met him on that occasion since he only came to the U.S. in

1964. It was only in May 1967 that Merton himself would encounter Nouwen at Gethsemani; and many years later that Nouwen would write his *Genesee Diary*.

Thérèse had already sent Merton funds to cover the postage for mailing his journals to her, but Merton told her they had already gone out in the mail before her note on "blue" stationery had arrived: "It was blue in more ways than the mere color of the paper, I thought, reading between the lines. Keep up your courage. Life is short but heaven lasts forever. What is there on this earth worth getting excited about? Or depressed about?"[178]

On September 11th, Merton's abbot, James Fox, wrote to Thérèse to tell her that he had received the notes she has sent on Merton's journal on September 4th along with some relics for Merton, but one of the "good, beautiful, angelic, contemplative, lost-in-the-cloud novice brothers" was cleaning up our room "and in his zeal for blind obedience he does not look at papers. — Scoops up everything off and away to the incinerator to burn."[179] He was hoping and praying she had made a carbon copy of the missing journal she could send him so he could have a copy made? He asks her not to tell "good Father Louis what happened. This is just between you and me, and Jesus."[180] Had Merton known what had transpired, he would have been far more understanding toward the Brother than the abbot, whom Merton felt often treated him like a child. This would surely have been one of those times.

A second letter from Fox to Thérèse on September 22nd asks for her personal reaction to Merton's publishing his journal while he is still alive. Noting that St. Thérèse's autobiography (*The Story of a Soul*) had only been published after her death, he was insinuating that, perhaps, Merton should do the same: "There is so much, necessarily and unavoidable of the I, I, I.... If Father waited until after his death, then there will be no criticisms or question."[181] He also expressed concern with Merton's exaggerated references to life at Gethsemani, no doubt for the sake of humor, but Fox felt they could easily be misinterpreted. Not surprisingly, Thérèse wholeheartedly backed the idea of journal keeping and of publishing it.

On August 25th, the feast of St. Louis of France, Merton's patronal saint from his name in religious life, he had received a note from Thérèse. His September 25th reply informs her he cannot send her a copy of *The Ascent to Truth* in time for her feast day on October 3rd, but he is sending her the manuscript of his early novel, *Journal of My Escape from the Nazis* that she had requested. *Escape* was a novel he had written when he was teaching and living at St. Bonaventure in Olean, New York, and the one novel he had not destroyed or given away. Since he does not intend to publish it, she is free to copy anything in it for her own use.[182]

By October 3rd, Merton had received the replaced typescript of the journal that had been accidentally destroyed from Fox's office in September. The abbot's ruse to keep Merton ignorant of the fact had succeeded. On October 8th, Merton apologizes to Thérèse for not acknowledging the typescript earlier, because he had only received it on October 3rd, although it had been received in September. The delay between September 11th when Fox asked Thérèse for another copy and October 3rd when Fox gave Merton the replacement, had given the abbot ample time to execute his secret plan without Merton being any the wiser.

In the October 8th letter Merton tells Thérèse that he had heard from Fr. Thomas, a monk at Piffard, of Thérèse's "lively visit," and thanks her for the photograph of Gerard she had sent. The large photograph of Merton he had sent her shows him as what he is, a perfect heel, he says, and asks her not to put any photographs on public exhibition or display them in print. He pleads with her again to "please stop calling me a saint. I can give you a good motive for doing so — you won't listen to reason… really you don't know me at all. I was grateful for your charity towards me in the article on Poetry and Education, but I am not a good poet either and it is really a waste of paper to write about me and a waste of breath to talk about me. Don't you think it is serious? Didn't Our Lord say He would judge every idle word?"[183]

In September 1951 Thérèse had published "Poetry in Education" in *Spirit*, where she compared Merton very favorably to other poets including the poet-convert priest, Gerard Manley Hopkins ("a kindred spirit"). Although she had submitted it as a letter to the editor, the journal published it as an article.[184] Merton, however, was not flattered or even pleased, and tells her bluntly on February 4th, 1952: "My general feeling is one of discomfort because when you put me up close to anyone like Hopkins it is quite evident that I am not much of a poet — although you strenuously insist that I am. Sister, I am just not that important — I wish for your sake that I were, since you think that I am."[185] She had recently reviewed his *Ascent to Truth* in *Books on Trial* with the usual extravagant encomiums and Merton asks God to bless her in her "stubborn generosity and interminable patience with these uncouth Trappists."[186]

Just before Christmas, Merton has what he terms "the gall" to send her what might not be an acceptable Christmas gift: his notes on St. Benedict for her to type. Undoubtedly, however, Thérèse must have thought it was the best possible Christmas present he could have given her! He then makes a "Scotch bargain" with her: she can keep a copy for herself if she will mimeograph about a hundred copies for him. He is working on reforestation in the woods and not writing: "The rest of my time is taken up with direction and conferences. I am really getting to know my children and love them more and more — hence they take up more of my time. But who has a better right to it?"[187]

Christmas 1951 brought Merton yet another relic (St. Augustine) from Thérèse and on January 4, 1952 he writes to thank her and answers her inquiry whether he had received her previous letter: "I know that correspondence from Milwaukee comes through especially slowly and I am not worrying. There is probably a letter from you around somewhere or on the way."[188] The students are still occupying most of his time: "My spiritual children are discovering more and more problems. I have them more and more in my heart, and in proportion as I do, I find Jesus in them, and live in Him, outside myself. That is another pathway to solitude — compassion. I scarcely have time for anything else.... A week ago today I took four of them who had been working overtime on Christmas mail out into the woods in the wildest and most beautiful spot I could find and it made them, I think, very happy."[189]

Thérèse's brother Gordon was in poor health and Merton prays that nothing serious will come of his illness: "I am sure every one of us in religion can profit by an enforced rest. Much as I hated to stay in the hospital last year, it helped me a lot both physically and spiritually. We all try to do too much.... One can still have the 'best part' in the midst of a certain activity, by being detached and free from care. But how much of our activity is useless. Forgive the meditation — for it is a meditation and not a sermon."[190]

Gordon had entered the Society of the Divine Savior in 1931 taking the religious name of Theophane, and studied theology from 1936 to 1939, earning a Bachelor's degree in theology at the Gregorian University in Rome. He was ordained on July 16, 1939 at the Minor Basilica of St. Anthony of Padua on the Via Merulana in Rome and celebrated his first Mass in the Papal crypt of the catacombs of St. Callistus on July 18.

From 1939 until 1949 Theophane was assigned to the Salvatorian Seminary in Lanham, Maryland as professor of the history of philosophy as well as superior of the community. He also studied at the Catholic University of America from 1939 to 1940, earning a Licentiate (Masters) degree in Theology. In March 1946, he was diagnosed with tuberculosis and sent for treatment to a sanatorium in Gabriels, New York, until 1947. After recovering, he was assigned to a Salvatorian parish in Menominee, Michigan, and also taught at the Salvatorian-owned Jordan Seminary there.

As has been noted already, Merton's handwriting was small, cramped and very difficult to decipher — something, he admitted, that even he often had trouble deciphering. Thérèse must have gained a great ability — a gift that Merton characterizes as "charismatic" — to be able to read it. Merton had not heard from Thérèse for some time and was wondering if she was ill with the same flu epidemic that had hit the Trappists in Utah and Gethsemani. On March 27th he continues to reassure her of his own good health in response to her regular inquiries: "Fr. Abbot watches me like a hawk and I am not allowed to keep the regular fast: eat rice and eggs. There are plenty of other ways of doing — or accepting — penance. I will not complain of the fact that I do not do enough: it always sounds silly to somebody else."[191] He mentions a "Negro priest," at Piffard, a Fr. Simon, who had died recently and asks if she had met him when she first visited there.

He reflects again on the spiritual suffering she seems to be experiencing: "The less you want, the less you suffer: but there always remains the fundamental suffering of realizing that there is something inside all of us which, though we are drawn by the love of God, still tends to oppose the love of God."[192] He goes on to describe the tension as a fight: "I suspect this lies somewhere at the root of the suffering you speak of: this ambivalence, in which you suffer, and cannot even persuade yourself that the suffering has value any more. Want it to have value: that is enough to give it value. And never expect to suffer with heroism: He won't let you. If you renounce that one desire…. You have done so, I suppose. But perhaps you expected that a return of 'heroism' would be the sign that it was accepted. Love Him without a sign: that is the best way. St. Thérèse was not given you as a patron for nothing."[193] Merton is very much aware of how much he has come to depend on her. Her saying she has found "consolation" in the St. Bernard notes she typed has assuaged his conscience: "for having imposed the labor on you. But if you go on doing such a good job, the temptation to give you more work becomes more and more irresistible."[194]

A postcard dated April 25th from Merton in Kentucky arrived in Milwaukee with a mistaken postmark of April 26th from the post office in Milwaukee. Thérèse, alarmed that Merton might have been in the city without her knowing about it, wanted to know if he had been to Milwaukee without telling her! He has no idea about the postmark, he responds on May 12th, but it really does not make any difference as long as it arrived. And, he adds jokingly, "If this one is post marked Buenos Aires — let me know."[195] She had offered to do some more typing for Merton and two months later, on July 12th, Merton suggests she might type the "Orientation" notes for his students again for the year, telling her it is a "privilege" for him to have her type his notes! He considers her both an editor and publisher. Perhaps she could do it during the summer, he suggests, but then realizes she would already be in the middle of summer school. Then, somewhat disingenuously, he writes: "I only permit myself to impose on you because you say the work is entertaining and that it amuses you. You have so many more valuable things to do: what about original work of your own?"[196] The *Journal* is ready for publication, but Merton has some fears about publishing it: "I began to worry quite a bit about the propriety of such a book. I feel like a hypocrite, writing about myself again. But the book itself is simple enough, and I suppose I was just worrying about what some people would say, and not about anything in the book itself, which, as far as I can see, is what God wants of me."[197]

Thérèse received one of the jewels of her collection on August 18th when Merton sent her the last of the original copies of *The Sign of Jonas*. He was at the time correcting the proofs and unaware that the book was headed for major problems with the Trappists' censors. She is still working on typing the conference notes for the students: "I hope you are not overworking with the notes and that you enjoy them as much as you say. It is good that <u>somebody</u> gets something out of them. But I mustn't exaggerate, either. Some of the scholastics seem to like the conferences well enough. (Please, no panegyric!)."[198]

Her letter of late August had assured him that the work she did for him was both interesting and helpful in her struggles, and he uses the occasion to comment again on her difficulties on September 2nd: "I am comforted again with the thought that the notes are of some interest to you and that they help you. Everybody <u>has</u> to have some difficulties. It is in our trials that we show our true merit and our love for God: and by that I do not mean that we show it by suffering in the grand manner, but by our poverty and our nothingness, accepted for love of Him. What can be better than His mercy? Our riches and our imagined virtues and strength tend to block the action of the one thing that makes us truly rich: the mercy of God. The religious life is full of that mercy. To receive it, we only have to be ourselves. That is — to be pretty small in our own eyes, and be glad of it. But to be ourselves. Do not imagine you have to have somebody else's humility. You have quite enough to suffer to make you humble in a way that will be uniquely your own... if only you will not let the darkness of your trial confuse you. If you get confused, you will let this great thing slip through your fingers. And if you fail to be true to yourself and to your God, you will be confused. You do not have to be a replica of some imaginary religious in somebody's pious book. You have to be the person God made you and — suffer accordingly, in order to be more and more yourself, which is to say more and more Christ in the eyes of the Father."[199] Here Merton touches on one of the fundamental themes of his own writings — the struggle each one has to experience authenticity in personhood, to get rid of the false self.

A month later, on September 18th, he thanks her for a gift of a book of English cathedrals she had sent for September 8th, the Feast of Mary's Nativity, also called Our Lady's Name Day. He recognized much in the book with certain poignancy, because he had lived in England, although when he writes of his time and impressions of England in *Mountain*, it is with anything but "poignancy." He explains this critical attitude to his experiences in England by saying that he had to be tough about it. He has a new series of notes in his own handwriting and he wonders if she still wants to keep the "privilege" of typing them. He continues to feel deeply for her in her trials: "It is easy to give advice and comfort. It was easy for Job's friends. God does not ask to be defended by Job's friends. His ways with Job are a sign of His transcendence: and in any case what happened to Job was not willed but permitted. This was something that neither Job nor his friends took into account. But since God is Who He is, even His permissions are the expression of an omnipotent mercy. Pray for me. I have some decisions to make and some graces I need."[200]

Thérèse had written to him on October 20th, about his problems over *Jonas* with the Trappist censors, but he was unable to set her mind at ease until November 6th. The Trappist censors had objected to *The Sign of Jonas* and the Abbot General had denied permission to publish it. Since it had already been printed and advertised, however, the decision had been reversed. Merton was unaware that Jacques Maritain, at the request of Bob Giroux, had written to the Abbot General in Rome protesting the decision to suppress the book. This was another instance when Fox thought it better not to inform Merton of what had really transpired. Merton thought the reverse of the decision had been brought about by a series of accidents!

In her October 20th letter, Thérèse told Merton she continued to experience tensions with her religious superiors. Merton tries to encourage her in a letter of November 6th: "I am sure that your superiors will continue to give due regard to the needs of your health, when you are such a valuable member of the Congregation. But if they should be less solicitous surely God would give you the strength to accept it and be happy about it. How can He possibly fail you? Is the religious life a trap that He draws us into in order to lead us to a point where we can go no further and where He abandons us to our fate? On the contrary, when we put ourselves in His hands we earn a right to very special helps and graces which never fail us, provided we do not fear to reach out for them. Do not be upset. His love is always with you, and He knows what human aids and consolations you need. Has He not provided for you in this respect, and sent you the advisers you need — especially in good Father Ellard?"[201]

Thérèse was coping with a nervous condition and stresses in her own life that aggravated the condition. Merton is quick to assure her that she is not to blame: "Your nervousness makes it morally impossible for you to handle your anxieties with perfect peace and with all the dispositions recommended by ascetic manuals: but that should be no source of <u>further</u> anxiety. Take your nerves as your cross and thank God for it and do the best you can with the situation."[202]

In May 1953, Merton tells Thérèse again how amazed he is at her miraculous power to decipher his illegible handwriting.[203] Without her help he could not write notes and prepare for conferences at the same time... "if I did not have you for a sister."[204] He does not capitalize the noun. By this time Merton's close friend from Columbia, Ed Rice has started *Jubilee* magazine with Bob Lax as a "roving editor" and Merton as an "advisor," since he had been forbidden to have his name appear on the masthead of any magazine. The abbot had given Merton permission to write something for the August issue of the magazine, but Merton has not seen a copy and asks Thérèse on May 20th if it has already appeared. If it has, he thinks that maybe the copy mailed to him "got into the ashcan instead."[205] Merton always felt that Fox's control of all the incoming mail meant that some publications like *Jubilee*, of which the abbot disapproved, never got through to him. Over the years many of Thérèse's own continual flow of book reviews and literary articles on Merton were published in the journal, *Renascence*, including one she had written around this time on the poet Rainer Maria Rilke, one of Merton's favorites. All of these did reach Merton.

In the summer of 1952, Thérèse was transferred to a Salvatorian-owned hospital in Wausau, Wisconsin, and was not happy with the move. She eventually returned to Milwaukee in January of 1953, briefly, to teach a class to the Salvatorian Sisters for one semester and then returned to Wausau. She taught psychology and sociology to the student nurses at St. Mary's School of Nursing during her time there and had her own office in the hospital. One Sister recalls her talking about Merton in many of the classes: "We were glad to have her as a teacher and eager to hear her because of the richness of her background."[206] She also met informally with a group of Sisters to discuss literature. While there she gave a poetry reading for a sodality of students, painted a picture of the Bishop of LaCross, John P. Treacy and some of the hospital chaplains, played the organ for special occasions such as the wedding of one of the doctors and wrote a poem for a Sister Mary Edward whose name she had chosen in a Christmas gift exchange. Virginia Erickson, who was at Wausau during Therese's time there and with whom she was on friendly terms, recalls Thérèse's negativity towards authority and provided her with a listening ear when she was unhappy and complaining about her superiors. She knew Thérèse was an artist and a dreamer in a very different culture, but thought she adjusted well. When the younger Sisters in Wausau wanted to initiate a formation program for "Junior Sisters" there similar to the "Salvatorian House" for Junior Sisters in Milwaukee, near Marquette, they had suggested Sr. Mary Edward to be its director. Thérèse told them they had chosen a "priceless gem."

Merton hopes she will profit by every minute of the new assignment and tries to console her: "Do not fret over anything that comes from me in the way of labor — it is only destined to serve as a recreation when better things pall.... I shall keep praying that all your troubles smooth out. Trouble outside of us need never disturb us inside: and if we have some ripples inside, we can ride them better by not being surprised."[207]

While she was trying to settle in with her new community and life in northern Wisconsin, Thérèse sent Merton a card from Wausau. Merton responded on June 6th: "You should abandon yourself with more and more confidence to Him, through her, even though you think your whole life is marked with anguish. That is only on the surface — but you are always aware of it because He gave you such a thin skin. It was in order to make you a saint that He did so."[208]

On September 26th Merton says he is happy to hear she is having a quiet year and is teaching psychology to the freshman nurses at the Wausau hospital. By this time she has a new superior, providentially appointed Merton suggests, who will take care of her. But even a provincial not appointed by Providence "who would not take care of you would still be providential, but not in such a nice way, and I think you are better off as it is."[209] Her return to reading the Book of Job is providing her with some consolation and Merton concurs: "the more I read the Book of Job the more I realize the dignity of suffering (which is such a new mystery in each individual in whom it occurs) and the indignity of those who have the gall to offer conventional explanations and palliatives for suffering. I hope you are well and resting and happy. Do take advantage of this rest and take care of yourself."[210] As for the photograph of herself in the woods that she had sent him: "The picture of you in the woods was a comfort: seeing is believing and I know now that you have a good place to go and be happy."[211]

He thinks the Trappists ought to send her Provincial some donation for all Thérèse's work, and plans to suggest it to Father Abbot when he returns. With Thérèse in Wausau permanently, mimeographing Merton's materials raised a logistical problem. On October 21st, he suggests that the Trappist novice Brothers at the monastery might do the duplication work there, but that will probably delay the work so the abbot thinks the work should be done outside the monastery. Another possibility is for Thérèse to make the copies in Milwaukee, but that means Thérèse would have to take the work there or pay someone to do it in Wausau: "Please do whatever is most convenient for you... whatever saves you trouble... just send the stencils here... it is about time we lifted a finger to help ourselves, after all."[212]

If Thérèse flooded Merton with relics, he sent her holy cards: "Is it really two years since I sent you any holy cards? I am ashamed of myself. Here are two or three. As a matter of fact, though, it is rather hard for me to find a decent one on the premises."[213]

Thérèse was still not happy with her new location and refers to it as being in "exile." And Merton tells her not to worry about the vacation it involves: "The wise providence of God establishes all things and orders them for the best. One of the most sanctifying things in your life is one that you like and understand least yourself: the feeling of emptiness and helplessness and fear in the depths of your heart. Learn to trust God when things seem most insecure. He does not want you to feel always sure of yourself. All that is necessary is to trust without seeing."[214] She might have been assigned to the new location because it would help her experience a more disciplined kind of community life. In Milwaukee her work schedule often interfered with her presence at community events. Perhaps the superiors thought she might not have been the best model for younger nuns in the formation community. She was a creative individual, a free spirit who needed to feel special or perhaps even important as many artistic types do. They are not always the easiest people to live or work with. A friend and former student described her as a very "layered" personality who could be quite stubborn about certain things and very fixed in her opinions on particular individuals and issues.

Thérèse not only typed Merton's notes and manuscripts, but also had the opportunity to offer suggestions now and then. On one occasion, for instance, she suggested his use of the phrase "sitting around" in a revision of one of his manuscripts was not appropriate, and offers what Merton calls, in a margin note, a more modest expression. On November 20th, Merton explained that he had to wire her with the corrections she wanted earlier because he had just received her request the previous day. He also writes in haste because, after hesitating for some time, he had received permission from the abbot to approach her about typing something that they would otherwise have to pay somebody for and, "why not you, who are the best and most cooperative typist I know."[215] This time she would receive more than just compliments, prayers and paper with his famous and illegible scrawl. He is referring to a sequel to *Seeds of Contemplation* to be called *No Man Is an Island* that he wants to get out in a timely fashion if she is willing to type it. As always, she could keep the original. There will also be financial remuneration that she cannot refuse: "...we would send some sort of remuneration for your time and work. No refusals, you have a vow of poverty and can't say no. I hope your superiors do not think I am too much of a nuisance by now."[216]

On January 21, 1954, just before Lent, he tells her that he enjoyed her review of *Jonas* because she had good words "for all my own secret favorite passages — including the Louisville junk wagon."[217] She was, at that time, typing notes for a manuscript called *Viewpoints* that was eventually published as *No Man Is an Island*. In February, she completed typing the manuscript and sent the original and a bound carbon to Merton. His only complaint was that she would not accept any kind of compensation. Thérèse was also busy with her own projects. She had contributed an article to *Jubilee* on Lourdes that Merton had read, and was lecturing locally at venues like the Sheil School of Social Studies in Chicago, and, nationally, from her "base of operation" in Wausau, as Merton called it in a letter of February 26th as Lent was beginning.

At the end of July, Thérèse sent Merton three poems she had written, but he did not respond with high praise for one of them until September 1st: "I can say at once that I am most enthusiastic about the one for 'Our Lady of Knock.' It is really inspired & your very best poem.... It has everything, and it comes from the depth, & it is universal.... It is much purer and more real than anything I have ever been able to say about her."[218] He hopes she will not be embarrassed to use it when she talks about Marian poetry. He was also fascinated by the poem about the "Chipmunk," though he thinks it could be shorter. This was the poem read at her funeral Mass by the Salvatorian priest homilist, André Papineau.

On November 29th, Merton replies to her description of her attending a Jewish Bar Milah: "Not only do you raise hawks, but you attend the rites of circumcision. It was an amusing description. When the little boy grows up and becomes a fervent Rabbi, and learns that his circumcision was attended not only by goyem but by religious goyem, the complexity of his spiritual life ought to be enough to produce something better than the novels of Kafka."[219] He also informs her that a friend of Dan Walsh, Anne Skakel, wants to do something for the monastery. Merton has agreed to let her type the new book, *Existential Communion* (later *The New Man*), because the abbot wanted to humor her. The Skakels, George and Anne (or "Big Anne" as she was known), were friends of the monastery and very generous benefactors to Gethsemani. When the new guesthouse for retreatants was built there, the chapel was named in honor of the Skakel family. Their daughter, Ethel, was the wife of Robert F. Kennedy. Anticipating her disappointment and being a bit defensive, he tries to explain: "I would not have done so if I had thought you would be eager for it. Still, I feel better in a way because it will be less of a burden for Mrs. Skakel — she has a couple of secretaries to take over when she gets tired," and a bit later attempts to placate Thérèse: "Do you mind?"[220]

Anne Skakel, being a collector herself, had four carbon copies of the Merton manuscript typed for Merton, but kept the original copy herself, knowing the value of such an item. Merton was well aware of this when he told his first bibliographer, Frank Dell'Isola in January 1955, "the big collection of such materials belongs to Sr. M. Thérèse now at St. Mary's Hospital, Wausau, Wisconsin. Mrs. George Skakel of Greenwich, Connecticut also has some of my manuscripts."[221] Surely Merton must have realized by now that Thérèse would have given anything to do the job for him. He attempts to compensate her with an offer that sounds like the proverbial crumb: "I can very easily let you have another little job I am supposed to do in the Spring."[222]

The year 1954 had been designated by the Pope as a Marian Year and Merton tells her that one of the great graces he has received would astonish people if he stated it publicly, which was his rediscovery of psychoanalysis: "I have read about all the books of Karen Horney. They are extremely good, very well balanced and sane and therefore really in accord with Catholic philosophy and ethics in the main — except for one or two details. But more than that, they seem to me to fit very well into the monastic tradition. Anyway, I think they are very fine books. You ought to try one. The best to start with would be 'Our Inner Conflicts.'"²²³

Merton's newly discovered interest in psychoanalysis and its usefulness in spiritual direction would lead to a traumatic event over an article he had written and his encounter with a noted Catholic psychiatrist. In December, he sent Thérèse something he treasures and knows she will like, perhaps to assuage her hurt feelings over having lost the job of typing the manuscript on existentialism to Mrs. Skakel — an old, beat-up magazine containing an article on his father's paintings with black and white photographs from Murat and Vieux Port in France during a Christmas holiday with his father, Owen.

# 5

## DIFFICULT YEARS FOR FRIENDS
### 1955-1959

For Christmas 1954, Thérèse had sent Merton a relic of St. Pius X whose encyclicals Merton was reading at the time. He is also preparing for a community retreat but not with any enthusiasm: "I am not terribly excited about the retreat. I made a private one over the Christmas vacation, and it was fine. I pray much better when I am not being talked at and when I can get longer periods alone in silence. Our community retreat is certainly a time of grace but there is so much running about from one exercise to another that it usually doesn't do much for me."[224]

Thérèse's letter accompanying the gift mentioned to Merton a painful experience in 1953, caused by words and decisions within her religious order that had negatively affected her life. The decision and the emotions surrounding it might have been her reassignment to the convent in upstate Wisconsin. He counsels her about it on January 18th, 1955: "It seems to me that the religious life contains fierce hidden sufferings, more for some than for others, but hardly anyone escapes unless he has a skin so thick that nothing ever gets through. Those sufferings are unavoidable. There is no explaining them rationally because they come from things that <u>should not be</u> — words that never should have been said, decisions that should never have been made. But the things were said, and made. And the ones involved stick to them blindly. Saints persecute saints, in the peace of the cloister. The suffering is all the more acute because one sees so clearly 'this should not be' — this is not what Christ planned for us. No, the abuses are not what He planned. But the bearing of them is something we can give to Him. The big thing is to get away without getting a martyr complex about it."[225] Most people, including Merton and Thérèse, he says, "just suffer and feel the whole thing terrifically and struggle vainly against it; and no rationalization is of any effect. It leaves deep wounds, too. But it is a great thing to be hurt by it all and still not be warped and spoiled. You have much to be thankful for: you are *you*. You are a person. So many others have gone through the mill and stopped being people after the first two years of it."[226]

She writes on St. Anne's Day, July 26th, and sends him the completed typed notes of his article titled, "Sacred Art." On August 6th he informed her he was taking a vacation from writing, and would not have time to rewrite the article. Nevertheless, the monk who lived to write, and complained constantly that all his writing distracted him from being a real monk, still wanted it to be published very badly — maybe *Jubilee* would take it as it is, he mused.

The abbot at Gethsemani at the time was in the process of appointing a new prior who is the second in command and responsible for the everyday running of the monastery. Merton, at least on the surface, says he does not want to be considered: "My health is all right, and they are certainly not making me Prior. That is not a job for me. I more or less asked to be considered 'out' when all Superiorship was concerned and Father Abbot and even the Abbot General have accepted this from me."[227] Merton had said there was a serious reason why he should never be elected. Some have speculated that it was because he had fathered a child during his student days in England, although the woman and child were supposedly killed in the Blitz.

He was still struggling with the need for more solitude and the possibility even of being a quasi-hermit: "I have been put in full charge of the forest. The state rangers are putting up a fire-lookout

## Difficult Years for Friends

post on our highest hill [Vineyard Knob]. I am supposed to take charge of it."[228] The agreement was that he would remain on duty in the tower for the entire day, coming to the monastery daily only for Mass and one meal. The abbot thought this might be somewhat of an answer to Merton's need for more solitude, and perhaps lessen his attraction to the eremitical life. Merton took his turn in the monastery fire watch but never as "fire watcher" at Vineyard Knob nor did he ever take up residence there.

He had made a private retreat after Christmas and confirmed his conviction that he had a solitary vocation of some sort: "Because solitary vocations do not fit into neat categories. And neither do I. All I know about it is that it is of 'some sort.' The big development has come since I gave up, myself, trying to fit it into too neat a category — 'Carthusian,' for instance. This, by the way, is all in confidence."[229]

Thérèse had written to describe a private retreat she had made with a Jesuit retreat master and he tells her he is glad she did not have the Jesuit who had given a community retreat at Gethsemani in January 1955 just after Merton's private retreat after Christmas. He describes Fr. Bruno, also a Jesuit, as a "stern disciplinarian, who scares people into being observant for a few months against their own secret desires, but does nothing to really change people from the inside. I wonder how much human understanding one would find in him?"[230] While acknowledging that the man might have accomplished some good, Merton compared him to the kind of director St. John of the Cross called a spiritual blacksmith. Each conference was an anvil chorus, but "for the love of heaven, don't quote me!"[231] Despite his trenchant criticism of the retreat master, Merton is willing to acknowledge, "I am fond of the dear good man. I had a couple of talks with him, and he means so well, and has such good aspirations and intentions, and after all God uses strange instruments... for all our human appraisal of his gifts, he must do a tremendous amount of good."[232]

In the fall, Ed Rice, a close friend of Merton, with whom

Thérèse had also cultivated a friendship, had sent her the original manuscript of *The Tower of Babel*, a gesture that pleased Merton, even though he had not yet seen the printed version that appeared in *Jubilee* magazine. Thérèse had once sent him a book about the Carthusians as a Christmas gift but it never reached him because "anything eremitical is considered bad for cenobites and it is kept outside the iron curtain."[233] In October 1955, the novice master at Gethsemani, Walter Helmstetter, was elected abbot of Our Lady of the Genesee Monastery in Piffard, New York at the young age of 34. Merton volunteered for the position of novice master just at the time the abbot was prepared to release him from his job as master of students, and allow him to live full time as a hermit under certain conditions. Ironically, this new position opened up just when he was anticipating more time for solitude since the position of fire warden had not been able to satisfy Merton's yearning for more solitude. Once appointed as novice master, however, Merton retained the position until 1965, when he finally was allowed to live as a full time hermit. Merton sent Thérèse a photograph of the novices on December 23rd as a Christmas gift rather than a monastery Christmas card, because the monastery cards were filled, he claims, with corny verses and a commercial tone he did not appreciate.

In January 1956, Thérèse had mailed Merton notes of his conferences she had typed with her suggestion for arranging them in sections. They arrived, he says, on January 28th during the Octave of the feast of St. Agnes (January 21). She had sent him earlier a relic of St. Clare, one of Merton's favorites, and he thanks her for it. At the time she was reviewing Merton's new book, *The Living Bread*, with a preface by Cardinal Gregory Agagianian. She heard from him on February 21st, but not again until May 26th: "You must think I am dead for sure, this time. Have you said a *De Profundis* for my soul? However I am alive and busy."[234] He had been occupied in the monastery fields with plowing and picking strawberries. He writes again on June 11th to thank her for a note on the anniversary of his ordination, May 26th.

*Difficult Years for Friends*

On September 25, 1956, Merton informs Thérèse that the ultimate "iron curtain" had descended on him and that his greetings for her feast day in October might be the last of his letters outside the official writing seasons (All Saints, Christmas, Easter and the Assumption) when the monks were allowed to send and receive mail. He relishes their correspondence and that of his other friends, though he has put on a show of being an ascetic. Since he had not gotten permission to write and inform Bob Lax and Ed Rice about the crackdown on correspondence, he asks Thérèse to inform them about the new restrictions. He has not written, or so he claims, or worked on anything recently but course lectures and "a little Christmas thing which, I believe, will come out this year."[235] *The Tower of Babel* will be published in the spring and *The Silent Life* is due out in the fall!

In the same letter he admits that a recently published bibliography by Dell'Isola "makes it quite evident that with me writing is less a talent than an addiction. Father Abbot hopes I can be cured of it now, and so do I. Nothing has been said about <u>never</u> writing again, but at least everyone wants to see how I get along without writing over a period of several years and I think it is certainly a necessary step to take."[236] Merton asks Thérèse to help Frank Dell'Isola (author of the first Merton bibliography) by sharing with him some of the orientation notes. Dell'Isola was one of the last persons to have seen Dylan Thomas alive when he visited him in the hospital and said that the real reason he died was that "when he came down with pneumonia and alcoholism, his friends could think of nothing better to do than call in a Christian science practitioner!"[237]

Taking advantage on November 8th of the permission to write during the octave days of the Feast of All Saints, he answers her letter of November 1st as among the four authorized letters he needs to answer. For some reason, a letter from his friend Bob Lax never got through. Merton says he actually enjoys receiving mail from friends rather than from complete strangers: "…one enjoys contacts more when the letters are from one's real friends, and not just a pile of ill-assorted business and other nonsense from complete strangers. It is indeed a relief not to be dealing with mail <u>all</u> the time.... I do hope Father Abbot will include you as 'family' now."[238]

Thérèse had sent him a collection of her poems, both old and new, which she hopes to have published (eventually as *Moment in Ostia*) and he critiques some of them in detail, but always with generous compliments. The poems contained in a section called "Monastery Detail," however, did not impress him: "Forgive me if I say that, all in all, I feel pretty well snowed under by that section, and I think you have said much too much: I mean it is all too fulsome, perhaps... I was wondering if the impression could not be counteracted or changed... will you forgive me, and consider it, at least? I do not want to force my opinions on you, and no doubt I am a little prejudiced. But it is uncomfortable to be so praised when I know so fully that I am not worth anything and such things should not be said about me. No, honestly, I am not just 'being humble.'"[239]

The abbot had finally stopped Merton from all writing. Thérèse had asked him for a Preface for St. Bernard's letters, but Merton cannot comply: "There is nothing I would like better, but I know you will understand. I even feel guilty for jotting down notes for the novitiate conferences still... I am not allowed to write poems, keep a journal, anything. This may sound pretty fierce, but actually it is wise. Writing with me was really turning into an addiction and I am glad of the respite.... It is certainly important for me to keep silent, above all about myself, at least for a while."[240] Thérèse had been told that this was a general cracking down on Trappist writers, but Merton clarifies: "It is true that the Abbot General is progressively tightening up restrictions and making the censorship tougher and tougher so that writers will be definitely discouraged in the Order. And that too is all right — it is really the spirit of the Order to keep silent!!! However not all the writers have been clamped down on and certainly not everybody has had their mail stopped.... I am the only one in the house that has his mail heavily censored and screened even on the four feasts when letters are allowed for all."[241]

*Difficult Years for Friends*

Merton writes only very sporadically during 1957. Between January 3rd and November 14th of that year, there are only 5 extant letters from Merton to Thérèse. At the conclusion of the post-Christmas letter-writing season, on January 3, 1957, Merton writes one of his four officially permitted letters to Thérèse. She had inquired about the exposition of the relics she sent. He assures her that they were exposed in the novitiate chapel on their various Feast Days, and thanks her for the latest relic of St. Anselm. His assistant and right-hand man, Fr. John of the Cross, had been made master of students. Merton describes him as "one of those who was closest to me among the students, a very talented and holy young priest…. I am glad of it — he will be a good one for the job…."[242] Ending with a postscript saying he will write at Easter, if he can, sounds as if Merton was taking the restrictions on letter writing seriously. One might wonder if he was not a bit relieved not to have to carry on such frequent and intensive correspondence. In any case, it did not dampen his correspondent's letter-writing enthusiasm.

In his August 21st letter he mentions a new novice, Ernesto Cardenal, a young Nicaraguan poet whose religious name at Gethsemani was Brother Lawrence. It was Cardenal who first aroused Merton's interest in and contact with prominent literary and political figures in Latin America. Cardenal and Merton formed a close friendship and even talked about the possibility of starting a new kind of contemplative community on Big Corn Island, off the coast of Nicaragua. Merton was still thinking of some remote location that would afford more solitude.

Nothing ever came of the project. Cardenal left Gethsemani in July 1959 and later founded a community of about a thousand fishermen called Nuestra Senora de Solentiname on an archipelago of islands on Lake Nicaragua. He pressed Merton through letters with pleas to join him there as a spiritual father. Later, Cardenal became the Minister of Culture in the Sandinista government in Nicaragua. As a kneeling, suppliant priest on the tarmac of Nicaragua's airport, he was the recipient of Pope John Paul II's very public finger-wagging and refusal to let Cardinal kiss his ring when the Pope arrived for a papal visit there in 1983.

During this period of exploring various locations that would provide him with more solitude, Merton was also in contact with Dom Gregorio Lemercier, the prior of an experimental monastic community in Cuernavaca, Mexico. Lemercier visited Merton in Gethsemani, and was trying to arrange a transfer of Merton from Gethsemani to Mexico. The experiment at Cuernavaca was later curtailed by the Vatican because of accusations involving the use of psychoanalysis by the monks, and other controversial innovations in the community. Lemercier eventually left the religious life after a protracted struggle with Rome and later married.

Merton was also in touch with several U.S. bishops about the possibility of a hermitage in some remote part of their dioceses. None of his plans ever came to fruition, nor would Merton have been successful in obtaining Rome's permission, though he made several efforts with advice and support from prominent clerical writers on monasticism such as Dom Jean Leclercq and Jean Danielou, SJ.

Cardenal, Fr. Tarcicius (Conner) and Fr. John of the Cross (Wasserman) were Merton's closest friends at Gethsemani. His relationship with Fr. John is mentioned many times and in some detail in Merton's diaries and journals. Merton was attracted by Fr. John's personality and intellect and took it very hard when the priest left Gethsemani. He was also Merton's confessor. After Cardenal returned to Nicaragua, Merton discovered that the abbot returned to Cardenal an unopened letter addressed to Merton and marked "Conscience Matter." Merton was furious, and told the abbot in a face-to-face meeting that Cardenal was a close personal friend. Grousing in one of his letters he says: "Now at that moment I noticed the expression on Dom James's face. He thought he'd won. To say that I had an 'intimate friend' was as good as confessing to a particular friendship.... It was all perfectly clear in his mind — I was a homosexual! — you see how he comes to his conclusions."[243]

In his August letter, Merton commends Thérèse on her project

## Difficult Years for Friends

of protecting the rabbits at Wausau and talks about some new birds he has spotted at the monastery. He also confirms what she had heard — that he had traveled to St. John's University, Collegeville, Minnesota the previous summer — to meet with the noted Catholic psychiatrist, Gregory Zilboorg.

Some commentators on this incident believe that the abbot misled Merton in order to set up a personal encounter with Zilboorg, but it seems as if Zilboorg himself arranged the meeting between Merton and himself at the conference, perhaps to confirm in person what he had already concluded through reading Merton's works. Merton had developed an interest in psychiatry in conjunction with his position as student master and the counseling it involved and had written a paper titled "Neurosis in the Monastic Life." Zilboorg had read it and objected strongly to its being published because he believed it would be harmful. The psychiatrist also thought he understood Merton's personality and problems in the monastery as if he had personally psychoanalyzed Merton rather than merely having read Merton's books and articles. Merton had first met Zilboorg at St. John's Abbey in July 1956, at a workshop on psychology and religion. The psychiatrist had some rather harsh criticisms of Merton, although Merton, at first, thought he was terrific.

Jim Forest recounts the meeting: "Zilboorg came to their meeting loaded with preconceptions about Merton largely based on reading *The Sign of Jonas*. At a private meeting Zilboorg told Merton that he was in 'bad shape,' a 'semi-psychotic quack' as well as a gadfly to his superiors, to whom he kept coming back until he got what he wanted. His attraction to fame revealed megalomania and narcissism. He was the kind of 'promoter type' who makes a killing on Wall Street one day and loses it on the horses the day after. His writing was becoming 'verbological' while his 'hermit trend' was pathological. As Merton listened, he couldn't help but think how much Zilboorg resembled Stalin. Yet Zilboorg was saying nothing worse than what Merton had written in his journal in his darker moments."[244] A second meeting with Zilboorg and Merton's abbot proved to be very traumatic for Merton who "flew into a fury and cried tears of rage."[245] Merton later accused the abbot of using this emotional outburst as evidence to authorities in Rome — to whom Merton had appealed for permission to leave the monastery — that Merton should not be allowed to become a hermit outside Gethsemani.

The flu epidemic that year hit both Gethsemani and Thérèse's community in northern Wisconsin. On November 14th Merton says her description of her illness sounds miserable, and that he is getting a cold himself. She was in the habit of sending him voluminous clippings about various people and events, but they were delayed in reaching Merton, since the abbot was reading each one personally as they arrived before he gave them to Merton: "It appears that I will indeed get some. It will be interesting to see which, I will let you know, and perhaps, that will be a barometer reading for future references. I am awfully sorry to subject you to our petty regulations like this. I hope you will forgive me."[246]

In spring 1958, Thérèse inquires once again about the possibility of a visit in one of two unanswered letters to Merton. Finally, he replies on April 18th: "Father Abbot is getting stricter all the time about correspondence and visits, the two things he is really strict about, and I just don't think it is possible that he will ever countenance visits of women who are not close relatives — or enormously wealthy benefactors. You are certainly a benefactor, but he doesn't look at it that way. You know how much I would enjoy talking over so many things: but as it is I am left in no doubt that he thinks I am way over my quota all the time, in these matters."[247] As for the color Kodachrome photograph of himself he had sent her, he would prefer to keep it out of sight, but she can do what she wants with it as long as it is not published. The good news was that his *Secular Journal* that had been blocked by the Trappist censors had finally been cleared for publication. In May he asks her to send clippings of Vice-President Nixon's visit to South America.

In the spring of 1959, Thérèse's new book of poetry, *Moment in*

*Ostia* was published. Merton commends her on April 3rd, and sympathizes with her distress at some printer's error: "*Moment in Ostia* is very fine.... I am most partial to the sonnets at the end. They are very womanlike and beautiful and I think they are absolutely your best work, much better than your free verse.... The work that seems to me less good reminds me of Merton.... So many thanks and compliments; it is a fine book with all the printer's carelessness."[248]

On May 14th Merton sends her copies of French and South American magazines for which he has written articles. It was during this period of his monastic life, and as a result of his friendship with Cardenal, that Merton pursued his interest in Latin America, and had begun corresponding with some of the leading poets and intellectuals. Thérèse had reminded him that he had not signed the materials he sent and he explains his policy: "I am not making a practice of automatically signing everything, it seems to be too mechanical, and I don't think that a signature dispensed like that would have any value. Mine doesn't have any value anyway, but there is no point in carrying things so far. But when the books come I will gladly sign them. A book is different."[249]

Thérèse's Congregation of Sisters was in the process of electing a Mother General and Merton was praying for its success, knowing the impact it could have on Thérèse's life and work: "It is so important to have understanding superiors and not ones who run the congregation like a machine. The religious life is for the souls of the religious, not for the 'outfit' — a thing that is often sadly forgotten. But the Holy Spirit will certainly take care of you."[250] On July 4th Merton responds to several of her "charming" letters, envying her descriptions of the rural beauties of the woods, deer and wildlife in Wausau. The results of the election of a new Mother General apparently did not make her happy: "I don't envy your General [major superior in Rome]. Whether in the world or in the Church, power corrupts. And it is a sad thing that obedience and authority, which are blessings in themselves, can in certain circumstances be used for the harm of souls. It is a thing that I am afraid I notice more and more, that the rigid institutionalism of religious life, though intended as a safeguard and a source of greater security, sometimes, or even often, ends up by stifling the spiritual life of souls that get 'caught in the machine'... of course we have to be discreet in saying these things, but we have to face them.... I hope that you or your Congregation will suffer no ill effects.... How is the new Provincial?"[251]

Commenting again on the fat packets of newspaper clippings she was sending him on a regular basis, Merton makes an attempt to curtail the amount. He prefers, he says, big outstanding stories he can post on the bulletin board for the novices, rather than the large number of miscellaneous and feature type items from the newspapers she is sending that are too small for the bulletin board and, probably too much trouble for her to send. He had sent her more of his own materials recently for her collection — notebooks, proofs, newspaper articles and some poems — items he calls another "package of junk." Thérèse is still anxious about the possibility of being assigned to another location, but Merton is optimistic: "I shall be praying that you will be happy wherever He places you, and at the same time I'll be hoping that it is still Wausau. It sounds so ideal for you."[252]

In July, Merton was at one of his low points, but none of this comes across in his letters to her during this period. His plans for a monastery with Cardenal somewhere in South America had not materialized and Cardenal will probably have to leave Gethsemani. Merton confides to his diary on July 5th some of his harshest criticisms of the abbot and the community, in which he does not even spare himself: "Here on the one hand you have the ones who believe in mechanical regularity — strict fidelity to the system in force... hardly able to produce any spiritual fruit excepting the satisfied sense of duty that warms the heart of a conformist — when he has conformed. For the rest it seems only to produce warped and eccentric personalities.... Dom James is not one of those who insist on regularity. His myth is vaguer and in the long run more harmful: that of the jolly, fervent, family of girl scouts and little boys... none of us are really monks. The top sergeants of regularity are only sergeants. Rev. Father is a girl scout. The others are frustrated scholars or businessmen or housemaids. And I — a frustrated intellectual, pseudo-contemplative, pseudo-hermit."[253]

He had promised Thérèse a special gift that she would certainly like, but on July 31st he informs her that Victor Hammer, a local artist and friend of Merton in Kentucky, is ill and cannot finish the special edition of *Sayings of the Desert Fathers*. As a replacement, he sends some of the proofs of the book along with other odds and ends. His prayers for a sympathetic Provincial have been answered, but the Mother General is another thing: "I am glad you have a good Provincial, but the news about the General makes me MAD. These authorities that love their own authority and pay not a bit of attention to Canon Law.... It gets to be authority for its own sake, sometimes. And they wonder why souls are broken under the burden.... I hope your Provincial will be very wise and guided by the Holy Spirit — and that you will stay up there in the quiet woods."[254] Lax and Rice are not frequent correspondents with Thérèse, but Merton calls them busy and crazy — both of which make them undependable correspondents.

Near the end of September, Merton is cleaning house and promises to send Thérèse whatever he decides to discard. The Soviet Premier, Nikita Khrushchev, had just visited the United States, and Merton wants clippings of both that event and President Eisenhower's return visit to Russia. At Gethsemani he gets bits and pieces of the news, but not enough to have any real idea of what is going on. From her November 1st, All Saints Day letter, Merton thinks Thérèse is sounding very well and happy and maybe, he suggests, it might have something to do with the packages of "waste paper" he had sent to her as promised.

Merton had written to Luis Somoza, the dictator in Nicaragua, with a plea that prisoners not be subject to torture. He had heard about the political situation there directly from Cardenal whose relatives had been imprisoned and tortured by the regime. He has received an unbelievable response from Somoza denying any torture in that country and it upsets him: "This whole business of political injustice and inhumanity is a tremendous problem and one to which we cannot blind ourselves. We are all getting more and more deeply involved in collective patterns of injustice without having the faintest realization of it. We are certainly to some extent responsible and implicated in what happens in Nicaragua since Spellman in person made a big speech down there boosting Somoza and saying what a fine leader, et cetera, et cetera... the problems get so vast and so intricate that no one can keep track of them, but still even a contemplative — rather most of all a contemplative — has no right whatever to ignore the issues."[255]

On October 27, 1959, Thérèse appeared on "Spotlight," a television program to talk about the life and work of Merton, broadcast from Waukesha, and sponsored by the Milwaukee-based Schlitz Brewing Company. While Merton joked about "the oodles of Schlitz" as very appropriate: "I used to drink plenty of beer, though now that is not even theoretically possible, since even if we had it I couldn't touch it, say the Drs. (Did have some in fact when one of the novices' parents visited, and it upset me badly)."[256] He also asked her seriously not to get him on television again "because for sure the news will get back to this place of contemplative austerity and the iron curtain will tighten still tighter and <u>nothing</u> will be able to get out. Honestly please be very circumspect, because there will be a frightful hullabaloo if this were discovered. Evidently Fr. Abbot didn't read your letter (<u>Deo Gratias</u>), but certainly he will not permit things like pictures, etc. to get out if he hears about it…. What do you think would happen if he heard about your misdeeds in that film??? With all due respect to Wausau, the Athens of the north, I am glad it wasn't Milwaukee or a <u>big</u> city. But I am still secretly laughing, especially at Schlitz. Somehow it is symbolic."[257]

If one wonders how Merton can get away with writing about the abbot in a letter that might have been read by the abbot, he clears it up in the following paragraph: "Incidentally Fr. Abbot is not here now, and that is why I can write this frankly to warn you to

## Difficult Years for Friends

be careful — which he would certainly want me to do anyway."[258] In the same letter he encloses cards for the television station technicians who worked on the program, but, "I think it would be better if I stayed far from TV, in every respect. Books, and talk about the author, ok, but not movies and not pictures of me, please, please. To me it is per se indifferent (though my personal preference is to stay out of sight). But on principle, and considering the ideas of the Order — it just has to be that way."[259]

Merton is very much aware that Thérèse had been traveling and lecturing on him: "I hope your lectures were a great success and did a lot to make people happy and interested in spiritual things."[260] By this time he has, seemingly, abandoned his attempts to convince her to stop her promotion of his life and writing. He asks for her prayers, as he always does, but especially at what he calls a "crucial time," but not because of his health, which is fine, including a minor operation, that went nicely. He concludes with one further request about her collection asking her to be circumspect about exhibiting his letters to her because it might encourage people to write to him. He has no secretary, just a monk who helps with the typing, and Merton hates to get letters that he cannot answer. His attitude to mail has changed dramatically from his early pious feeling about all the mail he had received after the publication of his autobiography.

# 6

## MATURITY AND GROWTH
### 1960-1964

On May 30, 1960, the Feast of St. Joan of Arc, Merton writes for the first time on a new Royal typewriter with foreign accent keys, but no question mark. Having selected the keys himself, he jokes that it is an indication of his own excessively dogmatic nature, prone to make declarations, but not ask questions. In response to Thérèse's inquiry about what relics he would like, he suggests St. Anthony of the Desert, but thinks there are probably no relics of that saint available since he was buried in an unknown place. St. Joan of Arc and the martyrs of Uganda are also on his list of favorites, but his devotion to saints, he comments, seems to be to the difficult ones whose relics are impossible to procure.

He apologizes for not having written at Easter not because of health problems, although he was having trouble with his eyes, but because he had had a lot of difficulties and distractions: "First of all with censors. You have no idea how absurd they have been. I wrote an article on solitude and anyone would think that it was an obscene novel, the way they landed on it. There is in the Order a kind of terror of any mention of the solitary life, no doubt because the tradition in this regard is unpalatable among us: we have decided that the cenobitic life is the ne plus ultra and we have to struggle by main force to keep ourselves convinced of this. Such absurdities arise from the arbitrary fantasies of institutional thought; thinking for the 'outfit' rather than in accordance with truth and the full tradition of the Church."[261]

A 1955 version of the same article had already been published both in French and Italian with no objections from the Order's censors in those countries. He had even re-written the original foreign version three times for publication in English, until he thought he had finally gotten it right. The Trappist censors in Rome, however, accused him of directly attacking his superiors and authorities of the Church, and preaching that people should be guided by the Holy Spirit and not by Church authority and spiritual directors: "This was for a sentence which ran something like: 'those who say interior solitude is sufficient do not realize what they are saying....' This was interpreted to mean superiors, as if no one else would ever think of saying such a thing. In another sentence, where I said that the principal anguish of the solitary life was that the hermit did not have anyone to guide him and the will of God pressed upon him with immediacy or something like that. Overlooking the fact that I said this was a source of anguish, they picked that up and said I was preaching against authority and spiritual direction and saying that everyone should seek to be guided directly by the Holy Ghost. You never saw such a stupid mess. The Abbot General Gabriel Sortais picked this up and flew into one of his rages, which can be very stormy, and I was all but consigned to the nether regions as a contumacious heretic."[262] The article in question was scheduled to appear in a new book, *Disputed Questions*, which was already in galley form.

*Jubilee* magazine, of which Merton was one of the originators, had recently turned down an Easter poem submitted by Thérèse. Merton tells her that the poem must have been too dense for *Jubilee* because it is a journal that only publishes poetry as an exception, and suggests she submit it to a more literary magazine. She told him she had been invited to Loretto Heights College in Denver, Colorado, to direct the poetry section of the Writing Workshop scheduled for June 25 to July 29. Merton is excited for her and encourages her to use the opportunity to introduce the students to both old and new poets.

Merton's last letter of 1960 is dated December 5th in which he responds to her raising the name of the controversial French Jesuit paleontologist, Pierre Teilhard de Chardin who had caused Merton some trouble. Ed Rice had sent Merton a copy of Teilhard's *The Divine Milieu* and Merton had written a review before reading the author's other work, *The Phenomenon of Man*. The review drew criticism from the Trappist censors who, Merton claims, "went into a panic, and the General took it up. They gave the article to some professor in Rome [who] said there was really nothing wrong with the article, but that Rome wanted Catholic magazines to keep silence about Teilhard de Chardin right now, and that it would be much better if I did not say anything. So it is not being published. It is all right with me, but do think that this is an unnecessarily cautious decision…. I don't know whether it is correct to say loosely that 'Rome' does not want anything said. Rather that certain elements in Rome do not want anything said in approval of T. de C."[263]

Merton claimed he had made it clear to the censors that it was only a review of one work of Teilhard and not an approbation of all his writings or his theology. Merton, however, was personally sympathetic towards Teilhard and, a few years later on June 10th confided to his 1967 journal: "I have the greatest liking and sympathy for Teilhard as a person and especially because of the treatment he had to undergo from his superiors — consistently silenced, removed from the scene, set aside, deprived of all recognition, all the usual petty machinations of a baroque, political Church to keep him quiet, and to prevent him having a 'bad influence.' And when one considers the approved illegible dullness that was encouraged and flourished instead!"[264] This, of course, should be read in light of Merton's own painful experience a few years earlier of being silenced by Church authorities on the topic of war.

He expresses his approval of the recent election of John F. Kennedy, though he thinks there was not much choice between the two candidates: "Kennedy is the better man, at least shows promise of much more development. And it is time to get the Republicans out of there; they have made a mess of things, especially foreign policy."[265]

Merton had initiated informal "conversations" with some local Protestant groups and the Abbey had constructed a small meetinghouse on the property for their gatherings and discussions. He refers to it as a "hermitage" where he can spend some time occasionally in the afternoon, but since he knows that he will not be permitted to live there permanently (he calls that a 'taboo') at the present time, he instructs Thérèse not to say too much about it. From December 1960 onward he had been allowed to spend, at times, half a day there. It was not until 1965, however, that he would be given permission to resign as master of novices and take up full time and permanent residency in the hermitage as an officially approved Trappist hermit, a goal toward which he been working for many years. The Abbot General is coming in January and Merton worries that he may veto the whole thing. He may not be able to write again before Christmas but will be sending more materials. He sends Advent greeting with the hope that God "will give you many special and wonderful spiritual gifts, though you may not fully realize what He is about. Let us trust Him always, and not rely on what people say about Him, because it is so often misleading, colored by their personality. I often wonder if we priests do more to hide God from men than to reveal Him. May he speak through us in spite of our limitations and failings."[266]

Thérèse was still pursuing relics for Merton. In early 1961 she sends him three new ones. On February 5th, he is still answering Christmas mail and responds to her question whether he likes the relics. By this time, it would have been rather awkward for him to say anything but "yes"! Merton, however, did have a genuine fondness for relics as one expression of his preference for some of the more traditional aspects of Catholicism. He replies that only icons are as precious and meaningful as relics — like one from Mt. Athos — but not "ghastly" like some of the modern icons. Thérèse had also sent him a relic of Pius X, but since he already had one, he passed it on to one of his assistants who had been promoted to the job of master of scholastics. The other two relics were those of St. Gregory Nazianzen and St. Thomas à Becket. As for a relic of St. Joan of Arc, he has given up on ever getting that one: "I don't expect to ever see more of her than a drop of water from the Seine at Rouen and that is not particularly sanctified... a lot of water has gone by Rouen since the ashes of the saint were thrown into it. Or were they?"[267]

Merton mentions *Sedes Sapientiae*, the 1961 letter of Pope John XXIII, stipulating that Latin should be maintained as the official language of the Church and that theology courses in seminaries should be taught in Latin. While some professors made valiant attempts, the document was honored more in the neglect than in the implementation. Some commentators suggested it might have been a compromise forced on the Pope to keep the curial traditionalists happy. Merton was scheduled to teach a course in mystical theology in the pastoral theology year, but does not comment on the prospect of teaching it in Latin.

Merton, pleading a vow of poverty, attempts on more than one occasion to dampen her enthusiasm for providing him relics. While he is delighted with each new saint she sends, he does not want to encourage her: "Though I love relics I am also supposed to be poor... but I don't mind acquiring spiritual riches for the novitiate as well as for myself. I just want to say I am always delighted with the presence of a new saint, but I feel I should not urge you on in this... it is after all a kind of possessiveness and I am not as much of a poor monk as I ought to be, with a room full of books and other things like that."[268]

He is still dealing with Teilhard because he has been required by the General to read "a book about T., an attack on him by a rather second rate theologian. I read it, and the whole controversy fills me with boredom.... I have thirty better things to do, I don't intend to argue. I'll wait until Teilhard is fully published and not misrepresented on one side or the other, and when reading him does not imply joining a movement. I still like him."²⁶⁹

Thérèse continued to send packets of newspaper and magazine clippings on a regular basis, but Merton tells her he does not really want any clippings about President Kennedy "because around here he [Kennedy] comes fourth, after the Father, the Son and the Holy Ghost, and everything he does is faithfully read in the refectory or posted on the cloister board."²⁷⁰ What he does want are clippings on literature, art, the Church in general for the novices and, for himself items on the Orient, Latin America and Africa. He is critical of his first bibliographer, Frank Dell'Isola because he had written that Merton's best work was *No Man Is an Island* and that Merton had not done anything good since then: "...which shows his perspective is all off. Not that I claim to be doing specially good work, but to pick *No Man Is an Island* which is so vague and not characteristic, and overlook something like the notes on solitude in *Disputed Questions* which is what I really have to say.... It shows he does not know who he is dealing with at all. He is not able to judge and discriminate between one thing of mine and another."²⁷¹

On March 3, 1962, Thérèse sends Merton a postcard of an angel by the painter Melozzo da Forli, thanking him for his pre-Lenten present of *Introduction to Christian Mysticism*. This is the first extant piece of correspondence from Lentfoehr to Merton. Though thrilled to receive the mimeographed notes, she expresses her sadness that she is not "in a position to do these things for you anymore as heretofore (and also perhaps some selfishness in the meantime as I used to fall heir to the precious manuscripts — which really form a wonderful part of the Mertoniana)."²⁷² There is still snow in Wisconsin, but Thérèse continues to feed her birds, including a one-legged starling who hops about pitifully, but innocent of his handicap. Her card is signed, "Your sister, S.M. Thérèse." The noun, "sister," is not capitalized — a practice that becomes more frequent over the years.

In the previous summer Merton had struggled with his feeling that he should be addressing contemporary issues: "I don't feel that I can in conscience, at a time like this, go on writing just about things like meditation, though that has its point. I cannot just bury my head in a lot of rather tiny and secondary monastic studies either. I think I have to face the big issues, the life-and-death issues: and this is what everyone is afraid of."[273] Between October 1961 and October 1962, Merton was writing on issues of nuclear war and peacemaking in a series of privately mimeographed "circular letters" that he sent to friends and correspondents. Since he had already run into criticisms for his writings on war, this was a way of getting his views circulated without having to submit them to a Trappist censor prior to publication. One of the letters, number 20, incorporated two paragraphs of a January 11, 1962 letter to Thérèse in which he comments on the tactics of some of the more extreme anti-war groups in the United States. In the same letter he mentions favorably Thomas Keating, the newly elected abbot at the Trappist Abbey in Spencer, Massachusetts. Keating later became a popular spiritual writer and a much sought-after speaker primarily on the concept and practice of centering prayer.

In the spring of 1962, Merton is still engaged with his writing and ecumenical dialogues with Protestant ministers, and entertaining a constant stream of other visitors. On the Vigil of the Ascension, May 10th, he commends her for being the guardian angel of the chipmunks in the north woods of Wisconsin where she is still living. He never sees any chipmunks at the novitiate, though, because the wild cats on the monastery property hunt them for food. That revelation must have saddened Thérèse!

In early June, Thérèse had sent Merton her catalogue of the materials in her collection and inquired about specific items. He thanks her on June 15th for what he thinks should really be called a book: "It was quite an 'experience' for me, too, and gave me much to reflect on. First of all the... perspicacity with which you have handled all that material. What splendid use you have made of every little thing: and I was agreeably surprised to find that long forgotten bits of scraps and poems or even essays I had thought long ago destroyed or lost, all turn up there. It's like the Day of Judgment and that can be taken two ways, since every idle word is to be judged! But seriously, you have done a marvelous job. I have been through it once, and will now go through it again more carefully and make all the observations you request."274

Merton's articles on peacemaking that had aroused opposition in some quarters routinely appeared in the pages of *Catholic Worker, Jubilee, Blackfriars* and *Fellowship* and he sensed, correctly, that eventually he might be forbidden to write. In fact in the letter of June 15th he informs Thérèse that he has finally been silenced on the issue of war and peace and that his Trappist superiors have also forbidden the publication of a new book, *Peace in the Post Christian Era*. Merton was very upset: "I was silenced, which I now am. Articles were in *Commonweal, Catholic Worker, Jubilee, Blackfriars* and *Fellowship*. I also have a book which was just typed and put on stencils when the order came in not to publish, because the 'material is too controversial.' This is from the General in Rome who does not read English and who has not seen any of the stuff himself. He is going on the reports of several rather obtuse censors in this country and especially the delation [an official complaint] of one of the American Abbots, I don't know who, who says I am writing for the Communists. Under separate cover I am sending you some of this material."275

On July 7th, Merton writes to Thérèse, but mistakenly postdates the letter by ten days — July 17th — the feast of Our Lady of Carmel in the liturgical calendar of the Trappist Order, and promises to pray for her on the anniversary of her vows, the 16th, the feast of Mt. Carmel in the universal Church's calendar. Actually, as mentioned previously, the date of Thérèse's anniversary of religious vows was July 15th — not the 16th — but for some reason Merton seems to have the 16th fixed in his mind. He calls the post dating a "slip of the mind and of the fingers." Her last letters to him, he says, sounded "happy and positive" and he speaks of "a great aura of fruitfulness about your life: as always, but now more so. Perhaps

## Maturity and Growth

I am prejudiced by the astonishing job you did with all that mess of papers and rubbish I have sent your way over the past years. To think that you could metamorphose it all into something that makes sense. You are certainly wonderful."[276] She is still preoccupied with the chipmunks and Merton tends to humor her, though probably in a way she would not appreciate: "...one often sees a chipmunk running around with no tail, which means he must have had a narrow escape. Not that we encourage cats, but the place is full of them, living in various cellars. I suppose they are tolerated on account of the rats."[277]

He encloses a photograph taken some time in 1960 with visiting Protestant retreatants describing it for some reason as a "funny one," and says he looks like a comedian. As an addition to her store of strange objects, he sends her a copy of a tape recording of his poem, "Tower of Babel," that had aired on the "Catholic Hour" radio program several years previously. "Someday, really," he suggests, "we might publish some of the materials you have there. There is enough for an interesting book of oddments, some day."[278]

In August 1962, Thérèse was in Washington, D.C. for a summer conference on poetry at Georgetown University where she met Daniel Berrigan, the Jesuit priest-poet and peace activist. He later told Merton about their meeting on one of his several visits to Merton at the hermitage. Among her poems are two about Berrigan, "Poet at Georgetown" and one called "A Time to Dance" written on the occasion of the twenty-fifth anniversary of his ordination to the priesthood. She was frequently in correspondence with Berrigan who at one time asked her to please "write bigger" and take pity on his aging eyes. Thérèse's own handwriting was small and cramped and, at times, difficult to read. In 1976 she was still pursuing him for any letters that he had saved from Merton, but Berrigan said he had only one of a personal nature in which Merton had spoken of "blind superiors," probably alluding to some of the problems that Berrigan had with his own Order over his anti-war protests.

Thérèse had also been selected to chair the poetry section of the Georgetown program for the following year. On August 19th her postcard to Merton came from the National Gallery of Art where, she says, she spends the best hours in D.C. She was also scouring the Washington bookstores to get Merton a copy of *Letters from Vatican City*, Xavier Rynne's immensely popular but unofficial (and a bit gossipy) behind-the-scenes account of some of the personalities and struggles of Vatican II. The writer used a pen name but was later unmasked as the Redemptorist priest, Francis X. Murphy. Given the official blackout on any substantial news, it was no wonder that his book was gobbled up by interested Catholic clergy and laity. The first printing had been completely sold out, and it just can't be had she informs Merton, somewhat with a sense of awe.

On September 20th, Merton responds to a letter she wrote to him once she was back in Wisconsin. Thérèse had visited a Carmelite Monastery in New York, perhaps on her return trip from Washington. Merton had been in contact with them previously when he was exploring possible new locations for an eremitical life. He suspects, however, that the abbot has kept the Carmelites' reply from him so as not to encourage him in thinking about relocating to another community. Since the abbot is away at the General Chapter in Rome, Merton feels free to share his frustration: "Your visits to Carmel consoled me. You know the Abbot pulled down the iron curtain on them, as far as I was concerned. Please give them my very best wishes when you write to them, and tell them I have not forgotten them or renounced them. I do not know if they ever understood what happened. Occasionally he [the abbot] does that. A whole batch of correspondents of mine just suddenly become nacht und nebel, [Night and Mist] as they used to say. With the New York Carmelites also disappeared the Benedictines of La Pierre qui Vire, and the Carmelites of Rio de Janeiro… others too. The trying part is that no one ever tells me who is on the blacklist. I just find out by writing until no replies and then I figure out what has happened. Another one is Damasus Winzen [Mount Savior, Elmira, New York], and some of the Benedictines at Collegeville. Benedictines seem to be bad, for some reason. Of course Camaldolese, etc., well, that is a foregone conclusion."²⁷⁹

Merton is reading Hans Küng having begun as soon as he could get *The Council, Reform and Reunion*. He describes it as a noble and courageous book, but worries about the possibility of the Council fulfilling all of Küng's expectations: "Küng of course I read as soon as I could get my hands on him. I thought it a noble, straight and courageous book. The vigor and honesty of the message was tremendous. But such books raise vain hopes, perhaps. The Council cannot possibly measure up to all he suggested. Yet precisely for that reason we must doggedly hope that it will. If we are too prone to resignation even before it all happens, then perhaps it will be far less of a Council than the Church needs. On the other hand, the vapid optimism and the 'victory communiqués' of the Catholic press give me cramps in the stomach. It is not that good at all. There is much hazard, and we must pray. The way they have consistently cut down on the work for unity and on the secretariat, which now ends up being a bunch of ushers to take care of the Protestant observers, is an indication of other trends which may be disastrous. But thank God we do not have to remain just at the mercy of men and trends. The Holy Spirit is there and the Church is still the Church. So we must pray hard."²⁸⁰

Thomas McDonnell was working on editing *A Thomas Merton Reader*, an anthology of various Merton writings. It was too late for Thérèse to send some of her materials to the publisher (Harcourt Brace) for inclusion, but Merton has another idea of how she might make use of some of the items in her collection: "…what I was really thinking was that there is every possibility they might want to make up a book out of the material you have, judiciously chosen here and there. I think there are faint possibilities, and you might want to think about it…. I think there are distinct possibilities for an interesting kind of grab bag project… they might even want to do your bibliography, though I don't know if that would be a smart idea."²⁸¹

A battle over the copyrights of Merton's works was brewing between two of his publishers — Farrar, Straus and Cudahy and Harcourt Brace. The former had refused to allow any of Merton's materials for which they held the copyright to be included in McDonnell's *Reader*, which was to be published by Harcourt Brace. Merton tells Thérèse: "FS and C absolutely refused to let Harcourt take anything from their books: wanted to make a horse trade between me on one side and Eliot and Lowell on the other, which was a bit sordid besides being preposterous (of course flattering, if it meant anything)."[282] In August 1962 he records in his journal his own evaluation of the *Reader*: "Proofs of the *Merton Reader*. This book is a good one. It lacks some of the best materials that should have gone into it. Farrar Straus and Cudahy refused to let Harcourt Brace have anything from their books. Hence three of the most important sources were excluded. *Thoughts in Solitude, Disputed Questions* and *The New Man*."[283] In 1964 the publisher's name was changed to Farrar Straus and Giroux when Merton's friend, Robert Giroux, became a partner in the publishing house.

Merton has read J.F. Powers' novel about a priest, *Morte d'Urban*, published in 1963, calling it a masterly job that is ruthless in the first part but gentle and merciful in the second: "The priest is an 'operator' a narcissist of the first water, and there is no let up in this appalling mediocrity until suddenly in the second half he becomes human and, though he remains an operator, he gains a real dignity and comes out with a certain nobility. Something happened to Powers himself in creating his character, a sort of breakthrough of some sort, apparently. But what a statement about the American clergy in the first half. Black, gloomy, of course a bit distorted, but devastating. It made me sweat. But funny, too."[284]

On November 19th, Merton sends Thérèse the correspondence surrounding the publication of the *Reader* for her collection, and suggests she contact Harcourt Brace about some of Merton's drawings she has in her possession. The people there are interested in doing something with the material, he says, and might even be envisioning

*Maturity and Growth*

a book of his early drawings. Merton's news about the local wildlife continues to be bad and must have distressed Thérèse: "Someone reported a deer on the property. I haven't seen it, but a deer doesn't have a chance in this part of the world. The Kentuckians are hopeless madmen with a gun. They shoot everything. It is pathological, really. The wild life around here ain't got it so good. I wish there was something that could be done about it."[285] Merton received a third extant post card from Thérèse on November 24th, the feast of St. John of the Cross. She was in Chicago, "Sandberg's [sic] city," as she calls it, where brilliant sunshine had replaced the fog "on little cat feet." She had received his letter and materials for her collection, she tells him, but she has not yet seen a copy of the *Reader*.

The Second Vatican Council, announced by Pope John XXIII in January 1959, began in October 1962 with its first official session in Rome of some 3000 bishops from around the world. In a December 20th letter Merton seems more optimistic about its outcome: "The Council was tremendous, wasn't it?... Really Pope John has been a great gift from God to all of us. What a superb Pope, and what a heart. The past few months have made me realize the greatness of the Church as I had never realized it before, not the stuffed shirt pompous greatness that some of the Curia people evidently want it to be, but the charity and the real concern for all men, the cura pastoralis.... And yet the Church is facing the same kind of critical juncture in thought that she faced with Galileo, and the fact that we have had enough sense to get vernacular in the liturgy is not a guarantee that we are going to automatically sail over this hurdle [the peace issue] without tripping up."[286]

The beginning of 1963 brings more gifts for Merton, and yet another relic of a saint (St. Bede) who was not on his list of favorites, and a book by Dante. Merton thanks her on February 19th and sympathizes with her about the intricacies of historical research she was involved in. Thérèse had been commissioned in 1962 by the Mother General of the Sisters of the Divine Savior to write an official history of the American Province, and was taking a course in history, to hone up on her research skills. She will struggle with the project for the next few years with Merton's prayers, encouragement, and advice, although such a project, he admitted in rather strong language, had no appeal for him.

She had, in the meantime, met both Berrigan brothers, Dan and Phil, a Josephite. Dan's book, as Merton already knew, had been stopped by the Jesuit censors because of the usual fear of someone speaking out and saying something. He was also aware of the controversy that had erupted at the Catholic University of America precipitated by the then Apostolic Delegate, Egidio Vagnozzi: "Did you hear about the faculty of Catholic U. forbidding the graduate school to invite four dangerous speakers: [John] Courtney Murray, [Gustave] Weigel, a third whom I forgot [Godfrey Diekmann] and, last, but not least, Hans Küng."[287] Merton had read Küng's book on the Council and reform with great enthusiasm and speculated that Küng might come to Gethsemani, but that never took place.

He had not yet, he said, received a copy of *Cross and Crown* with a review Thérèse had written. Maybe that particular magazine was one of those on the black list, he muses: "One never knows what will get stopped and what will get through."[288] He had also written a blurb for James Baldwin's *The Fire Next Time* that he fears might get him hanged. Both she and Merton were members of the Catholic Poetry Society and contributors to its publication. When she informs Merton that the organization had folded, he comments, somewhat, caustically: "I am a member of a defunct organization. Perhaps of more than one."[289]

The first extant, two-page, typed letter from Thérèse to Merton (apart from postcards) is dated St. Patrick's Day, March 17, 1963, written to congratulate him on the anniversary of his monastic vows, March 19th, the Feast of St. Joseph. She has just returned from Milwaukee where she had attended the annual Aquinas Lecture at Marquette University. While there, she visited the Merton calligraphy exhibit, "Signatures," which John Pick, the Hopkins scholar and professor of English, had organized in the new Marquette Memorial

Library. "He [Pick] is terribly excited about it all, and has been keeping clippings. However, since he told me that he would send you a 'batch,' I will keep the ones he sent me for the collection. OK? We are keeping our fingers crossed now, and our handed [sic] folded in prayer, so that some of the Milwaukee connosseurs [sic] of art will purchase some of them. They are absolutely thrilling! I went three times around and came back two days later to make the 'pilgrimage' once again. There were <u>many</u> viewers."[290]

On March 2nd Merton had mailed Thérèse a package of materials, including an anthology of Spanish poems containing four of Merton's own. What really "flipped" her out, however, as she records in her characteristically over-the-top March 17th letter, was when she began to read what she thought to be an article on the theologian Karl Barth, she "...found out that it was part of a diary, am I right? something on the order of *Jonas*. This is marvelous! This is the genre (right now) that readers will delight in. And it is so eminently <u>you</u>: simple, profound, wonderfully appealing."[291]

Thérèse had been in Rochester, New York, and returned home on February 27th, "happy and much better," she told Merton, after making her first air flight. At the time she was still working on typing her own manuscript for *Speak to Me, Sparrow*, a collection of her poems she still hopes to get published. Fr. Gerard Smith, SJ, a professor of philosophy at Marquette, had encouraged her to publish the poems in book form: "He seems to think I should hurry and get it out and whatever poems still come along (have some unfinished) use for another book — but <u>that</u> will be a 'New and Selected Poems,' and if I have only ten new ones — say in five years, were I to live that long, it should work out well."[292] She is, at the same time, still at work on the history of the American Province of the Sisters and also plans to finish the Merton catalogue and write some articles on her Merton collection — "as if there were any other," she adds in her own handwriting.[293] She also wants to write an introduction or preface for the Mertoniana catalogue that she hopes to have published and, "Perhaps an occasional recital."[294] More immediately there is an address she has been asked to give to the Wisconsin Fellowship of Poets on April 10th in Wausau. Reluctant at first to accept the invitation to the "great big secular (exclusively) affair!" she "later thought it over and it seemed <u>important</u> in a special 'ecumenical' way."[295]

Two of the psychiatrists [Dr. Carl Kline and Dr. George Andrews] at the Salvatorian hospital in Wausau had gone to Alabama to participate in the Freedom Marches. Thérèse, ever ready to credit Merton with some influence, surmises that his writings and those of the Berrigans, with which both doctors were familiar, might have prompted their decision, though neither was Catholic. Merton had written to Kline sometime in June 1962 and sent him a mimeographed copy of the book on war after he had received a letter from Kline.

Not to be outdone, however, Thérèse tells Merton about Milwaukee's own Freedom March, and her impressions of viewing it from a distance. Although she did not take part personally, she watched it "from the Public Library steps, and later from a large window of the Library — feeling guilty, really not to have been in it. But there were nuns and priests galore. The first view I had of it they were all coming out of the Episcopal church (St. James) across from the Library, from which they walked to City Hall, where a minister, a rabbi, and a priest, led prayers and readings. This they had also done in the Episcopal church, and the Sisters were very much impressed as they all prayed together. (I recall many years back, when we would scarcely dare to look up at that Church when passing along the street in front of it, much less think of entering and here were the nuns and priests, taking part in a 'prayer meeting.') Many Negroes, even children, were in the march; and it brought the tears to my eyes to see the huge crowd standing outside City Hall while they were addressed by the speakers! Yes, Salvatorians, were there in full force, Dominicans, Sisters of Holy Cross, and even the lovely ladies of the BVM, who have Holy Angels 'swank' academy. And Jebbies too, of course. Things are really happening."[296]

On May 1st, Merton writes a long delayed letter and acknowl-

## Maturity and Growth

edges that he had been too busy even to include a personal note with the last package of materials. Thérèse had noted that and did not hesitate to remind him! He was busy, he says, with the ever-increasing amount of correspondence, some of which has to be answered immediately. She had sent him another seasonal poem, though he offers no comment on it. He has, though, finally seen a chipmunk on the property: "I don't have the art of training them as you have. It is best they remain wild around here so the cats won't get them."[297]

In the meantime, he had been given permission to make a private retreat at the hermitage in June, but is still not allowed to stay there overnight. On June 12th, Merton recorded in his journal that he had received from Thérèse "a remarkably interesting (to me) list of the items in her 'collection.'"[298] By June 30th he is so busy with the details of publishing that he can't find her last letter. He does not even know when she wrote him, though he thinks it might be Easter, and he probably owes her more than one letter.

Between the first and second sessions of the Council, Pope John XXIII had died of cancer on June 3, 1963. Merton feels no one can replace him, but he does have a very favorable impression of the newly elected Pope, Paul VI, from his slight contacts with him when he was Cardinal Montini: bright, energetic, experienced and holy. John XXIII, though, was Merton's Pope: "I have no doubt he was one of the great saints of our time. Am very happy to have a beautiful signed picture of him... in the novitiate chapel. Pope Paul will, however, be good in a different way.... J.F. Powers sent a wonderful print of Pope John... it gets the spirit of his simplicity and love in a striking way.... I guess Pope John is, as far as I am concerned, 'my Pope.' I don't expect to outlive too many more of them."[299]

By November 1967, many progressives were expressing disappointment in Paul VI, but Merton came to the defense of the embattled pontiff: "Dan [Walsh] is evidently very much taken up with those who say Pope Paul is hopeless, etc., as if this meant anything particular! The whole institutional structure is questionable: why blame everything on the poor man who can't help being what he is — a curial official trained under Pius XII with a few lively ideas on Catholic Action acquired in the 20's and 30's. One almost feels that now the test of true Christian spirit is the willingness to say anathemas to Paul! One ought rather to be sorry for him — and for those who think it is relevant to curse him."[300]

In August, Thérèse returned to Georgetown for the summer poetry program, and is still working on the history of the American Province: "I am sure you are working hard, and can imagine that it is not easy. Yet the work itself will, I suppose, at moments sustain you. And when you think it is going to be hardest, there will be a strength that will come almost miraculously out of the difficulty itself.... I have known in my own heart the upheaval and repugnance I have felt at the mere thought of possibly getting associated with one such official project. It made me physically sick, and all such things do. We have to face the fact of our deep ambivalence about religious life and about the form of it we are in, with all the special little details that have been permitted by Providence (and that this permission by no means justifies or explains away!)."[301]

Evidently Thérèse had confided in Merton the difficulties she was experiencing with superiors and Merton reacts (or over reacts): "What you say about your General is shocking. The way people in such positions can latch on to power with a 'good conscience' and the way that power can be misused with an 'infallible rightness' is something wonderful to behold and not so wonderful to undergo. One must, I think, try to develop an immense breadth of understanding and pity even for people whose powers seem to make pity unnecessary in their case. But it seems to me that we should feel not only sadness and sorrow but also compassion for these things and these people, in an effort to bring into the Church the love that has to be there if it is to live as Church and if the legalism of some elements is to be counteracted. The fact remains that when things are in such shape, to be called upon to write a book which necessarily implies a full justification or at least a definite approval and acceptance of so many strange things, becomes an intolerable task,

## Maturity and Growth

and one's whole being cries out against not only the meaninglessness but even the potential dishonesty of it"[302] Merton suggests that one way to deal with such situations is simply to try to see things in perspective, which includes not being troubled by something that is really absurdly unimportant: "So we simply have to admit and reject the ridiculous element in our lives. Pious acceptance is no use. But by rejection I do not mean rebellion. I mean rising above it in a mature way that does not exclude a certain healthy scorn."[303] His response echoes, perhaps, the way he dealt with similar situations in his own life when he was prohibited by his superiors from writing or publishing. One can wonder if such strongly emotional language reflects more on his situation and feelings about religious authorities than hers.

On September 2nd, 1963 Merton sends her a card made for him by the novices for his feast day, August 25th, the Feast of St. Louis of France. The students' drawing shows Merton with a pipe, a hat, a gun and a beard. Merton rejects the gun since he is non-violent, but acknowledges that he shaves only every three days since the abbot is opposed to his growing a full beard. Other than that, he comments, the novices have a good eye and it might be an accurate character study of the man. In late September, Merton was hospitalized at St. Joseph's Hospital in Louisville for arthritis and a cervical disc problem that he was hoping to correct with traction without having to undergo surgery. While recovering he read Morris West's novel, *The Shoes of the Fisherman* and received a personal letter and an autographed photograph from Pope Paul VI, from whom Merton expected great things.

In the winter of 1963, Bellarmine University had mounted a one-week Merton exhibition and Merton writes to Thérèse on November 9th to clarify what he terms the "Bellarmine affair." The exhibit was to open on November 10th, he explains in a letter written the day before, and is only to last for a week while the Merton collection at Bellarmine is permanent. Merton had suggested to Dan Walsh, his former teacher at Columbia, and to Fr. John Loftus, the

Academic Dean of Bellarmine, that they ask Thérèse if she might be willing to lend some of her Merton materials for the event, but assures her that if she had lent some items, they would not be given for keeps, "...unless you thought they were worth becoming the 'ultimate' repository for your collection. But I thought you were planning to give it to Marquette."[304] He describes his friends Loftus and Walsh as younger and "lively and interested as anyone" in his work "second only to you."[305] Apparently Thérèse decided not to lend anything from her collection which she was in the process of cataloging and Merton seems to back down: "Of course you were perfectly wise and right to hold on to your material to finish your catalogue. It is certainly not a matter of giving anything away. And this exhibit is not too important anyway. In fact they seem to be interested in a few non-essentials, in connection with it. Medals and the Lord knows what. Who cares about that?"[306] Then he compliments her for her recently published poem, "Each Spring the Arbutus," that had appeared in *Commonweal* on September 27th.

As 1964 begins, Merton, who does not write until February and feels a little guilt for not having written sooner, assures Thérèse on February 1st, that he has not been ill and is concerned about the virus she had contracted. Nor has he gone to Europe with the abbot, because the abbot is not accustomed to taking people with him, least of all Merton. He does not want to be dragged around monasteries of the Order, he claims, having to perform. He would enjoy nothing less, though he adds a remark that might hint he would indeed have enjoyed it: "It is good of him to spare me this, not that there is any danger of it."[307]

He is still suffering from back problems that could only be corrected with a bone graft operation, and he wants to avoid that, if possible. Thérèse writes back that she had contracted a virus, but has recuperated. Merton, fearing that she was pushing herself too hard with writing "that old history," advises her to take care of herself. Towards the end of 1963, Thérèse had submitted a first draft of the history, *Three Came to Serve* to the Generalate in Rome for

*Maturity and Growth*

their consideration. She planned to incorporate their comments and suggestions in the text by the end of the summer of 1965.

The Salvatorian Sisters, meanwhile, are preparing for the election of a new Mother General in 1965 and Merton comments: "Something surely should be done. It is not God's will that people just sit around passively and take it, when the laws are repeatedly violated or got around. The Curia affair has shown to what extent these people are willing to keep the rules when it hurts <u>them</u> to do so. This is a crying abuse. It accounts for the zeal with which such people are always working to keep everyone else in a constant state of guilt and uncertainty. The unfailing torrent of reproaches, etc., etc."[308] The mention of the "Curia affair" no doubt refers to the Roman Curia and its well-documented opposition to some of the changes in the direction of the Church prompted by the decrees of the Second Vatican Council, though how it pertains to Thérèse's situation is not clear. Merton had read *The Pilgrim* by Michael Serafian that described the "beating" that Cardinal Bea took at the second session of the Council and wrote to Dan Berrigan: "This curial thing is really disastrous, and it threatens the whole structure of the Church, and maybe, one thing, this is providential.... I wonder if we are really going to have to get along without a structure one of these days."[309]

Promising to send her more material, he also suggests that she stop the cataloguing with what she has completed, and start again on the rest later: "...one must stop somewhere. Otherwise, it is just perpetual motion. It is good to have tasks, but not ones that are endless."[310] Needless to say, Thérèse was not about to heed his advice that she stop working on what by now had become her whole life's project! Dom Gabriel Sortais, Merton's Abbot General in Rome, died in 1963. The Trappists elected Ignace Gillet, whom Merton describes as a "standard, French, conservative, stand pat type, and I suppose an organizer."[311] He also expresses hope that the new superior might be more genial about censorship, and in 1964 under Gillet the ban on his writing was somewhat eased.

On March 20th, Thérèse writes that she will be traveling to Minneapolis for an art convention during Holy Week, driving first to Columbus (Wisconsin) and then taking a train to Minneapolis on Palm Sunday. Following the meeting she plans to visit her priest brother, Gordon (previously Theophane in religious life), and spend Easter with him at his parish, Sacred Heart, in Urbank, a small town northwest of Minneapolis. He had left the Salvatorians in 1953 and resumed his legal name. He became a diocesan priest of St. Cloud in 1955 and in 1957 became a pastor. This would be Thérèse's first visit to any of his parishes during his lifetime. She is nervous about having to give a poetry recital at St. Bonafacius, Minnesota, a Jesuit college, but it is really a novitiate for the Society of Jesus, she tells Merton. Connecting with Jesuit memories, she is reminded of another Jesuit, Louis Forrey, who had taught her short story writing at Marquette, but encouraged her to try writing poetry instead. It was Forrey who had suggested she submit her poem, "Dolor," to *Commonweal* magazine where it was published in the October 16, 1949 issue.

In February, Thérèse had sent Merton the "catalogue" she had completed, describing it as a fat one, but still not listing everything she has of Merton! For example, she had just found in her "hope chest" a copy of the Rule of St. Benedict that Merton had autographed and there are three packets of letters she has yet to catalogue: "That will not be difficult, if one keeps at the work continuously. I am not too consistent... and having my room in such utter tumult that to find a previous typed entry is almost impossible."[312] By April 1st, Merton has returned the bibliography to Thérèse expressing amazement at her patience in accomplishing such a tremendous job. There are items in the catalogue that he had either forgotten or never heard of: "There is no question that you are the one with the real collection. Where on earth do you keep it? It must be big enough for a couple of rooms by now."[313]

Once again on April 1st, Merton returns to the question of the permanent Merton collection at Bellarmine and Thérèse's plans for the future of her own materials. Claiming to be impartial to any solution she comes up with, he says she should feel free to make her own decision. He is not, he stresses, on anyone's side leaving the impression, of course, that sides have already been drawn. He suggests that the collection would be best situated in her geographical area in the north, rather than in the south. In any case, "...that is something we can put off to the distant future. But I wanted you to know for certain that I'm not committed in any way to anything and am completely indifferent myself. I would not quite know what to say. Naturally they [Bellarmine] are eager, but that is their affair. Do not interpret their eagerness as mine. But they are friends of mine, too, and so I am not against it either."[314] Merton inquires about her talk to the Jesuits in Kansas mentioned above and offers his own comments on Jesuits: "I hope the poetry reading to the Jebbies went off well. They are not as fierce as they claim to be, though I suppose they have to cultivate a professional toughness. Were they difficult? And if so, did it matter? There is certainly a great variety from one to another, or at least there are members of the society that stand out as quite different from the others. Dan Berrigan, for instance...."[315]

On July 12th, Merton notes with some surprise that "you will be reading poetry at Spencer [a Trappist monastery in Massachusetts]. I must admit this set me back on my heels. Unheard of things. Our Abbot would never countenance such things going on (he is away now, at the coast) but I think you know his policies. May those at Spencer be blessed for their liberality."[316] The Trappist abbots and novice masters from the American and Canadian monasteries were meeting at Gethsemani on October 4th. Merton is cautiously optimistic about their good will and desire to do right, and hopes that the meeting will bring about what he considers some much needed change in the monastic life.

Merton himself, however, was not always pleased with changes in the Church, especially in the area of liturgy: "Mostly desires of change are not always too enlightened. I am by no means a conservative, but I think that some of our Abbots in this country are a bit blind to real values that are primitive and still as good as new. They just want to be 'modern' and may end up by being nothing."[317] He sends her more uncorrected carbons of first drafts and prefaces for her collection and says he hopes she won't be "jealous" of the fact that he had given the letter from Boris Pasternak to the University of Kentucky. He felt he owed them something of value since they had given him an honorary doctorate of letters: "In any case," he consoles her, "you still have the best collection."[318]

Thérèse had been to Washington, D.C. for the summer workshop at Georgetown and had given him detailed reports about her time and experiences there. He is still trying to write something for Fr. Ray Roseliep's student magazine at Loras College, Dubuque, Iowa, but confesses he has so little time that it is difficult to get around to it. He is also battling poison ivy and plans to see a specialist because of the loss of skin on his hands and face.

Thérèse had written in a previous letter of her "intuitions" of passing time and, perhaps, of her own frailness in advancing age. Merton agrees: "I have them too. I am now pushing fifty and realize more and more that every extra day is just a free gift, and so I relax and forget about the past and future. The 'I' that goes from day to day is not an important 'I' and his future matters little. And the deeper 'I' is in an eternal present. If a door should open one day from one realm to the other, then 'I' (whoever that is) will be glad of it. I have no regrets except for sins that are forgiven in any case, and I forget the past, and don't get too excited about either the present or the future. For the rest, He Who is real will take care of what reality He has shared with us."[319] His Christmas note of December 13th is also a thank-you note for the clippings, poems and her review in *Renascence*.

She had sent him her poem about Kennedy that Merton thinks he has already seen in *America*. In return, he sends her notes on his drawings and a report on the racial situation in Mississippi. The abbot has asked him to remain the novice master for at least

## Maturity and Growth

another year, but he still feels he needs greater solitude, even a kind of semi-retirement, since he is approaching fifty in January. He had just read the galley proofs of Daniel Callahan's *Honesty in the Church* and is excited about it: "You must absolutely read it.... It strikes directly at the abuses you so often mention, the manipulating and politicking and the system that guarantees that the superiors are never wrong, no matter how they get around the law of the Church or violate the rights of their subjects.... Still, it is time for such things to be said. If they are not, there is no hope for a real renewal of the Church. And it becomes repeatedly more clear that renewal begins at the top."[320] We will, he suggests, see many more interesting and disturbing things in the Church in the next few years. By this time the third session of the Council had come to a close and Merton expressed mixed emotions: "The end of the Council session was not exactly encouraging. I know it was shattering for Fr. Häring, who wrote about it. He said it was shattering for Pope Paul also. I hear by all accounts that the Pope looks exhausted. His peace proposal at Bombay was impressive, however."[321]

Apparently, the initials of Thérèse's religious Congregation, "SDS" for Sisters of the Divine Savior, appeared as "DDS" in some publication. He jokingly promises to correct it: "With your new title of DDS I cannot quite make up my mind whether you are a bishop or just a dentist. Better to be neither. I will alert the publisher."[322]

# 7

## THE FINAL YEARS
### 1965-1968

Thérèse wrote to Merton on St. Patrick's Day, March 17th, 1965, but he did not get around to answering until March 27th, accusing himself of being a rather poor correspondent. He was gradually giving less time to letter writing and, as a result, has piles of letters, many of which never got answered, while others were delayed because he needed time to think about his responses. She had sent him a copy of the annual Aquinas Lecture at Marquette she had attended, and some poems by a young poet, Joel Keith. Merton has no time to read them, although he did read her clippings about the civil rights movement, including news about the recent racial tensions in Selma, Alabama. He was well supplied with news about Selma and expresses his belief that "for a lot of basically good people — white southerner — that the whole thing [civil rights movement] is a Communist plot and that this entitles them to react in any violent way they please. It is this failure of sense and loss of contact with reality that seems to be the most regrettable and dangerous thing of all. They are the ones who need help the most, and who can be reached least. I met a priest from Chicago who had been down there; he saw Dan and Phil Berrigan there. They also came out against the Viet Nam war, which I think was very good."[323] Phil Berrigan's book, *No More Strangers*, was ready for publication and Merton had written a Preface, but Dan Berrigan's contribution was not allowed to be included.

On April 10th Thérèse was scheduled to speak at an ecumenical gathering in Waukesha although she had been reluctant at first to take part. Merton encourages her: "And I think you will find that it is easy to get through to an audience as mixed as that. There is a blessing on every attempt at ecumenism that is true and sincere, and your desire to do this not for your own sake but for God and the Church and for them, will guarantee that it will be blessed in one way or another."[324] He was not doing any ecumenical work himself this year because "Fr. Abbot wanted me to withdraw from it as I am planning more and more to be in the hermitage and perhaps even live there eventually. I must meet his requirement, therefore, and am not sorry to."[325] There is more to the story than Merton shares.

On April 29, 1960, long before official encouragement of what would become known as the "ecumenical movement," he tells Dom Sortais, the Abbot General, that he had been given the go-ahead from John XXIII for a few discreet meetings with "distinguished guests" and "professors of Protestant theology." "These are discreet, rare contacts but which seem to help these souls to understand the Church, or else if they are Catholic, to deepen their love of God and their Christian faith."[326] In 1961, however, the Papal Secretary of State had written to Merton's abbot urging for Merton "a diminution of contacts with Protestant ministers and scholars."[327] Merton believed he had been reported to the Holy See because his ecumenical gatherings at the hermitage were regarded by some in the community with disfavor and suspicion. He concludes the letter saying he has the flu and is not keeping the strict fast, gets a small breakfast in the morning and meat for dinner.

In June, the Congregation of the Sisters of the Divine Savior elected a new Mother General, and Merton writes on the 16th to congratulate Thérèse: "I am so happy to hear at last things have leveled off and that there is hope of a real renewal. It is so important to break the awful log jams that build up in religious life and slow everything down to a dead stop. I hope that much good will come of it, and that things will move in the right direction."[328] He thanks

Merton and Thérèse in full habit (1951).
*(Courtesy Merton Legacy Trust)*

Thérèse with a book of Merton's poems.

Merton before his as yet unoccupied hermitage (1965).

Thérèse and her brother Gordon (Fr. Theophane, SDS) in Rome (1939).

Thérèse leaving the White House.

Thérèse at her desk writing.

Thérèse with her brother, Fr. Gordon, at his parish (1964).

Thérèse lecturing at Bellarmine Merton Center (1967).

Fr. Barry Griffin, SDS, and Merton display (1966).

Thérèse and Merton on a tractor (Nov. 7, 1967).

Picnic at Gethsemani (Nov.7,1967).

Thérèse and Merton clowning around (Nov.7,1967).

Thérèse's hermitage in Racine, WI (1976).

Thérèse at Merton's grave site (Sept. 16, 1980).

Thérèse reading poetry on the porch of Merton's hermitage (Sept. 16, 1980).

Obituary photos of Thomas Merton (+Dec. 10, 1968).

Merton at prayer.

Merton Exhibit following his death.

Official portrait of Thérèse (+Oct. 31, 1981).

Album photo, Marquette University.

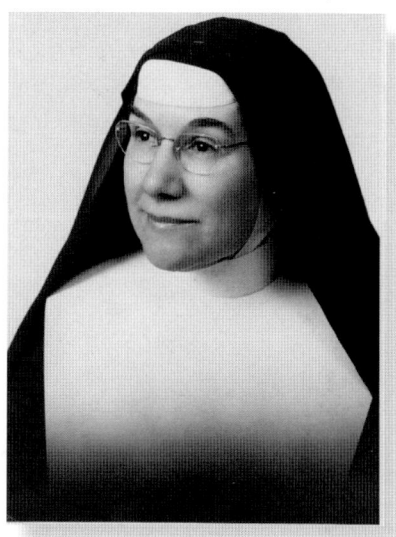

Thérèse before a favorite oil painting.

Thérèse with obituary photo of Merton before oil painting.

## The Final Years

her for sending Naomi Burton a catalogue of her Merton holdings. Burton was Merton's literary agent and an original member of the Merton Legacy Trust along with Tommie O'Callaghan and James Laughlin. The Trust had the responsibility of keeping track of the voluminous materials written by Merton — both published and unpublished — in the possession of others: "I suppose that the main thing is above all to keep track of unpublished material that is around in various collections or in the hands of friends or people I no longer know have it. The big job at the moment is for the trustees to get a good idea where everything is and <u>what</u> it is. You are the one who can be of most help in this, because you have the most complete collection and the one in which there are so many notes, sermons, unpublished pieces as well an original mss."[329]

Merton is now living semi-permanently in the hermitage dedicated to St. Mary of Carmel, and expresses hope that soon it will be his permanent residence: "It is wonderful to live so close to birds, etc. I want to get the woods around there made into a game sanctuary, but it is a problem to keep hunters out. They don't believe in signs and fences around here and short of having a sheriff around you can't do anything to protect the place. We have a lot of deer now, too."[330]

In the fall, apparently through the decision of her new Provincial in Milwaukee, Thérèse's "exile" to Wausau was ended, and she was assigned to live back in Milwaukee — "back in the swim of things" — as Merton terms it on September 28th. She had accepted a teaching position at Mount St. Paul College, in Waukesha, Wisconsin, a college owned and operated by the Society of the Divine Savior for students preparing for the priesthood. By this time she had completed the first draft of the history of the American Province of the Congregation of the Sisters of the Divine Savior. Her unpublished manuscript is on file in the archives of the Congregation's Provincial House in Milwaukee. Merton knows she will miss the woods and the animals of the north, but that she will also be glad to be in contact again with city life. He expresses his pleasure to be able to write to her again in Milwaukee, especially since his first letter to her there is one for her feast day, October 3rd.

In the summer of 1965, Merton had taken up permanent residence in the hermitage in a wooded area on Gethsemani's acreage that he had named "Mount Olivet Retreat Center," but goes down to the monastery once a day for Mass and dinner. Evening supper at the hermitage is a simple affair because, he says, he doesn't like to cook or wash dishes.

Merton often expressed some harsh criticisms of community life and even some of the other monks when he was under pressure, but he would usually come to regret what he had said in the heat of the moment and later present a more balanced view: "It is really a wonderful life, a revelation, even much better than I expected. It is so good to get back to plain natural simplicity and the bare essentials, no monkeying around with artificialities and non-essentials. It really gives a wonderful new dimension to one's life. I didn't realize, until I got out here, how… frustrated I really was in community, though of course I love the monks. I am afraid that community life has become terribly forced and artificial over the course of centuries, and there is no question that a new approach will have to be found if it is going to continue. So I like being a hermit, and I do have real solitude. There is never anyone around in the woods except an occasional hunter, and we are trying to persuade them to go elsewhere."[331] But living in solitude he also realizes he had no real news to share, and it was even sometimes difficult for him to think of what to write in a letter. Yes, he was working on journal material (*Conjectures of a Guilty Bystander*) he tells her, but it would not be published as a journal because of the objection in "high places" about a Trappist writing a spiritual journal. Their real fear, he thinks, is that the journal would be too frank about the Trappist life as it really is, so he was planning to keep it relatively impersonal.

Thérèse was still perplexed about where she would eventually place her extensive collection and frequently asked Merton for his suggestions. Most of the time he maintained a neutral stance, but in

## The Final Years

September he offers some concrete advice: "If you want a suggestion from me, I would say... divide it between Bellarmine and Marquette. There is much that you have that is also at Bellarmine, on the other hand the Bellarmine collection does not have some of the early material that you have. I would say perhaps a few of the important early mss. and other mimeographed material that is not at B. [Bellarmine] could go there, so as to make it more complete, but the bulk of your collection could still go to Marquette. Unless of course you yourself would badly want to keep it all in one piece."332

He knew her decision would be a complicated issue, and wants her to be clear about it well in advance of the actual bequest. On the reverse side of this letter from Merton there is a comment, written a few years later in Thérèse's handwriting, saying that Merton had changed his mind and was now of the opinion that she should not divide her collection, but keep it complete. He had stressed that the best plan for the various collections would be to have them in different parts of the country, rather than in one place. As for her collection: "Georgetown University," he thought, "would be a splendid place for my collection — if I so decided to make such a commitment."333

Merton writes on December 30th and sends a Christmas package with some invaluable items for her collection including photographs of the hermitage, two books, *The Way of Chuang Tzu* and *New Seeds of Contemplation*, in Italian with signed manuscripts and off-prints of other articles. In a two-page typed letter on February 1st, Thérèse gently chides him for not signing the two books — ("...how much more precious they would have been had you signed them") — he had sent, but finds in his letter an expression of peace and joy in his new life as a hermit. She is still searching for a publisher for *Speak to Me, Sparrow*, now titled *He Counts the Sparrows: New and Selected Poems*, for which Dan Berrigan had agreed to write an introduction. Merton had recommended Doubleday and provided her a contact name, but discouraged her from trying Bob Giroux at Farrar, Straus and Giroux. The problem is, he told her, that publishers don't like to publish poetry. Merton can get New Directions to publish his poetry in this country, but does not have a publisher in England.

She sends her warmest greetings to the hermit on his birthday that he is now spending in solitude, and wishes him graceful deer and some birds. Merton had mentioned in December that his breakfast consisted of coffee and toast on the open fire and that with a good hot fire he could get instant toast: "I'd love to see you making that 'instant toast!'"[334] One of her poems alludes to Merton's hermitage and life there in the winter:

> These days [winter] are come, as flying a synapse
> of sky your late letter flails
> with the storm and drops like snow
> to my hand. Breathless I take
> the page to my window to
> peer through the slim spokes of words
> for a glimpse of your cageling....[335]

In 1966, Thérèse was teaching full time at Mount St. Paul in Waukesha, Wisconsin, and serving as acting chair of the English department. One third of the students were Salvatorian religious seminarians and the rest were students from some thirty-eight different dioceses in the U.S.A. and Canada. The Salvatorian Fathers and Brothers who staffed the seminary college made Thérèse feel both needed and valued, and she formed many close and lasting friendships during her years there. Sometime after Merton's death she taught a course on Merton that included a film about his life and exhibited examples of his manuscripts from her collection and she spoke frequently about Merton both inside and outside of class in her conversations with the students, as many of them recall.

In 1966, she was also planning a Merton exhibit for the college from February 27th through the month of March with help from Fr. Barry Griffin, the school librarian and a committee composed

## The Final Years

of her own students. The venue, the college's lobby and parlor, Thérèse thought, was better even than Marquette and the planning committee wanted printed programs and lots of publicity. Barry had met John Pick, her professor of English friend at Marquette, and Pick had offered one of Merton's drawings belonging to the University for display at Mount St. Paul. Marquette had purchased one of Merton's drawings at the time they were on display at the Merton exhibit organized by Pick in 1965. At the time, Thérèse had expressed her disappointment that none had been sold and was delighted to discover that Marquette had purchased at least one of them. When Barry and the committee came to the convent to see "the collection," they really "flipped."

With her February 1st letter she includes an outline of a bibliography that a Salvatorian Brother, John Lyons, one of her students and a devoted Merton fan, was putting together for her exhibit. Thérèse asks Merton for his opinion of Lyons' bibliography project, which she thinks is far too pretentious. Frank Dell'Isola was the first scholar to publish a bibliography of Merton's works up to 1956. Lyons planned to update the Dell'Isola bibliography. Thérèse thinks that Lyons would also have to include in an updated version Merton's works in the collections at Bellarmine, St. Bonaventure and the University of Kentucky. Her contribution to the exhibit would be to track down and borrow Merton's notebook containing the first draft of *Seeds of Contemplation*. Merton had given it to Clare Boothe Luce who, in turn, gave it to the Trappist monastery at Moncks Corner in South Carolina.

Would Merton write a letter of congratulations and support, she asks, for the project at Mount St. Paul, as he did when the Merton room was inaugurated at Bellarmine in 1963? If so, the document would be framed and hung in the school library. She assures him that the Mount St. Paul exhibit would be a real ecumenical event, since it was being publicized to the local Protestants like the Presbyterian Carroll College in Waukesha. Merton wrote to the Mount St. Paul Library Club on February 6th: "I have been asked to make myself present personally by a word or, in the midst of the notes, the shadows and the glass cases in which I am dubiously present among you. I must count on the warmth and friendship of people like Sister Thérèse to do the real job… if there is something of Him in all this that is gathered here, fine. I hope you find it. If there is nothing of His, what use is the whole shooting match?"[336]

Thérèse had corresponded with a monk named Basil, a Trappist at the New Melleray Abbey in Iowa. Basil had lived for a time with Merton at Gethsemani and had heard of Thérèse's collection. He told her he knew where the first draft of Merton's poem, "Letter to My Friends," was, if she were interested. Apparently, Basil had borrowed some notes from Merton when they were at Gethsemani and had found the first draft of the poem on the back of them. Thérèse wanted that copy for her display and also to compare it with a second version of the poem Merton had written in one of his novitiate notebooks: "I had thought this was the first version — but this dear O.C.S.O. knew of the notes and wrote me about them. How kind and interested even strangers are — but I guess a monk is not a stranger," she says to Merton about Basil's unsolicited offer.[337]

Thérèse was still looking for a publisher for her poems (*Speak to Me, Sparrow*) and had taken Merton's suggestion and approached a representative from Doubleday, but they were not interested. Doubleday, however, at the time was associated with Hanover House, the publisher of her last book, and she was not sure if the rejection by Doubleday represented both publishers. She thinks it is a good manuscript and wants desperately to have it published: "(It's my 'swan-song' of poems, I know.)," she adds.[338] Writing to Naomi Burton for advice she downplays her own sophistication: "I'm so little of a business woman I hardly know where to start, and have really no connections with publishers. I would appreciate any suggestion or 'warnings' from you, since you are so skilled in the matter."[339] Her being out of circulation, she claims, makes it more difficult, since she has so little confidence and know-how. This was not the reality, since she had already negotiated the publication of several of her own

## The Final Years

books. This disarming appeal to her lack of ability or connections might be her way of involving Merton and his contacts.

In her February 1st letter she had forgotten to include Brother John Lyons' bibliography so she sends it on February 6th and tells Merton she is already thinking of another Merton exhibit at the Writers Conference at Georgetown University in August 1967. Thérèse's provincial had offered her the summer to "sit at any scholar's feet," she says, but she prefers instead to continue to rewrite the draft of the Province's history when she receives feedback from the readers, finish her work cataloging the Merton collection and then attend the writers' conference at Georgetown. A photograph of Merton in a working jacket had appeared in *Ramparts* magazine and, ever anxious to procure every photograph of Merton, she asks him the source so she could obtain a copy for her collection.

On February 14th, Thérèse writes in a panic to Merton about an incident in conjunction with the upcoming exhibit at Mount St. Paul's College that she had just learned about. One of the Salvatorian priests working on publicity for the event had taken three of Thérèse's personal snapshots of Merton and given them to the media along with the press release about the exhibit. When she discovered this, she called the priest immediately and told him to contact the papers at once and ask them not to print the photographs. She had already exhibited the photographs herself, but knowing Merton's restrictions on having his photograph published, she would never want them to appear in a newspaper. One of the photographs was of Merton sitting in a classroom teaching along with two other individuals from what she calls that "<u>special</u> group of <u>four</u>" [Merton, Bob Lax, Ad Reinhardt, a New York abstract painter and Sy (Seymour) Freedgood]. She thinks they might have been taken by Lax or Reinhardt, and is sick about the close call of having released unauthorized photographs of Merton: "Just <u>suppose</u> someone would not obey his [the priest's] request [not to publish them]?"[340]

The papers involved in the fiasco were the *Milwaukee Journal*, the *Catholic Herald Citizen* and the local Waukesha paper. Since photographs of Merton had already appeared in *Jubilee* magazine, one can wonder why she was so concerned about other photographs of him being published. She uses the fact of his already published photograph to plead for Merton's permission to publish the ones she has — and presses him to let her know quickly whether or not she could. A photograph of Merton had also appeared in the *Louisville Courier-Journal* in conjunction with a story of his entering the hermitage. That photograph was later picked up by *Time* magazine: "Since your photograph... has been published with our late article (of your having become a hermit) in papers all over the country... would you allow us to print them anyway?" she persists.[341] Merton replies on February 16th asking her not to show any photographs of the hermitage, but that it was all right to use photographs of him for publicity. By this time Merton's photograph had also appeared on the dust jacket of some of his books and most of his readers already knew what he looked like.

Merton agrees that Brother John Lyons should continue his work on updating the Dell'Isola bibliography: "My reaction is this: there is no hurry to get this all in print, and it might be a good idea to start on the most obvious work quietly, and see what develops. I may be pushing up the daisies in a few years... and then will be time enough to publish."[342] Yes, he recalls scribbling the first draft of "Letter to My Friends" that she is searching for, in the Guesthouse at Gethsemani, but has no idea where it is now. Her prayers for deer and birds for Merton have been answered: "I had a lot of friendly birds around, and fed them with crackers. The deer are around too. It is fine and silent — and lonely. I have no questions about this being the kind of life for me.... It is hard. You really have to face yourself, and believe me that is quite grim. ...it makes sense.... I often sense I had a very hard time convincing myself that the life down in the community did that. I always liked the other monks, but felt that the system itself was a bit artificial and unreal, and it seemed to be chewing so many of them into hamburger, so to speak."[343]

On April 5th he sends her a brief note and includes his retreat

## The Final Years

notes, but requests they be kept confidential, since they contain the personal case of a Sister in a Trappist community. He asks her also to be discreet with the letters from Evelyn Waugh he has sent her and is glad she is handling wisely all the personal letters he sends. On April 15th Merton says the long silence between February 16th and April 15th was due to the fact that he had been hospitalized for back surgery. His disc had deteriorated entirely — not just slipped as Thérèse thought — and had to be replaced with a bone graft from his hip. He is slowly recovering, but worries about further complications. Although he is still allowed to go to the hermitage during the day, he has to return at night to sleep in the monastery infirmary.

On March 23rd Merton had entered St. Joseph's Hospital in Louisville for spinal surgery and, while a patient, met and fell in love with a young nurse half his age known then to only a few at the time and later identified as Margie Smith, although Mott identifies her only as "S" in his account of the relationship. That was the start of a short-lived, four-month tumultuous, emotional and clandestine relationship that caused Merton both a major vocational crisis and, at the same time, growth in his emotional and spiritual life. This experience that shocked some Merton fans has been forthrightly and sensitively documented by Merton's official biographer, Michael Mott, in *The Seven Mountains of Thomas Merton*, and in other works such as John Howard Griffin's *Follow the Ecstasy: Thomas Merton the Hermitage Years, 1965-1968*, and Monica Furlong's 1980 *Merton: A Biography*, although she mentions the nurse relationship only in passing based on faint rumors circulating at the time when she was writing the biography. In a 1995 revision she recounts more of the details based on Mott's official biography, published in 1984.

Merton had confided to Thérèse something about the relationship, but we do not know precisely what since we do not have those letters. A close friend and former student of Thérèse, however, says that she was "most distressed about the Louisville nurse who she knew about chapter and verse," and that the revelation threw her into a royal tizzy so that she had wept almost hysterically when she told him about it.³⁴⁴ An envelope, post-marked September 14, 1966, by which time the affair with the nurse was coming to an end, has the following note on the back in Thérèse's own handwriting: "Three letters of this year — were destroyed. I thought it best, for in them Merton had confided a personal problem (the nurse, etc.) which I felt (should something happen to me), would not be 'safe' in the hands of others — though it is known (I believe) by a discreet group in Louisville."³⁴⁵

When Merton had to return again to the hospital in Louisville in October, he was sent to St. Anthony's Hospital, not St. Joseph's, but Mott claims that the nurse visited him there as well on two occasions and Forest claims that Merton spoke with her on the phone just a few months before his death. Merton had entrusted to James Laughlin a series of "nurse poems" that he had written and stipulated that they be preserved, but not published until they would not embarrass anyone. About the experience Merton wrote: "It needs to be known too for it is part of me. My need for love, my loneliness, my inner division, the struggle in which solitude is at once a problem and a 'solution.' And perhaps not a perfect solution either."³⁴⁶ In 1974 Laughlin told Thérèse that "at the request of the party concerned" they would not be printed in a new collection of Merton poems and that John Howard Griffin "will be dealing with this matter in the [Merton] biography, though in a very dignified way."³⁴⁷

On June 1st, Thérèse sends him belated ordination anniversary greetings explaining that her own tardiness in responding is due to the last two weeks of school, and to the fact that she had been commissioned to write a poem on St. Joan of Arc for the dedication of a new chapel in the saint's honor at Marquette University. She had recited the poem herself from memory at the formal dedication ceremonies on May 26th, although she had a copy with her for "psychological" security. Her only real fear, she recalls, was the wind. By this time she was not wearing the traditional habit, but a modified version: "I was really worried that my dress would parasol, and had to hold it down while speaking at the mike."³⁴⁸ The top brass of the

## The Final Years

University and City of Milwaukee attended the event and she was seated next to the Mayor's wife to whom she extended an invitation to visit Mount St. Paul's: "Did I ever tell you that I was elected or appointed to the Mayor's Council on the Arts?"[349]

She was shocked on hearing of Merton's operation, but was reassured now that she knew he was home and able to spend some time at the hermitage each day. And he *must* be very careful! The Merton display from Mount St. Paul had been taken down and was scattered around her studio, but soon she would put it in order and continue cataloging the new materials that continued to pour in from Merton. She informs him that she will be the poet-in-residence at Georgetown from July 15th to August 15th. The honor involves two lectures, one of which will be on Merton's poetry and a poetry workshop as she had done in 1963 — an experience she describes as strange, but does not explain why. Part of the Georgetown conference will be another Merton display — the *first* in the East — and Thérèse has been asked to arrange it: "I'm now expecting to hear just what facilities they have for the exhibit — I prefer glass topped cases.... It should get a lot of publicity, and draw many people... and that it is at Georgetown makes me very happy indeed."[350]

Before heading east, she will make her annual six-day retreat and take some vacation days at Wausau from June 13th to the 20th where she will be reunited with her animal friends, "and then miss them terribly afterwards!"[351] Then she would leave on July 14th for Washington and the Georgetown poetry conference. She seems upbeat and positive and, apparently, her difficulties in the community have been resolved: "I already have my [teaching] contract for next year, so I really am looking forward."[352]

Merton had recently published an essay, "Is the World a Problem?" in *Commonweal*. Thérèse was writing her June 7th letter to Merton when a copy arrived and she responds with her typical over-the-top enthusiasm: "How marvelous it is.... I walked the length of our garden for the last half hour absorbing — or trying to — this wonderful intellectual and spiritual feast. My, but this is excellent — the paragraph on 309 (second last) almost put me into the sky. And I went back and read it aloud! In this type of thing you are really at your best — this, and of course, your poetry. Your gift is your poetry — and still, one can't separate your various literary skills... to say nothing of the deep spiritual content."³⁵³

Merton was working on a contribution to a book called *Prophetic Voices* edited by Ned O'Gorman and published by Random House, and sends her a draft on June 7th. He had been asked by the editor to define seven words and be "revolutionary" in his contribution, because the book was to contain revolutionary thinking: "I don't know how revolutionary I was in the seven words, but anyway here they are. They might throw your retreat into turmoil. You can make a revolutionary retreat. I should have developed the one on war more, but have written so much on it I was fed up with the subject by the time I got that far. The first one on death is largely Rahner and existentialism and I think it is the best. The one on purity will make a lot of people sit up and some will reach for their anathemas."³⁵⁴ This essay was later republished in his book, *Love and Living* and was Merton's most extensive writing on sexuality.

He had published an article in *Commonweal* on secular Christianity but had not yet seen a copy in print: "I think that this fuss about secular Christianity is very superficial and short sighted. It is a silly pseudo radicalism that leads nowhere. I think if people are going to be radical they ought to go all the way. Secular Christianity is neither one nor the other, neither fully secular nor fully Christian, it is just a compromise which enables you to be nothing while pretending to be up to date."³⁵⁵

He tells her more about his back surgery that consisted in fusing the vertebrae, and, since he is still recovering, he misses manual labor. Even typing, at first was painful.

Gethsemani is taking over a foundation in Chile that the Spencer Abbey had founded, and, although Merton claims he knows Spanish well, he thinks the abbot wants him to stay at Gethsemani, so he does not suppose he will be sent. He is giving conferences on

## The Final Years

Christianity and the modern world that include details about Marxism, Freud and others. He continues to offer hope that her new book of poems will be accepted by Macmillan or, eventually, by some other publisher. He even offers to write "a line or two" if that will help, though it is not clear whether he is offering to contribute an introduction or write to a publisher on her behalf.

On July 23rd Thérèse is back at Georgetown, residing in Darnell Hall for the summer conference. She writes to Merton on college stationery thanking him for the items he had sent for the Merton exhibit at Georgetown. She had already started to work on the display in Healy Hall and discovered that the space was not as large as the lobby at Mount St. Paul, but the display cases made the materials stand out strikingly. She had to remove a picture of the French Jesuit explorer and missionary among the Native Americans, Père Marquette, to make room for Merton.

Her request this time is for Merton to tape some of his poems. It would be an exceptional experience for her students at Mount St. Paul, she says, to hear them in his voice. Her letter is full of descriptions of people and events on and off the Georgetown campus, including a trip to the National Theater to see *Barefoot in the Park* and encountering President Lyndon Johnson's daughter, Lucy and her husband, Pat Nugent — "a real ordinary person" — with whom she talked about Marquette. She had also been driven to Baltimore for a three-hour profession of thirty novices at the Motherhouse of the School Sisters of Notre Dame, toured the campus of the College of Notre Dame and the new Cathedral of Mary Immaculate, both on North Charles Street and saw the film, *A Patch of Blue*.

On July 31st, Merton replies that he has never taped any of his poems. He did not even own a tape recorder, did not want to bother other people and would never fool with one himself. Knowing of his almost disastrous attempt to learn how to drive the monastery Jeep, one wonders if he would have been anymore adept at using a mechanical device like a tape recorder. Just a year later, however, Merton had begun to use a tape recorder and in 1966 sent her one of his taped journals: "I have acquired a tape recorder and had to fool with it a little to make sure I know how to work it. It is a very fine machine and I am abashed by it. I take back some of the things I have said about technology.... The other night I ended by sitting up late and making all kinds of naive experiments with tape. I think I am getting on to it and that it has real possibilities if handled with care. One good thing about it: it may cool down my emphatic attitudes. I will do less underlining, do not have to try to be so definite, so decisive, a kind of freedom can come from being nicely relaxed, cool and open."[356] He describes Thérèse's recent letter from Washington as "very brisk and happy. I am delighted that you have a chance to get around and see people and things.... You need all that and it will be a great good for your work. We all need some kind of stimulation to keep alive."[357] Compared to her stimulating time in Washington, his only stimulation comes from bursitis in the elbow for which he has been getting cortisone shots. Eventually, he thinks, he might need an operation.

By September, Thérèse is back in Milwaukee working with the seminarians at Mount St. Paul College who, to this day, remember her as a breath of fresh air, although at times a bit flighty if not eccentric. On September 13th he affirms the students' esteem for her: "I can quite believe the seminarians when they say you are the best thing that ever hit their place. I am sure you are. You are their aggiornamento in person.... I am sure you are livening them up, because you are a very alive and alert person, and thank God for it."[358]

As for Thérèse's peculiar behaviors, one Salvatorian priest recalls her having told him that she often smelled the scent of roses in her apartment on the anniversary of Merton's death. Another Thérèse legend recounts that when she first moved into an apartment in Racine, she mistook the garbage disposal for a food processor, and wondered why nothing she put in ever came back. Her love for animals was well known, but at times bordered on the bizarre. She kept a hamster in her office who, when let loose, found its way into a bottom desk drawer where it proceeded to shred paperback books,

## The Final Years

creating quite a mess. Eventually she began to put more paperbacks in the drawer to keep it satisfied. Students who stopped by to visit her Waukesha apartment found her attempting to feed lettuce to a cricket trapped in the bathtub. Her students recall her being pulled across campus by her pet rabbit on a leash with her veil, piled atop her hairpiece, flying in the wind.

On the other hand, this naïveté might have been a practiced part of her charm. She always asked to borrow the "Victrola" from the school library using the Victorian designation. A friend recalls being at dinner with her in a group at a Washington, D.C. restaurant. When the waiter asked her what she wanted to drink before dinner, Thérèse paused as if perplexed by such a question. Then, without a moment's hesitation, she looked directly at the waiter and said, "I'll have a double Beefeater gin, straight up, with a twist." Some have attributed these idiosyncrasies to a certain quality of childlikeness they found in her: "Among the outstanding poets of today, there is one whose simplicity and candor, at once childlike and profound, captures our hearts and holds them spell bound… that separates her from our world, which has grown so sadly and strangely old in its evil. Only a 'shining mind' that has kept intact the lovely wonder of childhood could pen these lines, taken from the title poem of *Give Joan a Sword*."[359]

She still has had no success in getting her book of poems published, and Merton continues to sympathize with her. He recommends John Delaney at Doubleday, apparently forgetting that she has already tried them. He counsels her to be patient and fish around quietly for the right publisher since there is no sense rushing it. After her very positive summer experiences at Georgetown, Thérèse is thinking of leaving her Merton collection to the University that has treated her so well and, has, apparently, already made her an offer. Merton agrees: "…sounds like a good place if they are eager and urging. That is always a sign they will take an interest. There are several small collections on the east coast: Columbia, and two in Boston, Boston University and Boston College, which is something of a rival of Georgetown and I know they would be disappointed.... Then there is Bonas [St. Bonaventure]. But Georgetown sounds interested and that is a good point. I will go along if that is what you decide."[360]

He advises her to check with his friend and literary executor, James Laughlin at New Directions, to inform him of the collection and solicit his advice on the offer from Georgetown. From his own previous legal and personal difficulties with publishers, Merton is eager to make sure there are no complications between Bellarmine and Thérèse: "I thought I would mention this as I am hoping that this fall he [Laughlin] will get everything cleared up from this legal point of view and there will be no further complications about it. A matter of defining clearly the condition under which the collections exist and to protect publishing rights. This is important, and when it is settled everyone will be quite clear where we stand. It would be good to have a list at the time when all this is settled, but of course the list will not be final. There is always more coming, so I would not insist on trying to get it all perfect. What you have so far, typed up would be admirable."[361]

On March 23, 1967, Merton tells Thérèse that the Aquinas Lecture she sent him had not yet arrived. As an Easter gift for her collection, he sends her photographs of himself and Jacques Maritain, the noted French Catholic intellectual and philosopher taken by Merton when Maritain had visited the hermitage. They should not be reproduced, he tells her, without permission from John Howard Griffin. Griffin was the first official biographer of Merton, appointed in 1968. Some appeared in his book *Follow the Ecstasy* (1981), and others in *A Hidden Wholeness: The Visual World of Thomas Merton* (1970). While writing Merton's biography, Griffin was living in Merton's hermitage and was in contact with Thérèse soliciting her help. Due to illness, however, Griffin was unable to complete the biography, although some of his basic research was eventually published in the book cited above. After Merton's death Griffin had written to Thérèse to congratulate her on a poem that appeared in *America* magazine to say, "I wanted only to write and tell you how deeply I admired and loved your poem in *America*. John Moffit [*America's* poetry editor] said it was the finest thing they have done in a long time, and I certainly agree."[362] Thérèse still has not found a publisher for her poetry book, and Merton seems less and less encouraging: "...more and more good poetry is just not getting published commercially... the book business is pretty much of a racket."[363] She must have identified very much with his quip: "Other peoples' bad books get published. Why can't my bad book get published?"[364]

In the spring, Merton is working on getting his literary estate organized and on May 1st he asks Thérèse for a copy of her list of the materials she has — not a complete list, just what she has handy, even if unfinished — to give him some idea of what is there. There is also, he says, the possibility for publication of his early novel, *Journal of My Escape from the Nazis*, and he needs either the original manuscript or a copy of it. She responds on May 9th that she is still planning to complete the inventory of her collection by June, but she has been delayed because Naomi Burton did not return the copy of Part 1 that Thérèse had sent from Wausau in June 1965. Thérèse is finished teaching on May 28th, and plans to use her summer free time to work on her Mertoniana and have it completed and sent to Merton by mid-June.

She does not have the manuscript of his only extant novel, *Journal of My Escape from the Nazis*. She had borrowed the original from Bob Lax or Ed Rice for the first Merton display at Marquette in 1949, and had returned it to one of them afterwards. Ever vigilant and resourceful, however, lest some scrap of Merton material escape her collection, she had "made a hurried copy of it on very thin paper before I sent it back."[365] She can type that out and send him a carbon copy. She also had several chapters of the novel in its first draft "with some corrections in your handwriting, and especially precious because of that."[366] Also "precious" are the photographs of Merton and Jacques Maritain in the hermitage he had sent her in

March. Merton's photograph of Maritain is "simply stunning — that should go down in the annals of photography. Better by far than any Bachrach: thank you for all these things, which are cherished by me and so much enrich the collection with a special kind of human interest."[367] To Thérèse, even Merton's amateur photographical efforts far surpassed those of the recognized experts! In all fairness, however, Merton's photographic skills were recognized by John Howard Griffin, a professional photographer and also an admirer, who had high praise for them.

The question of who would get her collection surfaced again when she met Mark Van Doren, Merton's influential Columbia teacher and friend, two weeks previously at a dialogue between him and Archibald MacLeish at the Dominican College in Racine, Wisconsin. He was aware of her collection of manuscripts but she told him her secret: she was planning to leave the collection to Georgetown. Van Doren, however, favored Harvard, and even gave her the librarian's name. But her heart was set on Georgetown: "... you told me if this were my decision you would 'go along with it.' They are building a marvelous new library... where the Mertoniana would be suitably 'enshrined.'"[368] Georgetown appealed to her as the repository of the collection because at Harvard it would be only one of the many special collections. At Georgetown it would be the collection and, Washington being such an international city, more accessible to students from every part of the world.

The Congregation of the Sisters of the Divine Savior and most other nuns were continuing to experiment with versions of a more modern-dress habit, following the Second Vatican Council's call for renewal in religious life. She tells Merton that one of the young sisters is working at the *Milwaukee Sentinel* for the summer in secular garb: "We've made some interesting 'progress' too — as regards our veils, etc. Having discarded the coif we are piloting the following: Just a nylon stretch band over the hair — like the young girls wear — and over that — set on a bandeau, a short black veil.... It was a great humiliation... to enter my classroom the first day; but

## The Final Years

the seminarians were waiting — and stood up and clapped, saying it was 'sharp.'"[369]

Thérèse was always fastidious about her appearance. She once owned a fur coat someone had given her that had apparently been dry cleaned with chemicals. When someone accidentally spilled some kind of liquid on it at a party, the fur on the coat began to dissolve in front of everyone and she was devastated. She was also very particular about her hair. She blamed the veil that she had worn for so many years as a nun for her thinning hair. After the veil was modified and eventually abandoned altogether, she always wore a professionally coiffed hairpiece but never spoke about it.

At a June, 1967 Senior Day at Mount St. Paul's she recounts that John Yockey, a student and Cistercian monk, had brought a greased pig for what, she described as "rough games," and, given her sensitivity to animal life, it was not at all to her liking: "Some of us felt sorry for our very proper little Cistercian pig. At the end he looked so frustrated.... I can't see these things, can you?"[370] What she did not know, however, was that according to Yockey, the pig died shortly afterwards.

She had written a draft of a statement for a symposium she would be attending in June and asks Merton to edit it, but he questions the whole concept: "It seems to me that there ought to be some question about possible great differences between these 'minorities,' all embattled in slightly different, or very different, ways, and for different reasons: sometimes against each other. It is by no means clear that Catholics and Negroes are somehow fighting shoulder to shoulder for the same things. And also the 'Catholic' type minority in literature — what is it anyhow? Not Flannery O'Connor, or Jim Powers, surely. Catholic writers insofar as they are really good writers, tend to merge into the general picture, don't they? Of course there is the Catholic faith, but in specifically literary work that faith is not propounded as a self-conscious minority position? Or is it? It is just our faith, our kind of Christianity in a country that still calls itself Christian. Well, anyway, I know that is not clear but it is what occurred to me. The Jewishness question as it was discussed awhile ago seems to have been exaggerated somewhat."[371]

The spring symposium on "The Creative Artist and Christian Renewal" was being held June 9th and 10th at Rosary College in River Forest, Illinois where the Jesuit peace activist and poet, Dan Berrigan, will be on the program. After that she plans to spend a week in New York before heading to Washington for the annual Georgetown summer conference. She had initially decided to make her annual retreat at the Motherhouse in Milwaukee where she could continue her work on the Merton catalogue, but her superiors had a different idea: "…they thought I should get in the woods for at least a couple of days," so she went to Wausau for a five-day retreat from June 14th to the 18th.[372]

At the Chicago symposium Thérèse met Sister Corita Kent, the charismatic artist nun and had lunch with Dan Berrigan, whom she finds to be really a saint. She enjoyed Corita's "happening" when bubbles were floated down from the balcony all during her program. The religious exhibit at the New York World's Fair where people were whisked past the Pietà on a moving platform, Thérèse opined, was saved from being totally banal by Corita's drawings. She knew that "Corita," as she was always called, had worked with Berrigan and recalls some controversy involving Corita and the hierarchy: "…wasn't she 'campused' by Card. McIntyre on one occasion, for making drawings for one of Father's 'pacifist' books?"[373]

In 1967, the ferment of Vatican II was being felt in every part of the Church, especially in seminaries including Thérèse's own, and she tries to make some sense of it: "We lost some of our best seminarians at the close of the year — some of the 'intellectuals,' I mean, and I feel very sad about it. Apparently these people (being complex) are difficult to 'understand' and hence have difficult lives. But no doubt this is the case in all seminaries, especially in these times."[374]

On June 26th Merton begins to lay the groundwork for their first, substantial face-to-face meeting at Gethsemani since her

## The Final Years

spontaneous appearance at the monastery door in 1951. Bellarmine University was planning a program centered on their Merton collection sometime in November and Merton had suggested Thérèse as a speaker: "That would be in November. If you get down I'll try to work the Abbot over, in the name of Aggiornamento, and see if this time he won't let us have a decent visit, spend the afternoon and all. Friends in Louisville would be delighted to put you up. But don't let's discuss this in letters until it is assured: I think censorship of mail is starting up again and if the boss thinks you are too enthusiastic he'll say no. So let's play it cool. It is really sickening to have to perpetually go about things like this, knowing that if you start something it may suddenly get cut off and nothing come of it. That's why I seldom do make any suggestions. However, if Bellarmine sends an invitation, you might casually mention that and say sort of offhand what you think. 'I might consider it... etc.'"[375] Merton's implication seems to be that one of her conditions for accepting an invitation to speak at the Bellarmine event would be the guarantee of a meeting with Thomas Merton.

In July, Merton sent Thérèse a feast day letter and more materials, including the manuscript of *Mystics and Zen Masters*, some notes, a preface and more proofs. She is working on a monograph, *Marianne Moore: A Critical Essay*, for a series by Eerdmans, in Grand Rapids, Michigan, titled "Contemporary Writers in Christian Perspective" that is due on September 1st. Moore was a noted American poet who died in 1972 at the age of 84. She was a Pulitzer Prize winner and numbered among her friends Wallace Stevens, T.S. Eliot, Ezra Pound and W.H. Auden. Thérèse once said that the influences on her writing have been, for the most part, from her associations with other writers "such as a delightful afternoon with Marianne Moore in her Greenwich Village apartment."[376] It would be interesting to know if Thérèse's motivation for selecting Marianne Moore as a topic was her awareness that Moore knew and perhaps met Merton's artist parents, Owen the painter and Ruth the novelist, since they all moved in the same circles of artistic types like Alfred Stieglitz,

Georgia O'Keefe and Djuna Barnes in New York and Greenwich Village before and after the First World War. Gertrude Stein called them part of "a lost generation."

Thérèse will not be able to finish the cataloging job until after she returns from Georgetown. For the upcoming Writers Conference at Georgetown, she plans "to skip what I can of the writers' conference (isn't this a bad intention before I leave?) and confine myself to the monograph except for special things I much want to hear."[377] After six months at Wesleyan Press her poor "sparrow" manuscript of poems was finally rejected. Should she appear personally at some publishing house when she is in New York, she asks Merton? On August 4th, from Georgetown she reports to Merton that an official of the conference had gushed over her bringing Merton with her to the conference this time — all Georgetown had was their dull Masefield.[378]

The new library at Georgetown, the future home of the Merton collection in Thérèse's mind, was slated for completion in two years. She informs him she has been taken to dinner at a fashionable home in Bethesda and to a concert at the National Cathedral by two of her former Salvatorian students. By this time some of the students she had taught at Mount St. Paul were living at the Salvatorian house of studies in Lanham, Maryland, while pursuing theological studies at the Catholic University of America. The publisher of her planned monograph on Moore was also attending the Georgetown conference, and Thérèse plans to ask for an extension of the deadline. She was also hoping to visit Moore in New York on the way home but, because of Moore's illness, she told Thérèse that she was not receiving any visitors. A short time later, Thérèse discovered that Moore was receiving visitors but not everyone. In a rather piqued tone, she informs Merton that *Time* magazine recently carried a photograph of Moore "attending a baseball game with Mr. George Plimpton!! and he returned her to her apartment at 1:00 AM!!."[379] During the summer conference at Georgetown, Thérèse had met Maureen McManus, a public relations woman from Holt, Rinehart & Winston in

*The Final Years*

New York and one of the speakers on a panel of publishers. Thérèse gave her the manuscript of poems hoping they might be published: "I'm terribly disappointed about having these poems lying around for so long a time."[380]

In the summer of 1967, Milwaukee and several other major U.S. cities were the scenes of large-scale race riots. Thérèse, back in Milwaukee by September 2nd and still writing on Georgetown stationery, describes the city to Merton as the "Rioting City." The riots had started just the day after she left the city for the East Coast. She regrets the fact that things cannot be settled without violence and mentions the name of Father Groppi, a prominent and controversial priest who was on the front lines of the struggle for racial equality in Milwaukee and elsewhere. She had sent Merton "Mertoniana II," part of the catalogue she was trying to complete, but still had to list Merton's more recent publications. Thérèse's unpublished catalogue of Merton manuscripts includes those from 1938 to 1962 and volume two, 1962-1967, consisting of 500+ sheets. Her deadline for the Moore monograph had been extended to October 1st, and, in the meantime, she has been invited to speak on September 24th to the Wisconsin Regional Writers in Fond du Lac. Once again she repeats the *Time* magazine Moore story and adds, not surprisingly, that interviewing Moore personally was not absolutely necessary for the monograph, although she would love to have seen her.

On July 13th Merton comments in his journal on *Jubilee*, a review of Catholic thought and culture and one of the most respected Christian magazines of its time. It was hailed as the first national picture magazine for a Catholic audience. Rice and Lax began to publish *Jubilee* in 1953 and Merton was a frequent contributor, although he was not allowed to have his name on the masthead. In 1967, Rice stopped publishing the magazine and the company he had founded to finance it, AMDG Publishing, dissolved. Lax and Rice, friends of both Merton and Thérèse, had recently resigned and the magazine had been sold to the publishing house of Herder and Herder. Justus George Lawler was named publisher and Merton thought that Lawler "...should be good at it — but how disappointing it all is."[381] Thérèse liked Lawler because Herder and Herder's *Continuum* magazine had published a special edition devoted to Merton in 1969, but James Laughlin later expressed his belief that Lawler had exploited Merton because he used Merton's writings without obtaining permission from the trustees. Lawler tried to continue *Jubilee* for a year, but in December 1968, it was merged with *U.S. Catholic*, published by the Claretian Fathers.

Thérèse had in her possession a large black and white portrait of Merton by John Howard Griffin. She decided to color it with transparent oils, using the 1949 Kodachrome photograph of Merton, to get the color right: "...and it really came alive, blue eyes as well and all.... In a gold frame it will be striking. Belongs to the collection, of course."[382] Writing on September 26th for her October 3rd feast day, Merton has finally tracked down the manuscript of his novel, *The Journal of My Escape from the Nazis*, from Ed Rice, but he thinks that his literary agent, Naomi Burton, might not think it is the right time for publication. On September 10th he mentions in his journal the death of his Columbia friend, Ed Reinhardt. Thérèse had sent him a cutting with a letter on September 10th. On the 22nd he learned of the death of another close friend and his lawyer, John Slate, so he is searching for another lawyer. He has also lost contact with Bob Lax who has left Greece with no forwarding address.

Ed Rice and the *Jubilee* affair are still on his mind. In his journal entry for September 10th he described the way in which Herder and Herder took over the publication as "tragic" and laments "the awful dirty deal he [Rice] got from the Herder people."[383] Perhaps, as a result of what happened to Bob Lax and Ed Rice at *Jubilee*, Merton's negative view of publishing had been confirmed: "The whole poetry publication business is mysterious in the extreme: a gamble if ever there was one. The same is true of publishing as a whole. It strikes me as more and more of a racket. But publishers are getting rich, even though authors may not be. I am sure that if you keep after it you will find the right person eventually."[384]

## The Final Years

Finally, Thérèse received a formal invitation to Bellarmine to speak at its annual "Town-and-Gown" week. They wanted her to speak on Saturday, November 4th in conjunction with the official opening and dedication of the Merton Room. Part of the program would include a photographic exhibit on Merton by Ralph Eugene Meatyard, a photographer friend of Merton from Lexington. Merton phoned her in Milwaukee early in October to talk about the details of their meeting. A few days later, on October 13th, he writes: "I am probably as surprised as you are. I did not think I would be able to reach you, as I did not know the name of the convent, let alone the phone number."[385]

Merton assured Thérèse that no one was playing a joke on her by impersonating him when she received his phone call: "...of which there are plenty of people capable — I have been impersonated on the phone in all sorts of ways apparently."[386] In 1967, Merton heard that Frank Sheed, in London, had received a call from someone claiming to be Merton: "There are people around who are crazy enough to think that if they pretend they are Thomas Merton it means something."[387] Merton was looking forward to "having a good chat with you after all these years. The abbot is away now, but I am sure he will have no objections, and as I said he is about to retire. At least it is pretty sure he is. So we may well get a few significant changes around here, and things may open up somewhat. But it is still impossible for me to go anywhere, although I get all kinds of invitations, even one last August to come to New York and meet Cardinal Köenig and discuss his work with atheists, etc."[388]

In April 1967, Merton had spoken with friends about the forthcoming visit of Cardinal Franz Köenig to the States. In a journal entry for August 4th, he writes: "The thing that was really irritating me was the fact that Cardinal Köenig is coming to this country, and had invited me to meet with him, Norman Cousins, and some others in the East to discuss the business of his commissions and the [new] Archbishop [of Louisville, Thomas McDonough] urged me to go — and Dom James refuses."[389] Fox had written to Köenig saying that it would set a bad precedent with regard to the other monks and Merton's solitary vocation, but he invited Köenig to visit the monastery and offered to pay all his expenses.

Thérèse responds on October 16th to Merton's letter and telephone call. She has been living on "cloud nine" since she heard his voice: "You were the last person on earth I could have thought might call me! And there you were — your voice so warm and brotherly.... the day before, I had played your tape... as a feast day gift for my students on the feast of 'Mater Salvatoris.' They loved it, of course, and asked me if it were you — I said 'yes,' for that was my understanding when you wrote about the tape a month ago. But to me — who haven't heard you, of course, for *16* years — I wasn't too sure — it sounded a bit unlike that tape I heard you gave to the Sisters at Nyrinx [sic], and was circulated in some Sisters' communities."[390]

The day you called, she continued, "I had gone up to the 5th floor.... And I still do not understand how I heard the paging, for they do not call the 5th floor since some of the nursing sisters sleep there during the day, but I just happened to pass the window of my bedroom and thought I heard my name in the page. I rushed to the phone at the end of the corridor, and asked if she had called me — then I heard your voice."[391]

Merton had already informed her that she would be staying with Tommie O'Callaghan who lived in Louisville. The O'Callaghans, Frank and Thomasine, were old friends of Merton whom he often mentions in his journals. He got to know them and their children, six girls and a boy, through an introduction by Dan Walsh who had taught Tommie. Merton admits he was curiously fond of Diane, one of the daughters, who was nine or ten at the time, but was more complicated and vulnerable in Merton's view. In his frequent trips to Louisville for medical appointments he often stopped in for dinner with the family and met Tommie on different occasions to discuss matters having to do with the Merton Literary Trust. He gradually became part of the large family (he was "Uncle Louie" to the kids)

*The Final Years*

attending picnics and other gatherings and stayed there overnight on one occasion when his flight from the West Coast arrived late in the evening in Louisville.

He had asked the O'Callaghans to bring Thérèse out to Gethsemani on Tuesday the 7th, and writes to Tommie O'Callaghan on November 3rd: "Got a note from Sister. She is bubbling over with all kinds of expectations and I am sure will enjoy everything thoroughly: she is very much full of life, and appreciates very much being able to stay with you."[392] Merton says he will be busy until noon, but Frank, Tommie's husband, can show Thérèse the Church and whatnot: "It will be a good thing for him to meet Sister."[393]

Thérèse spent several hours with Merton at the hermitage on Tuesday, November 7th. Observers later commented that the monk and the nun, finally together after so many years of corresponding, did not know what to make of each other — Merton, ebullient, talkative, humorous, and Thérèse, shy, proper, retiring and probably awestruck by being, finally, in the presence of her beloved "Fr. Louis" in the flesh. Merton had worn a red poncho belonging to Tommie O'Callaghan while celebrating Mass for the group earlier in the hermitage before the outdoor picnic. It was a gift from a Jesuit priest friend of hers in Ecuador, perhaps her husband's brother who was a Jesuit. As the day became a bit chilly, Merton lent it to Thérèse and insisted that she put it on. She demurred, claiming she did not even know how to put it on, but Merton told her to slip it over her head just like a vestment. Before they left, Merton asked Tommie to "let her have it."[394] This is the garment she is pictured wearing over her religious habit in the now-famous photograph of her and Merton. The poncho and Mateus Rose wine bottle (shown in a photograph of Merton pouring wine at the picnic) are now in the possession of her close friend, Barry McCabe. After the picnic the celebration continued for some time back in the hermitage where, somewhat to Merton's annoyance, Thérèse insisted on putting some order into the contents of the hermitage. Merton later expressed some anger about the attempt, but Tommie O'Callaghan kept reminding him that Thérèse was his "first fan" and knew more about him and his work than anyone else. He should be patient with her, she urged.

Her feelings about the experience of the visit were expressed in July 1968, when Thérèse sent Merton a poem she had written ("A Hill is for Celebration/With Certain Apologies to Juan de La Cruz, for Tommie and Frank") describing the visit to Merton's hermitage.[395] The title reflects a Merton introduction, titled "The Street is for Celebration," to a book of photographs of Spanish Harlem by Msgr. Robert J. Fox. Merton's response to the encounter was much more subdued: "Your visit was really historic! I am glad it rectifies the austerity of the previous one which, as you know, was not my idea."[396] He was referring to her spur of the moment visit in August 1951, when Thérèse simply showed up at the monastery expecting to meet him. He mentioned the picnic visit also in a journal entry of November 12th in sparse words perhaps because he had not yet gotten over the incident in his hermitage after the picnic: "Sr. Thérèse, (here Tuesday briefly)."[397] A few days later, however, he wrote her: "I enjoyed having you here, and I hope you enjoyed it too."[398]

On her return from Kentucky, she was to be part of a panel on liturgy dealing with poetic expression in worship. Two other Salvatorians (a seminarian with a "hairdo like a hippie" and a drama teacher) were also to be part of the panel: "Some of our Masses are really grand — guitars, receive under both species, pretty gay words and rhythms, and we take the host in our hands… some even break their little hosts and communicate their next neighbor; he does the same for them. I guess I am an old lady who is very far-out, for I think it is marvelous."[399]

The sixties were a time of liturgical renewal and popular adaptations in the style of worship including innovations and experimentation, not all of which were carefully thought out let alone theologically sound. McCabe describes Thérèse as an "enthusiastic disciple of Vatican II."[400] She had participated in a Mass with Fr. Dan Berrigan in Racine that, no doubt, incorporated many of the emerging trends in more informal small group liturgies. In the sixties and seventies she commented that sometimes "religious authority figures were having trouble embracing Vatican II and that they still gave greater importance to blind obedience than to some of the more substantive messages of Christianity as clarified by Vatican II."[401]

Thérèse had sent Merton a copy of her will although, as he tells her on November 16th, she need not have done so since the more copies there are circulating, the more legal problems might arise. He has only two copies of his own will. The Trust agreement about his works has been signed and, although there is no official policy, all his unpublished material is restricted. Permissions must come from the Trust to copy any of it. As for the unpublished materials, such as those in other collections like Thérèse's, this material can be consulted, but permission for quoting in print must also be cleared through the Trust.

In the winter of 1967 Merton was soliciting contributions from various writers for a periodic, mimeographed publication of poems that he was calling *Monk's Pond*. He initially intended to publish just one edition, but later spoke about gathering materials for a second issue and finally settled on four issues, all of which appeared in the following year. He asked Thérèse for some short, unpublished poems that he could use in the magazine.

In January 1968, Merton sent her a copy of an official printed notice of the election of Flavian Burns as the new abbot of Gethsemani. Merton appended a note in his own handwriting: "A very good man — the best we have — years ago I spotted him for a future Abbot, young, alert, solid."[402] For Merton, the election of Burns was a kind of liberation. He described him as a person he could talk to and work with and even propose experiments.

By this time the Merton Legacy Trust was growing anxious about ownership and copyright issues surrounding Merton's prolific writings that were spread out over a number of collections. As a way of organizing the materials, the Trust drew up a set of rules for the Bellarmine collection and Merton sent Thérèse a copy on February 21st. The Trustees wanted some kind of uniform practice for authors when obtaining permission to copy or publish materials both from Merton's published and unpublished manuscripts. They wanted each institutional holder of Merton materials to enter into some kind of agreement with the Trust.

Thérèse had mentioned to Merton that she was thinking of changing her will and had been soliciting Merton's advice as to where she should leave her collection. She had thought of changing her will in order to leave it to Georgetown University, but never got around to doing it. By 1980, she finally decided to add a codicil to the 1974 version bequeathing her Merton holdings to Fr. Paul Dinter at Columbia University, as has been recounted above. Merton's new Louisville lawyer, John Ford, was naturally interested in her decisions about her collection and planned to contact Thérèse to discuss it. Merton apologizes on February 21st for all the red tape involved, assuring her that it probably won't affect her until scholars actually start using the collections. Merton is aware, however, from one of Thérèse's letters that at least one doctoral candidate, Dennis McInerny, had already been in touch with her about viewing some of the material.[403] One researcher who visited Thérèse to ask for some material relative to his dissertation research recalls how, when she opened up a closet containing her Merton collection it was almost as if she were opening a shrine for display. When she agreed to lend him the manuscript he needed so that he could photocopy pages locally, she first thrust it at him and then immediately took it back. This happened two more times before she finally and dramatically said, "Take it," allowing him to finally get hold of it.

His literary project, *Monk's Pond* or *"MPond,"* was not making much progress, because all the mimeographing equipment at the monastery was being used by people running off materials about the liturgy. The three poems she had offered for his magazine might be in the manuscript she had sent him somewhere in the monastery, he says, but he is not sure where. She should send him copies, but there is no rush, since he will probably not get to that project for several more months. Thérèse had expressed some concern about the classified materials in her collection, but Merton assures her that the only classified materials might be the *Sign of Jonas* holograph material: "...most of the classified stuff is letters — people with problems, etc. Or some of my own wrangling with the order, way back, about going elsewhere to be a hermit."[404]

The new abbot, Flavian Burns, is well liked by the monks, Merton reports. He is not wildly radical or progressive but just "frank and simple and you know where you stand. And he is willing to go along with anything fairly reasonable."[405] It was Burns who gave Merton permission to travel outside the monastery to places like California, Alaska and, eventually, to Bangkok. By March 6th Merton's literary magazine is in print with its first issue. He wants to use three of her poems in the fall issue — one about Lax and his Greek islands, one for Dan Berrigan, published in the *Catholic Worker*, and the "Salutation" about Buddhist incense at Mass published in *America*. He is working on getting his novel, *Journal of My Escape from the Nazis*, in shape for publication and he is grateful for her manuscript that Thérèse had sent which was proving helpful in putting it in some kind of order after another typist had mixed up all the pages. Merton said that Marie Charron, a friend of Tommie O'Callaghan and a typist for Merton at the time, had a difficult time with the stencils of the novel: "Marie C. must have dropped the ms. and got it back together wrong. Yet I carefully numbered the pages in pencil. Maybe not."[406] Charron, according to O'Callaghan, had a different version of the story and was not amused that Merton had blamed her for the mix-up that caused a delay.

A copy of his just published *Cables to the Ace* was also on the way to her and he was going to use three of her poems in the fall issue of his new, in-house publication. His brief note of March 6th to Thérèse is printed on plain white paper as usual, but in the upper right hand corner, is a simple black and white reproduction of a photograph of the hermitage taken after a snowfall. On March 19th, the Feast of St. Joseph and the anniversary of Merton's solemn vows, it was Thérèse who found herself uncharacteristically remiss in answering two of Merton's previous letters. She is still working on the unfinished Moore monograph (published in 1969) and had attended a Marquette lecture by Bernard Lonergan, an influential Jesuit theologian.

During her two-week Easter vacation she plans to develop her own research guidelines for use of her Merton materials similar to those in the Bellarmine document and put together her will regarding the collection. Tommie O'Callaghan, one of the original members of the Merton Legacy Trust, had suggested a paragraph for Thérèse's will that upset her very much. She interpreted it as meaning that her personal letters from Merton would become part of the Bellarmine collection. Thérèse was fearful: "When Tommie put together that little paragraph I sent you — she insisted I put the 'personal letters' in it, which frightened me a little since I thought they would be taking them away from me!! I surely won't part with them yet, and I don't think anyone should get hold of them yet either. Not that I expect to live 100 years, but maybe a little longer than, shall we say 70? Tell me what you think about the 'letters' angle? I had even thought previously I might like to entrust them somewhere else rather than with the collection, but Tommie felt they should be included in it."[407] It might have been this experience of feeling pressured by O'Callaghan to donate the personal letters from Merton to Thérèse to Bellarmine that precipitated Thérèse's resolve to do just the opposite. In all fairness, however, it should be pointed out that it was Merton himself who had first asked O'Callaghan to suggest to Thérèse that she leave her collection to Bellarmine. Apparently he did not want to do it himself, although she surely would have complied with his wishes had he but asked. Thérèse was determined, according to people who knew her, that the Thomas Merton Center would not get her collection.

Her friendship with Tommie, however, did not seem to be compromised, at least on the surface: "And Tommie? I think we have some ESP connection, she and I. At the Thomist lecture who should come over to me but Frank's Jesuit brother whom I had met in

## The Final Years

Louisville — in [fact] we had had breakfast together at Tommie's.... Naturally I thought of Tommie and re-lived some of my 'Kentucky experiences.' That evening, who should call me but Tommie!! I couldn't believe it was true. She told me all about her not going to Holland... but it is so good that she is well again. She told me of her visit with you too. I feel that I've known Tommie all my life."[408]

Hoping to have the summer free to finish the cataloging, Thérèse would like to write an Introduction that could be used were the catalogue eventually to be published: "I haven't said anything to Georgetown as yet... but will see them in late July and August."[409] Dennis McInerny, the doctoral candidate from Notre Dame, plans to visit her to look at Merton's drawings and other unpublished materials so the Bellarmine guidelines had arrived just in time.

Thérèse was teaching a small class of 12 senior drama majors at Milwaukee's Cardinal Stritch College on "Practical Criticism." She was using Merton's unpublished *Geography of Lograire* with its puzzling references to "Big John," "strangling chickens," "the factory that makes bathtubs," and "cancel the bottle of more redness," and she had likened the work to T.S. Eliot's *The Waste Land*. Since the class was not a public presentation, she thought it would be all right to use the unpublished manuscript for this special class. Her students, mostly seniors and drama majors, tried hard to unravel the work, with the girls, as she said, doing much better than her male seminarians. When the poem was eventually published Thérèse contributed to the "Notes" in the back of the book, explaining the meaning of the title.

In her *Words and Silence*, she offers a simpler explanation: "The name of the imaginative country of his poem, 'Lograire,' is Merton's own creation — a name derived from the family name of the French lyric poet François Villon (des Loges), with its references to the hut or cabin where, as a hermit, Merton spent the last three years of his life. By extension it applies as well to all the places in the world where he or anyone else has lived, and since, in a sense, each man has his own imaginative 'Lograire,' how does he or anyone else locate himself in the geography of all men?"[410]

In the summer Thérèse returned to Washington, D.C. for another program at Georgetown and Merton sends greetings to her there on July 13th in time for what he again mistakenly thought was her July 16th feast day of Our Lady of Mt. Carmel. John Ford, Merton's new lawyer, has already heard from Thérèse about her collection and Merton offers some advice: "The most practical thing to do would be for you to draw up the same kind of trust document with G'town as I did with Bellarmine, which would make the collections exactly alike. The Trust would be in full control of literary rights and the collection would be entrusted to Georgetown, definitely."[411]

Merton is on a "no-visitors policy," but people still get through to him. One of these was Mary Luke Tobin, a Sister of Loretto, whose Motherhouse is not far from Gethsemani. She often met with Merton, for example, to talk with him about the Sisters' upcoming Chapter. Tobin was one of the few women auditors officially invited to the Second Vatican Council and circulated Merton's banned manuscript on nuclear war among some of the Council Fathers.

Merton's penultimate communication from Kentucky to Thérèse is a brief note dated August 20th, in which he does not inform her of his planned trip to the East. The trip was to be kept strictly confidential so as not to feed the rumors that Merton was leaving the monastery, the Church or getting married which had circulated for years. She had sent him what he describes as a very "lively" new poem ["A Hill is for Celebration" mentioned above] for the winter 1968 issue of *MPond IV*. He thinks it is "safe" to include the poem because the only "tinkling" mentioned in the poem was that of teacups and that "can hardly shock anyone even if they figure out the 'action.'"[412] With poetic references to "the valley gate," "a lean-beaten path" and "dance of the tea mugs, Beatle-beat, and a pocket of poems," the "action" was probably drinking tea with Merton, listening to records and reading some poetry in the hermitage following the picnic in November of the previous year. Merton was

*The Final Years*

always concerned that too many people would know the location of the hermitage.

On November 21st Merton notes in his Asian journal: "Wrote the card to Milosz [Czeslaw Milosz, a Polish poet writer among those with whom Merton corresponded] this morning, sitting in the hot sun. Cards to Sr. Thérèse Lentfoehr, John and Rena Niles, Tom Jerry Smith."[413] This card from India was to be the last communication Thérèse Lentfoehr received from Thomas Merton. He has been mostly in the Himalayas, he tells her: "Your letter was forwarded from the monastery. Bro. Patrick [Hart] has been taking care of mail & all business. A mimeo newsletter should give a partial rundown on my 'news.' I am going on to Ceylon and Indonesia & expect to see many more interesting people. God be with you. Blessings and Joy in Xt Tom Merton."[414]

A Western Union telegram, dated December 10, 1968, was sent from Bardstown, Kentucky at 4:30 p.m. to "SISTER M THÉRÈSE 3516 CENTER ST MILWAUKEE WI" that reads: "WE REGRET TO INFORM YOU OF THE DEATH OF FATHER LOUIS MERTON IN BANGKOK."[415] It was signed: ABBOT OF GETHSEMANI and was a duplicate of a telephoned telegram that was, perhaps, the call that Thérèse received that day in her office at Mount St. Paul College. Paul Portland, a Salvatorian scholastic in his final year at Mount St. Paul, a student of Thérèse and her occasional driver when she needed transportation, was in her office when she got the news by phone. She became very upset, he recalls, and began to cry. At first he had no idea of what was wrong, but somehow figured out that Merton had been electrocuted in Bangkok. Eventually, he said, she settled down a little and began to make phone calls, probably to tell others of the tragic event.

Barry McCabe learned of Merton's death when Thérèse came to a Eucharist for a small group in the chapel of Mount St. Paul the same day. Thérèse stood with the group in a semi-circle, directly in front of McCabe, around the altar and began crying early on in the Mass. When McCabe asked her what was wrong, she stepped forward to the altar and said "Tom has died."[416] The small group continued the Mass, dedicating it to Merton and trying to comfort her as best they could.

Patrick Hart recalls sending numerous telegrams to various old friends of Merton, including Sr. Thérèse, notifying them of his death. A requiem Mass was celebrated at Gethsemani for the community on the 11th at which the homily was given by the abbot, Flavian Burns: "The possibility of death wasn't absent from his mind. We spoke of this before he set out — first jokingly, then seriously. He was ready for it. He even saw a certain fittingness in dying over there amidst those Asian monks, who symbolized for him man's ancient and perennial desire for the deep things of God."[417]

Thérèse asked if she might spend the days keeping vigil before the funeral on the 17th. She arrived at Gethsemani for the funeral Mass and burial well ahead of time since it took a full week from the time of death for the body to pass through all the red tape with the Thai government officials and arrive back in Kentucky aboard a U.S. military transport. She was allowed to stay in the family guesthouse at Gethsemani during that time and kept a daytime vigil on the porch of Merton's hermitage fortified "by a six-pack and sandwiches," recalls one of the monks, although she never wrote about it afterwards. After the funeral Thérèse went back to the O'Callaghan house where she spotted some four or five file cabinets in the dining room containing Merton material. Naturally, she was eager to get her hands on those documents, but O'Callaghan felt it was private and would not allow any access to the files. A few days later Patrick Hart, Thérèse and others were taken for a ride on the Ohio River in a boat owned by the O'Callaghans. The party stopped for lunch at the "Captain's Quarters," a well known and popular restaurant on the river's bank near Cincinnati.

In May, 1970 James Laughlin wrote to Thérèse asking her if she was going to do a book on Merton's poetry. He and Naomi Burton felt it was important that such a job should be done by a good critic who writes well and can do a serious job. Laughlin was

## The Final Years

willing to reserve Merton's notebooks for 18 months so that Thérèse could have first crack at them in preparing her manuscript. He also informed her that a student from Columbia University was preparing a dissertation on Merton's poetry. Apparently, Thérèse had some reservations about someone else working on a similar project. In a letter from Adam Horvath to James Laughlin, the scholar tries to calm Thérèse's uneasiness: "I feel confident that if she had a chance to meet me and talk about our mutual interest in Fr. Merton's poetry, any sense of uneasiness on her part concerning my ambitions would be dissolved... the trustees could... hold in abeyance their decision concerning which items in the Merton Room at Bellarmine I would be allowed to see until they had a chance to learn Sister Thérèse's own feelings after she had met me."[418] Eventually, Horvath did meet with Thérèse and she was willing to help him.

In January 1972, Thérèse went to Bellarmine to examine Merton's poetry books and had requested access to his private journals that she had not seen before, but was not permitted since she had not been named by Merton as one of the people who could have access to all his papers. It might have been at this time that a strange incident occurred when Thérèse was staying in Louisville at St. Agnes Convent with the Sisters of Charity while doing research at Bellarmine. One night the sisters on the floor where the guest rooms were located heard an emotional outburst from her room, including some angry remarks directed at Merton. The sisters later asked Frank O'Callaghan about the Sister who was heard banging around in her room, shouting and swearing. The episode probably resulted from a combination of her lingering grief over his death and her frustration at not having access to the materials she knew existed when she had seen them at Tommie O'Callaghan's following the funeral.

Laughlin wrote to Thérèse on March 24th apologizing for the fact that she could not have access to all the restricted Merton materials: "I still feel badly about these, and think that Tom was just daydreaming when he wrote that part of the trust Indenture, and did not name you as one of the persons who should have access to all his papers. Certainly, I'm sure that would have been his wish, if he had thought about it at the time."[419] He expressed the hope that there was nothing in the restricted journals that would be absolutely necessary for her work on the book.

In September 1973, she was in discussion with New Directions about publishing her book on Merton poetry. Laughlin told her that other publishers might charge her for certain fees, but if the book were to be published by New Directions since "you are one of Tom's oldest friends and have done so much for him and about him, we just wouldn't feel right 'sticking' you for commercial fees."[420] Thérèse did send the manuscript to New Directions but on May 18, 1974 Laughlin informed her that the publishing house was booked up for several years and would not be able to publish her work on Merton. In the meantime she tried several other publishers. In May 1974, she sent Sheed and Ward two manuscripts entitled *Beautiful Cellars* and *A Hill is for Celebration*, but in September received a rejection of *Beautiful Cellars* which might have been another title for *Words and Silence. A Hill is for Celebration* was an alternative title for *Speak to Me, Sparrow* (see endnote 28).

On October 9, 1975 Patrick Hart promised to discuss her manuscript with the Director of Cistercian Publications since he had recently been appointed to the Board. She had consulted Hart for advice on where to leave her Merton collection. Apparently, Thérèse had also been contacted by Bellarmine officials who wanted to visit her personally to discuss her collection. She informed Hart who offered his own analysis: "Your surmise about the reason for the Dean and the 'Reverend Fathers' visit to you may be right... now and then I hear people saying: 'Oh, how wonderful it would be if we had Sr. Thérèse's collection here, etc.' So, I would not be at all surprised if they have some such plan up their sleeves. Or on the other hand, and maybe not independent of this, they may wish to offer you a position at Bellarmine.... I wonder just what their real motives might be?"[421] The Dean was Robert Whitmann and the Director of the Merton Center was Father Clyde Crews, a Merton

## The Final Years

scholar and diocesan priest of Louisville, whom Hart describes as young, energetic and the Archbishop's right-hand man.

On June 3, 1976, Laughlin asked Thérèse to send him her manuscript again and he will have a second look at it. Eventually, the book was published by New Directions, but not until 1979. She did not capitalize on her long relationship with Merton in the book: "Probably no other person could have brought to this first study of all of his poetry the precise combination of spiritual insight, knowledge of the craft of poetry, understanding of and respect for Merton that is found in the 'author's note' and the nine chapters of *Words and Silence*. Though once past her 'note,' S. Thérèse has avoided overt personal comments, her readers should be prepared for a highly favorable evaluation of his poetry."[422] Although the work met with mixed reviews as noted earlier, Thérèse continued her writing and speaking about Merton until her death in 1981 and her name and life are forever associated with Thomas Merton.

# AFTERWORD

When I entered the Congregation of the Sisters of the Divine Savior in 1959, Sister Thérèse Lentfoehr was already one of the "living legends" among the professed members. We youngsters knew her as a published poet and something of a mysterious figure that "floated" into the motherhouse on very rare occasions. I also recall being awed one evening during a province gathering when she and Daniel Berrigan, SJ, sat among us, read their poetry and spoke of their participation in the Catholic Writers Workshops around the country. Heady stuff, to say the least! So, I first knew Thérèse as a poet in her own right and someone accepted as a peer among American Catholic poets of her time. Only later would I learn of Thérèse's 20-year-long correspondence with Thomas Merton and her commitment to preserving the written manuscripts he had entrusted to her.

All of this came to mind when friend and brother Salvatorian, Fr. Robert Nugent, SDS, asked if I would write an Afterword to his soon-to-be published book: *Thomas Merton and Thérèse Lentfoehr: The Story of a Friendship*. I said yes, determined to work closely with our Senior Archivist, Sister Aquin Gilles, who had known Thérèse well and had assisted Bob with his research, even critiquing his early drafts. Much to my dismay that plan was thwarted by the unexpected and early death of Sr. Aquin shortly after I said yes. Therefore what follows is more distanced from Thérèse as a person than I suspect the author had hoped. Nonetheless, I am grateful for the opportunity to comment on the life and work of one of my Salvatorian Sisters.

There is no doubt in my mind that Nugent's book will be

welcomed by those who are dedicated to a full understanding of Thomas Merton. Clearly, Merton's letters to Thérèse add color and perhaps even some depth to a portrait of this gifted and complex man. However, in reading through Nugent's manuscript, I am struck by a number of things that offer insight and make this book an interesting read for those not already fascinated by all things Merton.

First of all, this correspondence allows to us see aspects of Thérèse's generation in a new way. Her life as a Catholic and as a Salvatorian Sister was shaped by two world wars and the coming of age of Roman Catholicism in the United States. By 1946, Old World Europe had been devastated by bombs, exhausted by death and shamed by concentration camps. American Catholics participated fully in the war efforts. By the war's end, Catholics who served the country abroad and at home were no longer intimidated by their immigrant experience. The words "American" and "Catholic" fit together in a new way. It was into this atmosphere, that Thomas Merton and his *Seven Storey Mountain* conversion epic emerged. His story would epitomize all that was vibrant and exciting about being Catholic in the "New World." Thérèse was not the only one caught up in the enthusiasm around this European-born "bohemian" free thinker, who turned his back on the past, embraced Catholicism and then became a monk. Thérèse's often fanatical commitment to Merton and his work may seem a bit "over the top" to some of us today. However, as I recall discovering my own GI father's underlined version of Merton's conversion story, I realize that who he was and what he wrote was very important to that generation. Merton's embrace of American Catholicism in one of its most radical forms spoke of a new time in history. This new understanding would be crystallized fifteen years later in the presidential election of John Fitzgerald Kennedy.

A second insight that Nugent's work offers relates to the changes that occurred in the Church and in religious life during these years. It is clear from the selected correspondence Nugent has chosen that both Merton and Lentfoehr entered their respective

## Afterword

religious communities at a time when age-old traditions were taken for granted and change was rare. In some ways, both of them were grounded in the old ways. Their shared interest in relics and holy cards is just one example of this. However, in other ways, both of them also rode the crest of the new with their concern for social issues and their struggles with what they perceived as heavy-handed authority. Nugent's work allows us to see how these times of change were experienced by these two as unique individuals, but it also gives insight into what was happening to members of both contemplative and apostolic religious communities in the wake of the Second Vatican Council.

Lastly, I would like to say that as a Salvatorian, I find some key aspects of our founding charism tucked within Nugent's treatment of the correspondence between Thérèse and Merton. Our Founder, Francis Mary of the Cross Jordan, felt strongly that Salvatorian apostolic work should never become a list of jobs or tasks in the Church. We are to be open to "all the ways and means the love of Christ inspires" at any particular time in history. It is clear that the unique gift of Thérèse as artist-poet was one of the means through which her ministry expressed itself over the years. While it is never easy for the free artistic spirit to soar within any structure, there is no doubt in my mind that Thérèse's spirit belonged in the Salvatorian world.

Another aspect of the Salvatorian charism that this correspondence shows is our call to work collaboratively with others for the sake of the mission. Thérèse sensed that Merton's writings were important and that she could make a difference in their preservation. She devoted herself to making that happen. At times, the project seemed to become greater than her personal professional objectives. We sense in Thérèse a certain selflessness for the sake of the mission that is not often seen in artists of any age. I would posit that this collaborative drive within her was at the heart of her vocation as a Salvatorian.

There is also no question that Thérèse's time with the Salvatorian Seminarians at Mount St. Paul College and later at Dominican College contributed significantly to the evolution of collaborative work between the Congregation of the Sisters of the Divine Savior and the Society of the Divine Savior (Fathers and Brothers). Thus, Thérèse became a "living legend" for both branches of the Salvatorian Family in the United States. While much has changed since Thérèse's time in the 1960s and 70s, it is good to recall that what we experience today came into being through the collaborative work of many over the years.

In closing, I want to thank Fr. Robert Nugent for his invitation to contribute these few words to his work. Thanks Bob, for the work you have put into these pages and for the collaborative spirit you have shown throughout.

*Sister Carol Thresher, SDS*
*Provincial Leader of the Sisters of*
*the Divine Savior (Salvatorians)*
*May 2011*

## Song for a Marriage

(For Kathryn and Nicholas on your Wedding Day)

God's ways are mystery –
There is no searching
Into the seasons of his providing
Who dares to break our careful patternings
To weave his own design
As he maps each life a new creation.

This day of sacrament is the *kairos*
Of his inscrutable planning –
Like a luminous page of a Book of Hours
Wherein under gold branchwork of the chant
Each word of text is eloquent:
*Ecce sic benedicetur omnis homo*
*Qui timet Dominum,*
And the medieval artist's dream
Of a radiant bride
Stands like a lily of the field
With all the margins bright with flowers.

This page has come alive for us today –
When He who singularly gifted you
In the pristine rites of music
Now drops his peace upon you
Like the crystal notes
Of your harpsichord's Scarlatti;
A joy textured of madrigal
You placed on the lips of children,
And love, a never-ending chorale,
Deep and resonant
As a surprise of bells
In the silence of a great cathedral.

And always, may the Christ-light shine
Over your rooftree like a great star;
And should a shadow come
Let it be only that of bird-wings
In swift flight.

Kathryn, Nicholas –
You who have brought us to your sacred sharing
Will follow you with our love
As you run together in wind of the Spirit who
In an unpredictable moment
Left on your doorsill
A love-flower
Petaled splendidly
As Dante's perfect rose.

*Sister Thérèse*
*December 14, 1974*

# ENDNOTES

1. Kathryn Freund to Mary Rouse, November 9, 1981, Archives of the Sisters of the Divine Savior, Milwaukee, Wisconsin.
2. James Laughlin to Thérèse Lentfoehr, January 31, 1972, Thomas Merton Papers, Columbia University.
3. Thérèse Lentfoehr, *Words and Silence: On the Poetry of Thomas Merton* (New York: New Directions, 1979), vi.
4. William H. Shannon and Christine M. Bochen (Eds.), *Thomas Merton: A Life in Letters* (New York: HarperCollins, 2008), xiii.
5. Roger Lipsey, "Merton, Suzuki, Zen, Ink" in Bonnie Bowman Thurston (Ed.), *Merton and Buddhism* (Louisville, KY: Fons Vitae, 2007), 41.
6. Kevin Sullivan, review of "Give Joan a Sword," *Spirit*, Vol. XI, No. 1 (March, 1944), 25.
7. Margaret E. Schoeverling, "Sister M. Thérèse, Sor.D.S.– Poet Laureate to the Holy Father," *The Magnificat*, Vol. 8 (January, 1949), 120, 125.
8. *Contemporary Authors Online* (Detroit: Gale, 2002).
9. James Laughlin to Thérèse Lentfoehr, August 20, 1969, Thomas Merton Papers, Columbia University.
10. Robert E. Daggy, "Sister Thérèse Lentfoehr, S.D.S.: Custodian of 'Grace's House' and Other Mertoniana. A Memoir," *The Merton Seasonal*, Bellarmine University, Vol. 6, No. 3 (Autumn, 1981), 2.
11. Roy Larson, "Tribute to a lasting model for religion seekers," *Chicago Sun-Times*, December 9, 1979, 40.
12. Daggy, "Sister Thérèse Lentfoehr, S.D.S.," 5.
13. Christine Bochen in her book review of Mark Shaw's *Beneath the Mask of Holiness*, in *The Merton Annual*, vol. 23 (2010), 313.
14. "To the Memory of my Father."
15. *Contemporary Authors Online* (Detroit: Gale, 2002).
16. "Spirit of Place (In memory of my mother)."
17. Transcript of interview with station WTMJ Milwaukee on January 9, 1945, Archives of the Sisters of the Divine Savior, Milwaukee, Wisconsin.
18. Violet E. Dewey, "Poetic Inspiration Pops Up Everywhere for Sister Thérèse," *The Milwaukee Journal*, December 11, 1966, 3.
19. Ibid.
20. Ibid., 3.
21. Kevin Sullivan, Review of "Give Joan a Sword," *Spirit*, Vol. XI, No. 1 (March, 1994), 25-26.
22. William H. Slavick, "Sr. M. Thérèse Lentfoehr" in *Biographical Dictionary of Contemporary Catholic American Writing*, Daniel J. Tynan (Ed.) (New York: Greenwood Press, 1989), 164.
23. Schoeverling, 123.
24. Kathryn Freund to Mary Rouse, November 19, 1981, Archives of the Sisters of the Divine Savior, Milwaukee, Wisconsin.

25 Victor Hamm, "Sr. M. Thérèse: In Memoriam, poetic reflections at the Mass of the Resurrection," November 4, 1981, Archives of the Sisters of the Divine Savior, Milwaukee, Wisconsin.
26 Ibid.
27 Schoeverling, 123,
28 It is not clear in the sources what this unpublished manuscript of new and selected poems was titled. She seems to have changed the title several times including *He Counts the Sparrows, Speak to Me, Sparrow, Letter to Avila*, and *A Hill is for Celebration*.
29 Freund to Rouse, November 19, 1981, Archives of the Sisters of the Divine Savior, Milwaukee, Wisconsin.
30 Ibid.
31 Michael Mott, *The Seven Mountains of Thomas Merton* (Boston: Houghton Mifflin Company, 1984), xxi.
32 Freund to Rouse, November 19, 1981, Archives of the Sisters of the Divine Savior, Milwaukee, Wisconsin.
33 Keith J. Egan, "Epilogue" to Thérèse Lentfoehr's "Poetry of Gervase Toelle," in *The Sword*, Vol. XLII, No. 1 (April, 1982), 21.
34 Personal e-mail to author, May 26, 2011.
35 Daggy, "Sister Thérèse Lentfoehr, S.D.S.," 3.
36 Jane Marie Richardson, "Sturdy Shelter," *The Merton Seasonal*, Vol. 14, No. 4 (Autumn, 1989), 14.
37 Lawrence S. Cunningham, *Thomas Merton and the Monastic Vision* (Grand Rapids, MI: Eerdmans, 1999), 139-140.
38 Another review made the same observation: "Robert Lowell's 'Our Lady of Walsingham' which is a section of his poem 'The Quaker Graveyard at Nantucket,' might well have been used." Isabel Harris Barr, *Spirit*, Vol. XV, No. 1 (March, 1948), 28.
39 Robert Lowell, "The Verses of Thomas Merton," *Commonweal* 42 (June 22, 1945), 240-242.
40 Thomas Merton, "(Review of) *I Sing of a Maiden*, compiled by Sr. Thérèse Lentfoehr," *Commonweal* 47, No. 19 (February 20, 1948), 477-478.
41 Robert E. Daggy (Ed.), *Thomas Merton: The Road to Joy/Letters to Old and New Friends* (New York: Harcourt Brace and Jovanovich Publishers, 1989), 189.
42 Daggy, "Sister Thérèse Lentfoehr, S.D.S.," 3.
43 Book review in *The Milwaukee Journal*, April 13, 1975, 10.
44 Thérèse Lentfoehr, *Words and Silence: On the Poetry of Thomas Merton*, vii.
45 Kevin Lewis, review of *Words and Silence* in the *Journal of the American Academy of Religion*, vol. 48, number 4, December, 1980, 637.
46 Ibid., 638.
47 Jay Martin, review of *Words and Silence* in *American Literature*, Vol. 51, No. 4 (January 1980), 584.
48 Ibid.
49 Leonard Allen, review of *Words and Silence* in *Best Sellers*, University of Scranton, Vol. 39, August, 1997, 187-189.

# Endnotes

50 Robert Lax to Lentfoehr, June 25, 1981, Thomas Merton Papers, Columbia University.
51 Thomas P. McDonnell, review of *Words and Silence* in *America*, Vol. 141, No. 7 (September, 1979), 131.
52 Ibid.
53 Ibid., 132.
54 Christine M. Bochen (Ed.), *Learning to Love: Exploring Solitude and Freedom* (San Francisco: HarperSanFrancisco, 1997), 264.
55 Dewey, "Poetic Inspiration Pops Up Everywhere for Sister Thérèse," 9.
56 Robert E. Daggy, "Question and Revelation: Thomas Merton's Recovery of the Ground of Birth," Speech delivered at the First General Meeting of the International Thomas Merton Society of Great Britain and Ireland, May, 1966.
57 Nugent to Lentfoehr, August 18, 1981, Archives of the Sisters of the Divine Savior, Milwaukee, Wisconsin.
58 For a description of the "Merton industry" that a prominent Merton scholar claims was founded and supported by Merton himself, see Paul M. Pearson, "Thomas Merton: Preserving His Own Memory," in *U.S. Catholic Historian*, Spring, 2003, 47-62.
59 Interview with Patrick Hart by the author, July 6, 2010.
60 For Dinter's personal account of his time at Columbia until 1988, see *The Other Side of the Altar: One Man's Life in the Catholic Priesthood* (New York: Farrar, Straus and Giroux, 2003).
61 Paul E. Dinter to Lentfoehr, October 24, 1980, Thomas Merton Papers, Columbia University.
62 Daggy, *The Road to Joy*, 301.
63 Mrs. Melville E. Stone [Naomi Burton] to Lentfoehr, May 25, 1972, Archives of the Sisters of the Divine Savior, Milwaukee, Wisconsin.
64 Ibid.
65 Patrick Hart to Mary Rouse, November 31, 1981, Archives of the Sisters of the Divine Savior, Milwaukee, Wisconsin.
66 Robert E. Daggy to Kathryn Freund, February 15, 1982, Archives of the Sisters of the Divine Savior, Milwaukee, Wisconsin.
67 Robert A. Wilmot to Paul E. Dinter, January 22, 1982, Archives of the Sisters of the Divine Savior, Milwaukee, Wisconsin.
68 Copy of codicil to Lentfoehr will, September 22, 1980, Archives of the Sisters of the Divine Savior, Milwaukee, Wisconsin.
69 Excerpts of some of Merton's letters to Thérèse are also included in *Thomas Merton: A Life in Letters* edited by William H. Shannon and Christine M. Bochen. See footnote 4 in the author's Introduction.
70 Thérèse Lentfoehr, "To the Members of the Catholic Poetry Society of America," *Spirit*, Vol. VI, No. 5 (November, 1939), 157.
71 Maglione to Lentfoehr, September 6, 1939, Archives of the Sisters of the Divine Savior, Milwaukee, Wisconsin.
72 Ibid.
73 Ruben L.F. Habito, "Hearing the Cries of the World: Thomas Merton's Zen Experience" in Bonnie Bowman Thurston (Ed.), *Merton and Buddhism* (Louisville, KY: Fons Vitae, 2007), 115.

74 Draft of Lentfoehr letter to Raphael Simon, October 20, 1974, Archives of the Sisters of the Divine Savior, Milwaukee, Wisconsin.
75 McCabe to Nugent, personal e-mail, March 29, 2010. For a critical view of Merton's understanding of Zen Buddhism and D.T. Suzuki see John P. Keenan, "The Limits of Thomas Merton's Understanding of Buddhism" in Bonnie Bowman Thurston (Ed.), *Merton and Buddhism* (Louisville, KY: Fons Vitae, 2007), 118-131.
76 John Eudes Bamberger to Lentfoehr, October 20, 1976, Thomas Merton Papers, Columbia University.
77 Donald Grayston to Lentfoehr, n.d., Archives of the Sisters of the Divine Savior, Milwaukee, Wisconsin.
78 Schoeverling, 124.
79 Thérèse Lentfoehr, "Thomas Merton and His Hermitage," *Sisters Today*, Vol. 50, No. 4 (December, 1978), 240.
80 Daggy, "Sister Thérèse Lentfoehr, S.D.S.," 5.
81 Daggy, *The Road to Joy*, 188.
82 Ibid.
83 Merton to Lentfoehr, December 27, 1948, Thomas Merton Papers, Columbia University.
84 This letter was published in Arthur W. Biddle (Ed.), *When Prophecy Still Had a Voice: The Letters of Thomas Merton and Robert Lax* (Lexington, KY: University of Kentucky Press, 2001), 106.
85 Daggy, *The Road to Joy*, 189.
86 Montaldo, *Entering the Silence*, 261. Merton mentions Thérèse by name no more than a few times in his journal entries over the years.
87 Daggy, *The Road to Joy*, 189.
88 Merton to Lentfoehr, December 27, 1948, Thomas Merton Papers, Columbia University.
89 Montaldo, *Entering the Silence*, 266.
90 Merton to Lentfoehr, February 19, 1949, Thomas Merton Papers, Columbia University.
91 Daggy, *The Road to Joy*, 191.
92 Daggy, ibid.
93 Merton to Lentfoehr, February 19, 1949, Thomas Merton Papers, Columbia University.
94 Merton to Lentfoehr, April 26, 1949, Thomas Merton Papers, Columbia University.
95 Ibid.
96 Ibid.
97 Montaldo, *Entering the Silence*, 146.
98 Merton to Lentfoehr, April 26, 1949, Thomas Merton Papers, Columbia University.
99 Daggy, *The Road to Joy*, 192.
100 Merton to Lentfoehr, May 13, 1949, Thomas Merton Papers, Columbia University.
101 Ibid.

# Endnotes

[102] Ibid.
[103] Daggy, *The Road to Joy*, 193.
[104] Ibid., 194.
[105] Gladstone Augustine Ellard, a Jesuit priest with whom she had developed a close friendship. He wrote her on a regular basis from 1937 to 1969 and served as a quasi-spiritual director and sounding board until his death in 1970. He taught at St. Mary's College and seminary in Kansas from 1932 until 1969. His brother, Gerald Ellard, was one of the influential leaders in the liturgical movement in the United States.
[106] Merton to Lentfoehr, July 15, 1949, Thomas Merton Papers, Columbia University.
[107] Ibid.
[108] Mark Shaw claims that Merton's heavily censored autobiography was not the whole truth because it did not convey the picture of Merton as a "sinner of the first degree" and was actually "a watered-down version of what really occurred." Shaw argues that the misrepresentation was intentional and part of a "quiet conspiracy, a cover-up." Cf. Mark Shaw, *Beneath the Mask of Holiness* (New York: Palgrave Macmillan, 2009). For critiques of Shaw's thesis by recognized Merton scholars see Jim Forest, "Beyond the Shadow and Disguise," *The Merton Seasonal*, Vol. 34, No. 4 (Winter, 2009), 40-42, and Christine Bochen, *The Merton Annual*, Vol. 23 (2010), 306-314.
[109] Naomi Burton Stone to John Mulryan, July 21, 1981, Thomas Merton Papers, Columbia University.
[110] "Evelyn Waugh has edited the London edition and tells me he cut a great deal more... what he cut seemed to be more or less 'local interest' to Americans. I am perfectly willing to see anything go out of a book. It will take a lot to move me to object with what editors want to do with any ms. of mine," Daggy, *The Road to Joy*, 190.
[111] Merton to Lentfoehr, July 15, 1949, Thomas Merton Papers, Columbia University.
[112] Ibid.
[113] Daggy, *The Road to Joy*, 195.
[114] Ibid.
[115] Merton to Lentfoehr, August 28, 1949, Thomas Merton Papers, Columbia University.
[116] Ibid.
[117] Ibid.
[118] Ibid.
[119] Merton to Lentfoehr, October 3, 1949, Thomas Merton Papers, Columbia University.
[120] Ibid.
[121] Lentfoehr to Irenaeus Herscher, November 11, 1949, St. Bonaventure University Merton Collection.
[122] At Christmas, 1968, Patrick Hart sent Merton's breviary to Thérèse.
[123] Lentfoehr to Herscher, November 17, 1949, St. Bonaventure University Merton Collection.

124 Biddle, *When Prophecy Still Had a Voice*, 110.
125 Montaldo, *Entering the Silence*, 390-391.
126 Mott, *The Seven Mountains of Thomas Merton*, 150, 251, 253, 254, 299, 405, 493.
127 Ibid., 204.
128 Merton to Lentfoehr, January 7, 1950, Thomas Merton Papers, Columbia University.
129 Thomas Merton, *A Search for Solitude: The Journals of Thomas Merton*, Lawrence S. Cunningham (Ed.), (San Francisco: HarperSanFrancisco, 1996), 4.
130 Ibid., 6.
131 Mott, *The Seven Mountains of Thomas Merton*, 503.
132 Merton to Lentfoehr, January 7, 1950, Thomas Merton Papers, Columbia University.
133 Ibid.
134 Ibid.
135 Merton to Lentfoehr, January 21, 1950, Thomas Merton Papers, Columbia University.
136 Toelle, *Spirit*, Vol. XVI, No. 3 (July, 1949): 84-89.
137 Merton to Lentfoehr, May 6, 1950, Thomas Merton Papers, Columbia University.
138 "Two Letters on 'The Merton Problem'" 1 by Sister M. Thérèse, S.D.S, *Spirit*, Vol. XVI, No. 7 (March, 1950), 20-21.
139 Ibid., 20.
140 Ibid., 21.
141 Ibid, 20.
142 Sr. Thérèse Lentfoehr, "The Poetry of Gervase Toelle," *The Sword*, Vol. XLII, No. 1 (April, 1982), 20.
143 Daggy, *The Road to Joy*, 198.
144 Lentfoehr to Herscher, March 7, 1950, St. Bonaventure University Merton Collection.
145 Lentfoehr to Herscher, n.d., St. Bonaventure University Merton Collection.
146 Merton to Lentfoehr, April 8, 1950, Thomas Merton Papers, Columbia University.
147 Ibid.
148 Daggy, *The Road to Joy*, 201.
149 Ibid., 201-202.
150 Ibid., 202.
151 Ibid.
152 Merton to Lentfoehr, July 10, 1950, Thomas Merton Papers, Columbia University.
153 Ibid.
154 Merton to Lentfoehr, July 31, 1950, Thomas Merton Papers, Columbia University.
155 Daggy, *The Road to Joy*, 203.

# Endnotes

[156] Merton to Lentfoehr, July 31, 1950, Thomas Merton Papers, Columbia University.
[157] Daggy, *The Road to Joy*, 204.
[158] Ibid.
[159] Ibid.
[160] Daggy, *The Road to Joy*, 205.
[161] Ibid.
[162] Merton to Lentfoehr, November 29, 1950, Thomas Merton Papers, Columbia University.
[163] Daggy, *The Road to Joy*, 206.
[164] Merton to Lentfoehr, March 1, 1951, Thomas Merton Papers, Columbia University.
[165] On February 27, 1981, John J. Ford, the attorney for the Merton Legacy Trust, wrote to Thérèse about the *Jonas* manuscript that Merton had sent to Thérèse as an "inter vivos loan," and then later asked to borrow it back for research. Merton had it in his possession when he died and Thérèse wanted it back. Ford acknowledged that it was a loan from Merton to Thérèse, but said he could not return it unless she had documents from Merton proving that he had requested it back as a loan. Columbia University has the original, handwritten, autographed manuscript in the Merton collection, so apparently it was returned to her before her death in October.
[166] Merton to Lentfoehr, April 28, 1951, Thomas Merton Papers, Columbia University.
[167] Daggy, *The Road to Joy*, 206-207.
[168] Merton to Lentfoehr, April 28, 1951, Thomas Merton Papers, Columbia University.
[169] Daggy, *The Road to Joy*, 207.
[170] Merton to Lentfoehr, May 21, 1951, Thomas Merton Papers, Columbia University.
[171] Ibid.
[172] Daggy, *The Road to Joy*, 207.
[173] Ibid., 207-208.
[174] Merton to Lentfoehr, June 5, 1951, Thomas Merton Papers, Columbia University.
[175] Ibid.
[176] Ibid.
[177] Merton to Lentfoehr, July 7, 1951, Thomas Merton Papers, Columbia University.
[178] Merton to Lentfoehr, July 13, 1951, Thomas Merton Papers, Columbia University.
[179] Fox to Lentfoehr, September 11, 1951, Thomas Merton Center, Bellarmine University.
[180] Ibid.
[181] Fox to Lentfoehr, September 22, 1951, Thomas Merton Center, Bellarmine University.

[182] His novel, *The Journal of My Escape from the Nazis* would eventually be published in 1969 as *My Argument with the Gestapo*.
[183] Merton to Lentfoehr, October 8, 1951, Thomas Merton Papers, Columbia University.
[184] "Poetry in Education," *Spirit*, Vol. 18, No. 4 (September, 1951), 113-122. The article was a talk she had given at Hunter College, NY in 1950.
[185] Daggy, *The Road to Joy*, 210. Thérèse said that Merton had seen the article and sent her one of the "little sermons" she occasionally received from him.
[186] Ibid.
[187] Merton to Lentfoehr, December 19, 1951, Thomas Merton Papers, Columbia University.
[188] Merton to Lentfoehr, January 4, 1952, Thomas Merton Papers, Columbia University.
[189] Ibid.
[190] Ibid.
[191] Merton to Lentfoehr, March 27, 1952, Thomas Merton Papers, Columbia University.
[192] Ibid.
[193] Ibid.
[194] Ibid.
[195] Daggy, *The Road to Joy*, 211.
[196] Merton to Lentfoehr, July 12, 1952, Thomas Merton Papers, Columbia University.
[197] Ibid.
[198] Merton to Lentfoehr, August 18, 1952, Thomas Merton Papers, Columbia University.
[199] Merton to Lentfoehr, September 2, 1952, Thomas Merton Papers, Columbia University.
[200] Merton to Lentfoehr, September 18, 1952, Thomas Merton Papers, Columbia University.
[201] Merton to Lentfoehr, November 6, 1952, Thomas Merton Papers, Columbia University.
[202] Ibid.
[203] From March 10, 1953 until July 17, 1956 there is a gap in Merton's journals, although he continues his regular professional and personal correspondence during this period.
[204] Merton to Lentfoehr, May 20, 1953, Thomas Merton Papers, Columbia University.
[205] Daggy, *The Road to Joy*, 213.
[206] Maryanne Englehardt, SDS, personal conversation with author, August 21, 2011.
[207] Merton to Lentfoehr, May 20, 1953, Thomas Merton Papers, Columbia University.
[208] Merton to Lentfoehr, June 6, 1953, Thomas Merton Papers, Columbia University.

# Endnotes

[209] Merton to Lentfoehr, September 26, 1953, Thomas Merton Papers, Columbia University.
[210] Ibid.
[211] Ibid.
[212] Merton to Lentfoehr, October 21, 1953, Thomas Merton Papers, Columbia University.
[213] Ibid.
[214] Ibid.
[215] Merton to Lentfoehr, November 20, 1953, Thomas Merton Papers, Columbia University.
[216] Ibid.
[217] Daggy, *The Road to Joy*, 215.
[218] Ibid., 216-217.
[219] Merton to Lentfoehr, November 29, 1954, Thomas Merton Papers, Columbia University.
[220] Daggy, *The Road to Joy*, 217.
[221] Merton to Dell'Isola, January 17, 1955, Thomas Merton Papers, Columbia University.
[222] Merton to Lentfoehr, November 29, 1954, Thomas Merton Papers, Columbia University.
[223] Ibid.
[224] Merton to Lentfoehr, January 18, 1955, Thomas Merton Papers, Columbia University.
[225] Ibid.
[226] Ibid.
[227] Daggy, *The Road to Joy*, 219.
[228] Merton to Lentfoehr, August 6, 1955, Thomas Merton Papers, Columbia University.
[229] Ibid.
[230] Ibid.
[231] Ibid.
[232] Ibid.
[233] Merton to Lentfoehr, October 22, 1955, Thomas Merton Papers, Columbia University.
[234] Daggy, *The Road to Joy*, 223.
[235] Merton to Lentfoehr, September 25, 1956, Thomas Merton Papers, Columbia University.
[236] Daggy, *The Road to Joy*, 225.
[237] Merton to Lentfoehr, November 8, 1956, Thomas Merton Papers, Columbia University.
[238] Merton to Lentfoehr, November 8, 1956, Thomas Merton Papers, Columbia University.
[239] Ibid.
[240] Ibid.

[241] Ibid.
[242] Merton to Lentfoehr, January 3, 1957, Thomas Merton Papers, Columbia University.
[243] Mott, *The Seven Mountains of Thomas Merton*, 617.
[244] Jim Forest, *Living With Wisdom: A Life of Thomas Merton* (Maryknoll, NY: Orbis Books, 2008), 127.
[245] Mott, *The Seven Mountains of Thomas Merton*, 297.
[246] Merton to Lentfoehr, November 14, 1957, Thomas Merton Papers, Columbia University.
[247] Daggy, *The Road to Joy*, 229-230.
[248] Merton to Lentfoehr, April 3, 1959, Thomas Merton Papers, Columbia University.
[249] Merton to Lentfoehr, May 14, 1959, Thomas Merton Papers, Columbia University.
[250] Ibid.
[251] Merton to Lentfoehr, July 4, 1959, Thomas Merton Papers, Columbia University.
[252] Ibid.
[253] Merton, *A Search for Solitude*, 302-303.
[254] Merton to Lentfoehr, July 31, 1959, Thomas Merton Papers, Columbia University. The book was published as *The Wisdom of the Desert*.
[255] Daggy, *The Road to Joy*, 234.
[256] Merton to Lentfoehr, November 20, 1959, Thomas Merton Papers, Columbia University.
[257] Ibid.
[258] Daggy, *The Road to Joy*, 234.
[259] Merton to Lentfoehr, November 20, 1959, Thomas Merton Papers, Columbia University.
[260] Ibid.
[261] Daggy, *The Road to Joy*, 235-236.
[262] Daggy, *The Road to Joy*, 236. In 1963, Sortais was the Abbot General who had decided to close a Trappist monastery in Algeria whose martyred monks became the subject of a highly acclaimed 2011 French film, "Of Gods and Men," until the local Bishop Duval protested strongly: "'I have made my decision' was his [Sortais's] cold reply. That night... Sortais died from cardiac arrest.... With Sortais dead, so was his decree." Cf. John Kiser, *The Monks of Tibhirine* (New York: St. Martins Griffin, 2002), 20.
[263] Merton to Lentfoehr, December 5, 1960, Thomas Merton Papers, Columbia University.
[264] Bochen, *Learning to Love*, 247.
[265] Merton to Lentfoehr, December 5, 1960, Thomas Merton Papers, Columbia University.
[266] Ibid.
[267] Merton to Lentfoehr, February 5, 1961, Thomas Merton Papers, Columbia University.

## Endnotes

[268] Ibid.
[269] Ibid.
[270] Ibid.
[271] Ibid.
[272] Lentfoehr to Merton, March 3, 1962, Thomas Merton Papers, Columbia University.
[273] Shannon, *The Hidden Ground of Love*, 139-140.
[274] Daggy, *The Road to Joy*, 240-241.
[275] Merton to Lentfoehr, June 15, 1962, Thomas Merton Papers, Columbia University. For a more detailed account of Merton's silencing, see Robert Nugent, "Thomas Merton: The Silenced Monk," in *Silence Speaks* (New Jersey: Paulist Press, 2011), 73-93.
[276] Merton to Lentfoehr, July 17, 1962, Thomas Merton Papers, Columbia University.
[277] Daggy, *The Road to Joy*, 241.
[278] Merton to Lentfoehr, July 17, 1962, Thomas Merton Papers, Columbia University.
[279] Merton to Lentfoehr, September 20, 1962, Thomas Merton Papers, Columbia University.
[280] Ibid.
[281] Ibid.
[282] Ibid.
[283] Victor Kramer (Ed.), *Turning Toward the World* (San Francisco: HarperSanFrancisco, 1996), 238.
[284] Merton to Lentfoehr, September 20, 1962, Thomas Merton Papers, Columbia University. Merton later asked Thérèse to contact Powers and ask him for copies of his book so that he could use it to help "humanize" the novices. It was perhaps for the same reason that he once took the unprecedented step of taking his students swimming in the monastery lake.
[285] Daggy, *The Road to Joy*, 242.
[286] Ibid., 243.
[287] Ibid.
[288] Merton to Lentfoehr, February 19, 1963, Thomas Merton Papers, Columbia University.
[289] Ibid.
[290] Lentfoehr to Merton, March 17, 1963, Thomas Merton Papers, Columbia University.
[291] Ibid.
[292] Ibid. See endnote 28 for more about this manuscript.
[293] Ibid.
[294] Ibid.
[295] Ibid.
[296] Ibid.
[297] Daggy, *The Road to Joy*, 244.
[298] Kramer, *Turning Toward the World*, 227.

[299] Daggy, *The Road to Joy*, 245.
[300] Patrick Hart, *The Other Side of the Mountain* (San Francisco: HarperSanFrancisco, 1998), 8.
[301] Merton to Lentfoehr, August 9, 1963, Thomas Merton Papers, Columbia University.
[302] Ibid.
[303] Ibid.
[304] Daggy, *The Road to Joy*, 247.
[305] Ibid.
[306] Merton to Lentfoehr, November 9, 1963, Thomas Merton Papers, Columbia University.
[307] Merton to Lentfoehr, February 1, 1964, Thomas Merton Papers, Columbia University.
[308] Ibid.
[309] Shannon and Bochen, *Thomas Merton: A Life in Letters*, 313. "Michael Serafian" was a pen name of Malachi Martin.
[310] Merton to Lentfoehr, February 1, 1964, Thomas Merton Papers, Columbia University.
[311] Ibid.
[312] Lentfoehr to Merton, March 20, 1964, Thomas Merton Papers, Columbia University.
[313] Merton to Lentfoehr, April 1, 1964, Thomas Merton Papers, Columbia University.
[314] Ibid.
[315] Ibid.
[316] Daggy, *The Road to Joy*, 249.
[317] Merton to Lentfoehr, September 17, 1964, Thomas Merton Papers, Columbia University.
[318] Ibid.
[319] Ibid.
[320] Daggy, *The Road to Joy*, 250.
[321] Merton to Lentfoehr, December 13, 1964, Thomas Merton Papers, Columbia University.
[322] Ibid.
[323] Merton to Lentfoehr, March 27, 1965, Thomas Merton Papers, Columbia University.
[324] Ibid.
[325] Ibid.
[326] Shannon and Bochen, *Thomas Merton: A Life in Letters*, 31.
[327] Kramer, *Turning Toward the World*, 187.
[328] Merton to Lentfoehr, June 16, 1965, Thomas Merton Papers, Columbia University.
[329] Ibid.

# Endnotes

[330] Ibid.
[331] Merton to Lentfoehr, September 28, 1965, Thomas Merton Papers, Columbia University.
[332] Daggy, *The Road to Joy*, 252.
[333] Ibid., 252-253.
[334] Lentfoehr to Merton, February 1, 1966, Thomas Merton Papers, Columbia University.
[335] "The Firebird (For a monk in winter)."
[336] Photocopy of original in the Archives of the Sisters of the Divine Savior, Milwaukee, Wisconsin.
[337] Lentfoehr to Merton, February 1, 1966, Thomas Merton Papers, Columbia University.
[338] Ibid. See endnote 28 for a list of the many alternative titles of this unpublished manuscript.
[339] Ibid.
[340] Lentfoehr to Merton, February 14, 1966, Thomas Merton Papers, Columbia University.
[341] Ibid.
[342] Daggy, *The Road to Joy*, 254.
[343] Ibid., 255.
[344] Steve Avella, personal e-mail to author.
[345] Handwritten on the back of an envelope from Merton dated September 14, 1966, Thomas Merton Papers, Columbia University.
[346] Bochen, *Learning to Love: Exploring Solitude and Freedom*, 1967.
[347] Laughlin to Lentfoehr, July 19, 1974, Thomas Merton Papers, Columbia University.
[348] Lentfoehr to Merton, June 1, 1966, Thomas Merton Papers, Columbia University.
[349] Ibid.
[350] Ibid.
[351] Ibid.
[352] Ibid.
[353] Ibid.
[354] Daggy, *The Road to Joy*, 256. For a discussion of Merton and sexuality see Robert Nugent, "Thomas Merton and Sexual Wholeness," *The Merton Seasonal*, Vol. 17, No. 1 (Winter, 1992), 9-15.
[355] Merton to Lentfoehr, June 7, 1966, Thomas Merton Papers, Columbia University.
[356] Bochen, *Learning to Love*, 222-223.
[357] Merton to Lentfoehr, July 31, 1966, Thomas Merton Papers, Columbia University.
[358] Merton to Lentfoehr, September 13, 1966, Thomas Merton Papers, Columbia University.
[359] Schoeverling, 120, 122.

360 Merton to Lentfoehr, September 13, 1966, Thomas Merton Papers, Columbia University.
361 Ibid.
362 Griffin to Lentfoehr, December 11, 1969, Thomas Merton Papers, Columbia University. James Laughlin had also written Thérèse: "Of the various memorial poems that I have seen so far, I like yours the best of all. There is so much of him in it, the way he was, it is deeply moving." (November 13, 1969, Thomas Merton Papers, Columbia University.) Since her poem appeared in *America* on December 13th, however, and these letters predate the publication of the poem, it might be that they saw it before publication.
363 Merton to Lentfoehr, March 23, 1967, Thomas Merton Papers, Columbia University.
364 Forest, *Living With Wisdom: A Life of Thomas Merton*, 63.
365 Lentfoehr to Merton, May 9, 1967, Thomas Merton Papers, Columbia University.
366 Ibid.
367 Ibid.
368 Ibid.
369 Ibid.
370 Ibid.
371 Merton to Lentfoehr, May 12, 1967, Thomas Merton Papers, Columbia University.
372 Lentfoehr to Merton, June 13, 1967, Thomas Merton Papers, Columbia University.
373 Ibid.
374 Ibid.
375 Merton to Lentfoehr, June 26, 1967, Thomas Merton Papers, Columbia University.
376 *Contemporary Authors Online* (Detroit: Gale, 2002).
377 Lentfoehr to Merton, July 19, 1967, Thomas Merton Papers, Columbia University.
378 John Masefield (1878-1967), British poet laureate since 1930, whose works included poems about the sea and World War II.
379 Lentfoehr to Merton, August 4, 1967, Thomas Merton Papers, Columbia University.
380 Lentfoehr to Merton, September 2, 1967, Thomas Merton Papers, Columbia University.
381 Ibid.
382 Ibid.
383 Bochen, *Learning to Love*, 287.
384 Merton to Lentfoehr, September 26, 1967, Thomas Merton Papers, Columbia University.
385 Daggy, *The Road to Joy*, 260.
386 Ibid.
387 Daggy, *The Road to Joy*, 104.

# Endnotes

[388] Merton to Lentfoehr, October 13, 1967, Thomas Merton Papers, Columbia University.
[389] Bochen, *Learning to Love*, 272.
[390] Lentfoehr to Merton, October 16, 1967, Thomas Merton Papers, Columbia University.
[391] Ibid., 267.
[392] Daggy, *The Road to Joy*, 268.
[393] Ibid., 267.
[394] Author's phone interview with Tommie O'Callaghan, October 13, 2010.
[395] "When a leanbeaten path
outbranching held us — toward a sky —
hung light we three together
laddered that happy mountain.
At a stumble stair a door blazed
open and under
the icon light we found our guru who thundered
us out of our sky with the parable
of his house: dance of the tea-mugs,
Beatle-beat, and a pocket of poems....
Late we left that singing hearth all in
a joy as, lit by this swami's hand,
we shook out our cares lightly
under the great moonflower
along the downtrail pines."
[396] Merton to Lentfoehr, November 16, 1967, Thomas Merton Papers, Columbia University.
[397] Hart, *The Other Side of the Mountain*, 11.
[398] Merton to Lentfoehr, November 16, 1967, Thomas Merton Papers, Columbia University.
[399] Lentfoehr to Merton, October 16, 1967, Thomas Merton Papers, Columbia University.
[400] McCabe to Nugent, March 29, 2010, personal e-mail.
[401] Ibid.
[402] Merton to Lentfoehr, January 1968, Thomas Merton Papers, Columbia University.
[403] Dennis Q. McInerny was the author of *Thomas Merton: The Man and His Work* (Washington, DC: Cistercian Publications, 1974).
[404] Daggy, *The Road to Joy*, 261-262.
[405] Ibid., 262
[406] Hart, *The Other Side of the Mountain*, 50.
[407] Lentfoehr to Merton, March 19, 1968, Thomas Merton Papers, Columbia University.
[408] Ibid.
[409] Ibid.
[410] Thérèse Lentfoehr, *Words and Silence*, 115-116.
[411] Merton to Lentfoehr, July 13, 1968, Thomas Merton Papers, Columbia University.

[412] Daggy, *The Road to Joy*, 263.
[413] Hart, *The Other Side of the Mountain*, 289.
[414] Daggy, *The Road to Joy*, 263.
[415] Archives of the Sisters of the Divine Savior, Milwaukee, Wisconsin.
[416] McCabe to Nugent, personal e-mail, March 29, 2010.
[417] Copy of homily in possession of the author.
[418] Adam Horvath to James Laughlin, June 29, 1970, Thomas Merton Papers, Columbia University.
[419] Laughlin to Lentfoehr, March 24, 1972, Thomas Merton Papers, Columbia University.
[420] Laughlin to Lentfoehr, September 10, 1973, Thomas Merton Papers, Columbia University.
[421] Hart to Lentfoehr, October 9, 1975, Thomas Merton Papers, Columbia University.
[422] Sister M. Linnea, O.S.B., review of *Words and Silence* in *Sisters Today*, Vol. 51, No. 2 (October, 1979), 127-128.

ST PAULS

This book was produced by ST PAULS/Alba House, the Society of St. Paul, an international religious congregation of priests and brothers dedicated to serving the Church through the communications media.

For information regarding this and associated ministries of the Pauline Family of Congregations, write to the Vocation Director, Society of St. Paul, 2187 Victory Blvd., Staten Island, New York 10314-6603. Phone (718) 982-5709; or E-mail: vocation@stpauls.us or check our internet site, www.vocationoffice.org